Police Use of Excessive Force against African Americans

Policing Perspectives and Challenges in the Twenty-First Century

Series Editor:

Jonathon A. Cooper, Indiana University of Pennsylvania

In many respects, policing has evolved over the last two centuries; yet issues that concerned policing in the nineteenth and twentieth centuries continue to be salient to contemporary law enforcement. But how these challenges are manifest to the police today are distinct, as society and politics, too, have evolved. And so understanding the role of police in society, the behavior and organization of law enforcement, the relationship between officers and civilians, and the intersection of theory and praxis remain important to the study of police. To this end, volumes in this series will consider policing perspectives and challenges in the twenty-first century, around the world, and through a variety of disciplinary lenses. Ultimately, this series "takes stock" of policing today, considers how it got here, and projects where it might be going. *Policing Perspectives and Challenges in the Twenty-First Century* will be of interest and use to a variety of policing scholars, including academics, police executives, and others who study law enforcement.

Titles in the series

Police Use of Excessive Force against African Americans: Historical Antecedents and Community Perceptions, by Ray Von Robertson & Cassandra D. Chaney

Police Use of Excessive Force against African Americans

Historical Antecedents and Community Perceptions

Ray Von Robertson and
Cassandra D. Chaney

Afterword by
Earl Smith

LEXINGTON BOOKS
Lanham • Boulder • New York • London

Published by Lexington Books
An imprint of The Rowman & Littlefield Publishing Group, Inc.
4501 Forbes Boulevard, Suite 200, Lanham, Maryland 20706
www.rowman.com

6 Tinworth Street, London SE11 5AL

British Library Cataloguing in Publication Information Available

Library of Congress Cataloging-in-Publication Data

Library of Congress Cataloging-in-Publication Data Available

ISBN 978-1-4985-3918-0 (cloth)
ISBN 978-1-4985-3919-7 (electronic)

Contents

Preface

Police. Law Enforcers. Cops. "Arm of the Law." Law Enforcement Agents. Crime Squads. "The Man." Five-O." "The Fuzz." "The Popo." Regardless of the name used to describe them, the image of the men and women who swear, "To Protect and Serve" evokes various thoughts and feelings. Currently, there are 744,674 police officers in the work force and 86.7 percent of police officers are male, making them the more common gender in the occupation.[1] In addition, 79 percent of police officers are White, making them the most common race or ethnicity in the occupation. Representing 13 percent of police officers, Black or African American is the second most common race or ethnicity in this occupation.[2]

During the sixth GOP Presidential Debate, nominee Donald J. Trump boldly declares, "The police are the most mistreated people in this country." While some perceive police as facilitators of societal law and order, others perceive police as contemporary bullies who murder without consequence. Those who perceive police through the lens of the former, no doubt, immediately think of particular members of law enforcement that conduct their jobs with respect, dignity, courage, and honor.

In the article, *"If Most Police Officers Are 'Good' Cops, These Are Even Better,"* Nick Wing[3] acknowledges many of these individuals. Some of them include Chief Chris Magnus (Redmond, California), Police Chief Steve Anderson (Nashville, Tennessee), Police Officer Adyl Polanco (New York City), Police Chief Cameron McLay (Pittsburgh), The Sanford Police Department, Police Chief Scott Thomson (Camden, New Jersey), and Police Sgt. Bret Barnum (Portland, Oregon). However, those who perceive law enforcement as contemporary bullies and murderers immediately reflect on the faces of people of color (in particular African Americans) who lost their lives to police. The intense media attention given to Freddie Gray, Samuel

vii

Dubose, Philando Castile, Terance Crutcher, Alton Sterling, Jamar Clark, Jeremy McDole, William Chapman II, Walter Scott, Eric Harris, Tamir Rice, Akai Gurley, Michael Brown, Eric Garner, and others, leads to negative perceptions of police. Our article, "Racism and Police Brutality"[4] is one of the most nationally and internationally cited academic works related to this subject, which clearly suggests the intense interest scholars and lay members have in this topic. On page 482 of that article, we write, "Police brutality is improper and unjust. So a plausible concern becomes how in a society that ostensibly emphasizes egalitarianism, can a milieu exist which allows police malfeasance to thrive?"

The purpose of this book is to provide the historicity of law enforcement as well as how that history directly relates to the current relationship between communities of color and law enforcement. This book consists of five chapters. In the first chapter, we discuss how Critical Race Theory (CRT) relates to the treatment of African Americans. The second chapter will explore early antecedents of police brutality against African Americans. This history includes, but is not limited to, plantation overseers, the lynching of Black males, early race riots, and incidents such as the Los Angeles Rampart Scandal and the Rodney King incident. The third chapter provides qualitative commentary from African American college students regarding their perceptions of police as well as their recommendations regarding how members of law enforcement and colleges and universities can help communities deal with issues of police brutality. The fourth chapter will discuss the qualitative commentary provided by participants as well as how these perspectives support and extend existing scholarship. The final chapter will examine the policy implications and efficacy of better training, community policing, body cameras, citizen efforts to reduce the problem of police brutality, and strategies to reduce the problem that have shown promise. Furthermore, we summarize the major outcomes of the study. We conclude with the theoretical contributions of the study, the potential policy implications, and recommendations for future research.

We dedicate the book to the men, women, and children who lost their lives by members of law enforcement as well as the men and women who lost their lives while serving our communities with dignity, integrity, and honor.

NOTES

1. There are 645,936 males in the workforce and 98,738 females in the workforce.

2. Data USA, Police Officers, 2018. Accessed on July 15, 2018, https://datausa.io/profile/soc/333050/.

3. Associated Press (December 8, 2017). 14 high-profile police-related deaths of U.S. blacks. Retrieved from https://www.cbc.ca/news/world/list-police-related-deaths-usa-1.4438618.

4. Chaney, Cassandra, and Ray V. Robertson. "Racism and Police Brutality in America." *Journal of African American Studies*, 17, no. 4 (2013a): 480–505.

Acknowledgements

We would like to acknowledge the African Americans who have lost their lives to street violence. Most of these individuals began their day, expecting to come home alive, yet they never did. Some of these African Americans recently lost their lives by police violence, while others have been gone for some time. Regardless of the length of their departure, these males and females remain in the memory of their loved ones. The names of those lost are too great to list. However, we specifically acknowledge Orlando Barlow, Sean Bell, Cedric Chatman, Amadou Diallo, Samuel Dubose, Malcolm Ferguson, Eric Garner, Prince Jones, Dante Price, Tamir Rice, Alberta Spruill, Timothy Thomas, and Ousmane Zongo. We wish these families peace as they daily cope with the loss of their loved one.

We also thank members of law enforcement who serve their communities with honor, dignity, professionalism, and respect. These men and women vow to "serve and protect" and willingly enter dangerous situations to help citizens. We also wish peace for the families who have lost an officer in the line of duty. In particular, we thank the families of the fallen officers in Dallas for their courage: DPD Officer Michael Krol, 40, who had been with the department since 2007. DPD Sgt. Michael Smith, 55, a former Army Ranger who had been with the department since 1989. DART Officer Brent Thompson, 43, a former Marine who had been with the department since 2009. Thompson was the first DART officer killed in the line of duty since the department's inception in 1989. DPD Officer Patricio "Patrick" Zamarripa, 32, a former Navy sailor and Iraq War veteran who had been with the department since 2011. In addition, we thank the families of the fallen officers in Baton Rouge for their courage: Deputy Brad Garafola, 45, who had been with the East Baton Rouge Parish Sheriff's Office since 1992. Officer Matthew Gerald, 41, a former Marine who had been with the BRPD for four months. Corporal Montrell Jackson, 32, who had been with the BRPD since 2006.

We would like to express gratitude to scholars who paved the way and have been instrumental in our professional and personal development. In particular, we would like to thank Professor Robin L. Jarrett (University of Illinois at Urbana-Champaign), Dr. Laurie Kramer (Northeastern University), Dr. Angela L. Wiley (Auburn University), Professors Isiah Warner, Roland Mitchell, Lori Martin, Stephen Finley, Herman Kelly, and Dereck Rovaris (Louisiana State University), and Professor Eduardo Bonilla-Silva (Duke University).

Last, but not least, I thank my friend and colleague, Ray. Through this process, I have learned so much from you. In addition, I deem it an honor to work with you as we do the important and much-needed work of bridging the acrimony between our communities and law enforcement.

To my co-author, Dr. Cassandra Chaney. I feel honored to have the opportunity to work with the most intelligent and hard-working scholar ever. Your high standards and integrity represent something every scholar should strive to achieve. You are the best, hands down!!

To My Mom and Sister: Thanks Mom for everything and R.I.P. (Rest In Power) to my sister Wendy. After a long battle with multiple sclerosis, you deserve some rest. I will always love you!

Sincerely,
Ray V. Robertson and Cassandra D. Chaney

Chapter One

Black People in America

A Legacy of Maltreatment

On Sunday, February 7, 2016, the Denver Broncos defeated the Carolina Panthers 24-10 during Super Bowl 50. An estimated 167 million persons worldwide viewed the game, which was one of the most watched Super Bowls in the history of the game. However, many would argue the halftime show overshadowed the game. The halftime show immediately becomes controversial when African American crossover entertainment sensation, singer Beyoncé Knowles, premieres her video for the single "Formation" which includes a tribute to Black women who were members of the Black Panther Party for Self Defense. The women of the Black Panther Party play a prominent role in the activist group, which seeks to not only defend the African American community against unchecked police brutality/excessive force, but also provide much-needed social services for the Black community such as free lunch programs and free clinics.[1]

In the same way, it is debatable as to the political nature of the halftime performance and the song itself (this is a topic that we explore at length later in the book), and there were clear political messages in the music video for "Formation." Specifically, the video includes a thought-provoking scene in which the words "STOP KILLING US" are visible on a wall almost simultaneously as Knowles is perched atop a sinking police car. Both the halftime show and video drew the intense ire of many ultra-conservative groups, most notably among these former New York City mayor, Rudolph Giuliani who during an episode of *Fox & Friends* the following day calls the performance an "attack" on police officers.[2]

Interestingly, Giuliani was not alone in perceiving the performance as an attack on cops, yet at the time of this statement in 2016, White men execute

1

seven of eight police officers in the line of duty.[3] Nevertheless, social movements like Black Lives Matter (BLM), recording artist Beyoncé Knowles,
and Black activists who are increasingly concerned with police use of excessive force have been unfairly labeled as anti-police.[4] In addition, the aforementioned seems even more spurious when juxtaposed with findings from a
2015 Guardian study. The 2015 study finds that among 1,134 documented
deaths at the hands of officers, young Black men were nine times more likely
to be a victim of murder by police officers than males of other races.[5] In
addition, the study is important when noting African American males comprise only 2 percent of the U.S. population but account for more than 15
percent of all deaths logged during 2015 in an ongoing investigation into
police use of deadly force.[6]

Our work focuses on how African American college students attending a
historically Black college/university (HBCU) in the South perceive law enforcement. Initially, readers may wonder given the disastrous interactions
between police and African Americans of all ages, why focus specifically on
Black college students?

There are four reasons why this book focuses on African American college students. First, African American college students have a long history of
not only activism but also strained relations with police.[7] In *The Black Campus Movement: Black Students and the Racial Reconstitution of Higher Education, 1965–1972* (2012),[8] renowned race scholar Ibram X. Kendi impres-
sively chronicled the history of the Black campus movement. Moreover,
Kendi (2012) touched on how the Black student movement, which was pivot-
al in the development of Black/African American/African studies courses
and improving the conditions for Black students at both historically Black
colleges and predominantly White ones alike, frequently involved instances
of police using excessive force, namely at Southern University (1972) and
Jackson State University (1970).

Second, African American college students are members of an age cohort
that has recurrent negative encounters with police.[9] Case in point, Landers et
al. (2011), in their study of police contacts and stress involving 83 African
American college students (66 females and 35 males), yields several findings
that provide credence to an exploration of the thoughts of Black students
regarding law enforcement. Foremost, the researchers find that adolescents/
young adults ages 15–24 account for the largest percentage of arrests made
by police. Next, the study cites individuals in the 18–24 age group as reporting greater fear of arrest despite innocence than older cohorts report.

Third, both African American male and female college students report
contacts with police as stressful, with males affirming contacts with police as
more stressful than their female counterparts do. Stress levels among college
students, particularly African American collegians, are important to note
because they can lead to produce serious problems.[10] In their study of the

connection between mindfulness, stress, and blood pressure, Wright et al. (2018) reveal: (1) stress can produce hypertension; (2) stress can also lead to mental health and cardiovascular problems; and (3) African American college students experience stressors beyond those encountered by White students related to racism, discrimination, and negative life events.[11]

Lastly, a concentration on African American collegians is warranted because research has shown that middle class African Americans are more likely to report positive views of the police than working class African Americans of lower socioeconomic statuses. Further, although not every college student comes from a middle class background, research reveals a college degree is a pathway to middle class standing for African Americans.[12] Thus, we feel that developing an understanding of how Black college students feel about police in college could not only improve their interactions with law enforcement officers while pursuing an education but also could provide hope for better interactions with police and those Black students who matriculate and enter the middle class.

This chapter will examine how the legacy of maltreatment of people of African descent in America relates to the excessive force police use against African Americans, which is currently at the apex of public consciousness. This topic is important for two major reasons. First, although scholars are beginning to increase their coverage of the brutal treatment of African Americans by law enforcement, this topic has generally received little scholarly attention.[13] Second, there is a lack of adequate attention to remedying disparate treatment of African Americans by police officers, which emerges from a larger subtext of marginalization. Given the promulgation that America is now a post-racial society, in which race no longer matters,[14] the following questions were foundational to the current work: (1) What are the socio-historical roots of the "othering" of African Americans?; (2) How can the aforementioned serve to de-sensitize the public to the increased use of excessive force by law enforcement against African Americans?

In the section that follows, we situate our objectives within the extant literature. To accomplish this, we examine several intellectual precedents to the maltreatment of African Americans. In other words, we look into social and historical events in which Black people are victims of unfair treatment in order to buttress the historical mistreatment of Black people since their modern contact with Europeans. First, we will delve into the marginalization of African Americans in America. Then, we explore the racial and social control of Black bodies as well as why this problem persists. Third, we provide an overview of Africa as the birthplace of humanity. The aforementioned will highlight the socio-historical importance of the fall from grace experienced by people of African descent across the diaspora. Fourth, we look at European colonialism and imperialism. It is here where one can find some of the first examples of the use of excessive force against Black people by law

enforcement outside of the United States. Fifth, we review the tumultuous
enslavement of African Americans. This history is important because plantation overseers (which we will cover more extensively in chapter 2) are the
predecessors of modern police officers.

CRITICAL RACE THEORY (CRT)

Critical Race Theory is the theoretical framework for this erudition. This
theoretical foundation is appropriate as our study investigates the excessive
force categorically used against African Americans by police officers and
recognizes excessive force as a social problem that fosters racial and social
inequity. Derrick Bell, the late legal scholar and father of Critical Race
Theory (CRT) believes racial discrimination weakens the quality of African
American life. In his seminal work, *Faces at the Bottom of the Well*, Bell[15]
says the following regarding the perniciousness of racism against African
Americans:

> Indeed, the racism that made slavery feasible is far from dead in the last
> decade of the twentieth century America; and the civil rights gains, so hard
> won are being sadly eroded. Despite undeniable progress for many, no African
> Americans are insulated from incidents of racial discrimination. Our careers,
> even our lives, are threatened because of our color (Bell 1992, 3).

Thus, racism undergirds the racialized control of Black bodies through
excessive police force. Thus, if one comprehends the extent of racism and its
manifestations, then the rationale behind excessive force is more coherent.
Further, CRT is amenable to the treatment of maligned groups due to its five
areas of focus: (1) the primacy of race and racism and their interconnected-
ness with other forms of subordination; (2) a questioning of the dominant
belief ideology/status quo; (3) a commitment to social justice; (4) the central-
ity of experiential knowledge; and (5) an interdisciplinary perspective.[16]
Moreover, we use CRT in this book to discern why police frequently are
involved in yet not severely punished for engaging in acts of excessive force
against African Americans, how African Americans view police, and how
both African American and White college students view police in general.

Why Are African Americans Marginalized?

Marginalization is denying an individual or group complete social acceptance. It encompasses treatment as an "other" or being subject to "othering"
accompanied by treatment outside the norm.[17] As recipients of historical
stigma and discrimination, African Americans rarely receive the empathy
and deference given to other groups, especially during tragic situations.

Thus, when a law enforcement officer executes an unarmed African American, it does not engender widespread outrage outside of the African American community.[18]

As we previously allude, the marginalization of African Americans has an extensive history. The marginalization of Black Americans is so visceral that when participating in studies designed to identify the color of a criminal, Blacks and Whites report seeing a Black criminal when there was no criminal present.[19] Sadly, even after knowing African Americans are disproportionate heirs of capital punishment, Whites are still more likely to approve of this form of punishment.[20]

In their 2016 study of homicides involving police against unarmed Black males, Pratt-Harris et al. offer findings that crystallize the many problems that can emerge, given the disparate treatment of African Americans. Specifically, these scholars place in context, biased assessments of law enforcement, practices, and descriptions of their contacts involving lethal force with Black males. First, such encounters strengthen society's racist views of Black males. Second, it increases the institutionalization of deadly force against Black males. Third, it greatly minimizes the likelihood that discriminatory practices against African Americans are evidence of systemic racism, discrimination, and White supremacy.

What is White Supremacy? White Supremacy is defined "as an historically based, institutionally perpetuated system of exploitation and oppression of continents, nations, and peoples classified as 'non-White' by continents, nations, and peoples who, by virtue of their White (light) skin pigmentation and/or ancestral origin from Europe, classify themselves as White."[21] Essentially, White Supremacy is the notion that the values, beliefs, attitudes, and behaviors of White people are superior to those of non-White people.

The appalling treatment of people of African descent in America is not a new phenomenon. However, the Black community frequently dismisses the extent that school textbooks support the marginalization of Black people.[22] Linter's[23] examination of American textbooks finds these books generally communicate the narrative of African Americans, along with those of other relatively powerless groups, in a manner that foments biases and stereotypes. He postulates that history represents an amalgamation of fact and fiction and classrooms and curricula become invaluable tools to promote hegemony and supremacy. Thus, since Whites control most American school systems, most teachers, and most school curricula, the aforementioned reinforce White Supremacy.

In her fascinating work, *Right to Be Hostile: Schools, Prisons, and the Making of Public Enemies,* Erica Meiners[24] critically examines how schools disregard Black children and place them on a trajectory culminating in a "school to prison" pipeline which feeds mass incarceration, and the prison industrial complex (PIC), decimates families, and weakens communities.

The destructive process of mistreatment in schools, along with the reciprocal relationship between schools and jails produces what Meiners[25] refers to as "ontological choreography." The phrase "Ontological choreography" illustrates the creation of a "disposable" species, which is expendable to the extent their extermination is natural. Consequently, this is what schools do to Black students, precipitating a "right to be hostile."

Similar to schools, the mass media is a powerful agent of socialization. In fact, the mass media wields such power that even when the projected images of a group do not align with official statistics (e.g., arrest statistics of Blacks) they are believed and accepted as real.[26] Negative depictions of Blacks in the media support beliefs in the minds of Whites that Blacks are predisposed to criminality and deserve ill-treatment from law enforcement.[27]

One of the most widely cited examples of the beginning of pejorative depictions of African Americans was D. W. Griffith's *Birth of a Nation* (1915). In this film, lauded as a cinematic masterpiece of its day, depicts Black men as brutes, lazy drunkards, and criminals whose sole intent was to engage in deviance and rape White women.[28] Hence, according to the film, the salvation of America can only occur via the Ku Klux Klan. Not surprisingly, both Klan membership and the lynching of Blacks increase after release of the film.[29] The undesirable delineations of Blacks, and Black men in particular, were so widely accepted that reportedly in a private screening of the film (*Birth of a Nation* 1915), then President Woodrow Wilson characterized it as history written in lightning.[30]

In a random survey of non-student adult residents to determine whether exposure to network news has an effect on racial attitudes and perceptions of African Americans, Dixon[31] reveals startling findings. Specifically, his research elucidates that network news programming reinforces the view that African Americans are intimidating which correlates with higher racism scores in a sample of Whites, Blacks, and Latinos. Finally, the author suggests that the reactions of respondents to news coverage of African Americans were possibly the product of selective exposure and perception. Selective exposure and perception refer to the notion that viewers selectively focus on information that supports their prejudicial views of African Americans.

Sadly, the "Big, Black, Criminal Brute" trope exists today. Recently, "Mission Impossible" actor Ving Rhames said California police officers pulled a gun on him in his own home after a neighbor called 911 to report a "large black man" breaking in. This Black actor, who has an accomplished resume in television and movies,[32] said he was in his Santa Monica home wearing basketball shorts when officers confronted him with their guns drawn. According to Rhames, "I open the door [and] there's a red dot pointed at my face from a 9 mm, and they say, 'Put up your hands!'" What was especially noteworthy about this incident was that Rhames' neighbors called police because "they noticed a large African American man entering the home" and assumed that he was burglarizing the home.[33]

Research by Dixon[34] lends support to Armour's[35] notion of Negrophobia, which is an unreasonable fear of African Americans. First, since America is still residentially segregated, interpersonal contact between Blacks and Whites in non-occupational settings is often nominal at best. Second, because substantial interpersonal contact is minimal, the actual communication to negate trepidation is absent.[36] Third, since crime is an intra-racial phenomenon, Whites may be less likely to experience alarm at the sight of other Whites, who are actually more likely than Blacks to inflict harm on them than Blacks are. Finally, reality-based crime shows (e.g., *First 48, Lockdown*) depict Blacks as criminals at levels disparate to their actual levels of criminality in the larger society. This is important because media images are often real in the minds and hearts of viewers.[37] Consequently, society becomes desensitized to Black deaths.

Disproportionately negative media images substantially contribute to perceptual divides regarding the treatment of Blacks by police. "According to a Pew center poll, twice as many Blacks as Whites say African Americans are subjected to mistreatment by police."[38] The discernment gap also exists in regards to views of mistreatments within the American court system. Pejorative media images of peoples of African descent (i.e., Black people), extend outside the continental United States. Feagin[39] cites research from Sociologist Nestor Rodriquez who conducted in-depth interviews with recent immigrants to the United States from Latin America. The results of the study elucidate the impact of the U.S. mass media machine's portrayal of its Black citizens. Particularly, when he queried his subjects on their anti-Black views, they reveal they learned about Blacks from U.S. movies.

In his tome, *Racist America: Roots, Current Realities, and Future Reparations*, Joe Feagin[40] provides a poignant examination into the effect of the pernicious mass media caricatures of Black people on the American psyche. He posits that such representations amount to what he refers to as "sincere fictions."[41] Sincere fictions are synonymous to the promotion of negative stereotypes while simultaneously advocating romanticized ideals of Whiteness. The former dehumanizes Blacks while the latter reinforces White supremacy. To illustrate, he delineates the portrayal of these "sincere fictions" in movies. For instance, between the 1920s and 1940s more than seventy-five films present the enslavement of African Americans as morally-beneficial for them. Examples of American classic movies that endorse the aforementioned are *Gone with the Wind* (1939) and the *Littlest Rebel* (1935) which disseminates images of Blacks as "happy" in subordinate, demeaning, or subservient roles.

In "The Invisible Weight of Whiteness: The Racial Grammar of Everyday Life in America," sociologist Eduardo Bonilla-Silva[42] contends less than favorable portrayals of Blacks in movies and television sitcoms is consistent with a racial grammar that essentially "others" African Americans, which in turn, makes it difficult for them to attain social acceptance. Thus, racial grammar manifests itself in several ways. First, the prevailing racial grammar upholds the underrepresentation of Blacks in movies and television in self-affirming roles. Second, when minorities appear in movies they frequently appear as what Bonilla-Silva[43] characterizes as "magical negroes" or Blacks who are endowed with some sort of special power. However, the only time the special power the "magical negro" possesses is to help traverse White lives. For example, Will Smith plays the role of a "magical negro" in the movie *Hancock*.[44] In the movie, Smith is a superhero, who although being a flawed alcoholic, makes it his mission to help a White couple with their problems.[45] Another example of how Blacks maintain a 'racialized grammar' is by appearing as "buffoons" or "thugs" (Bonilla-Silva 2012). An illustration of the buffoon character is present in the commercially successful film, *The Blind Side*.[46] In this movie, based on the book *The Blind Side: Evolution of a Game* (2007), Michael Lewis relates a semi-biographical tale of the life of current professional football player, Michael Oher. To summarize, all tribulations Oher encounters in his life receive immediate resolution when his White family legally adopts him. Thus, reinforcement of the helpless "buffoon" and "White savior" tropes are inherently prominent.

Finally, Bonilla-Silva[47] asserts the plots of film and television shows: (1) reinforce racial boundaries; (2) uphold the racial status quo; and (3) present a felicitous view of racial affairs. As a result, the marginalization of Blacks becomes normal; a part of the "social fabric" of American life, and thus, Black life becomes expendable.

Why "White on White Crime" Is Not Criminal

A familiar phrase to most Americans is "Black on Black crime," however; the term "White on White crime" is rarely used. This paradox becomes even more complex when one recognizes that crime is largely an intra-racial phenomenon. Despite the fact that "Black on Black crime" is a common theme in criminological literature (i.e., that crime is an intra-racial phenomenon, even when it comes to violent crime), "White on White crime" is generally not part of the American lexicon.[48]

In terms of violent crimes, despite stereotypes and implicit biases, studies reveal that even though Blacks tend to represent the prototypical violent criminals, Whites have only themselves to fear regarding violent crime victimization.[49] Case in point: A study by Becker[50] posits when crimes are intra-racial, economics is the motivation. The study showed when examining racial salience scores, 37.3 percent of robberies were intra-racial while 72 percent of aggravated assaults were intra-racial. Consequently, despite these scholarly findings, Whites still have an irrational fear of being victims of a violent death, at the hands of Blacks.[51]

To elucidate the disparate impact of not crediting Whites with their fair share of criminality and, its associated stigmatization, a 2010 survey displays White Americans overestimate the proportion of crime committed by people of color by embellishing their share of burglaries, illegal drug sales, and juvenile crime by 20 to 30 percent.[52] In "Crime, Bias, and Statistics," *New York Times* writer Charles Blow[53] highlights two disheartening realities concerning why the non-criminalization of Whites is so problematic. First, although Whites are the least likely racial group to be victims of violent crime, they are more likely to support more punitive crime policies. Second, policy makers' merge of crime and race in their policy initiatives disproportionately affects non-majority group members.

Media characterizations of Black and White victims are starkly different. In their study of the differential media coverage of White crime victims as "angelic," Chaney and Robertson[54] share very interesting findings. First, the authors bring attention to when White male Adam Lanza killed twenty children and six adult staff members at Sandy Hook elementary school in Newtown, Connecticut on December 14, 2012, television and social media promote characterizations of White victims as "angels." Although it is appropriate to grieve the tragic loss of human life, the authors contend Black lives in society do not have the same value. For instance, when the lives of Michael Brown, Trayvon Martin, Jordan Davis, Rekia Boyd, and countless other Black males and females were cut short, media, television, and social media platforms did not characterize them as "angels."[55] In fact, the criminalization and dehumanization of Brown and Martin were so great that many wonder if they were victims. Contrarily, the White perpetrator of the Sandy Hook elementary massacre, Adam Lanza, a twenty-year-old White male, has never been described as a "thug," nor was there widespread speculation regarding how he was reared. Most importantly, the stigma from his heinous crime does not extend to other White men, as is generally the case when a Black person commits a crime.[56]

Second, Chaney and Robertson[57] compare words the media uses to describe the eight Black child victims who died in Chicago in 2012 to the twenty Whites killed in the Sandy Hook Elementary School tragedy. The authors draw attention to how various forms of media (e.g., print, internet, etc.) frequently depict the Sandy Hook victims as "angels." On the other hand, no such words were used to characterize the eight Black fatalities in Chicago, who were age seven or younger. The findings of this work strongly suggest that if loss of White lives evokes an "angelic" nomenclature, Black lives are on the opposing end of that position, and thus, deserving of death.

To add, even professionals indirectly blame Blacks for their criminalization. For instance, the Federal Bureau of Investigation (FBI) director James

B. Comey appears to be guilty of such an offense. In an article published in the *Washington Post,* Comey posits the overall increase in violent crime over forty states in 2015 was at least partially the result of the "Ferguson Effect."[58] The "Ferguson Effect" is essentially the inability of police officers to engage in effective policing because of the protests and formation of the *Black Lives Matter* movement after the murder of unarmed teen Michael Brown in Ferguson, Missouri. The "Ferguson Effect" also encompasses a recalcitrant attitude by officers when citizens videotape them as they perform their duties, which can discourage less aggressive policing, the video going viral, and possibly more protests by citizens across the United States.[59] Conversely, what receives far less support is that fewer police officers lose their lives in the line of duty than in years past and when murdered, Whites kill them.[60] Finally, although the "Ferguson Effect" is a phrase that has gained traction among law enforcement agencies, it did not affect violent crime after the murder of Michael Brown in Ferguson, Missouri. However, after Freddie Gray died in police custody in 2015, there has been an increase in violent crime, which aptly has the term, the "Gray Effect."[61]

Black Children Do Not Have the Luxury of Being Children

Throughout this chapter, a consistent theme is that Black lives have less value than White lives. Evidence for this assertion has support in statistical research relating to the following disparities between Blacks and Whites: (1) mass/hyper-incarceration; (2) income/wealth inequality; (3) school quality; and (4) drug arrests, etc.[62]

In a study of perceptions of 176 police officers, Goff et al. (2014) reveals officers are more likely to view Black children as older as and less innocent than they do White children. Ostensibly, viewing Black children in such a manner justifies in the minds of some why Black children are disproportionately more likely than other ethnicities to be on the wrong end of police violence. Moreover, researchers established the Black/ape trope predicts actual disparities in police violence toward children. Likewise, it should not come as a surprise that when Black youths commit crimes, they are eighteen times more likely to receive sentences as adults than White children are.[63]

A poignant example of the devaluation of Black life is the case of Harambee, a 450-pound silverback Gorilla, shot to death on May 28, 2016 by a Cincinnati, Ohio zoo official after a three-year-old African American boy fell into his enclosure.[64] The child's mother, Michelle Grey, 32, shortly turned her head while tending to her other young children who accompanied her to the zoo, when her three-year-old son fell into the enclosure and into the exhibit.[65] After falling into the exhibit, this gorilla pulls the child across a moat, which reportedly gave the child a slight concussion. Furthermore, for ten minutes, the gorilla tossed the boy, stared at him, and ignored the special calls from his handlers to leave the area. To ensure the safety of the child, zoo director Zane Maynard makes the decision to kill seventeen-year-old Harambee. While many Americans question why Harambee was not simply tranquilized by zoo officials, most are unaware that attempting to sedate an irritated silverback could have easily resulted in the animal killing the child. Stated another way, the tranquilizer would have taken too long and the child could have been fatally injured before the drug took effect. [66]

On the surface, the Harambee incident may not appear to be an example of the disregard of Black lives. However, when we examine the enormous amount of public sympathy for Harambee, a gorilla, compared to virtually no sympathy for Black parents and their endangered children, we have ample evidence of the lack of collective public concern for Black adults and children. However, in an article that appeared in the online publication, the *Root*, journalist Kirsten West-Savali presents compelling information to buttress the assumption that Black children's lives have more value than that of a silverback gorilla. Savali [67] makes several thought-provoking points to give credence to the devaluation of Black life. First, the author elucidates how parents of all races have criticized both parents of the three-year-old African American child for their perceived negligence. What makes the aforementioned even more insidious is that although the child's father was not even present during the zoo visit, the media saw fit to publish his criminal record. Second, Sheila Hurt, resident of Cincinnati, went to great lengths to create a Change.org petition to garner support for filing charges against the parents, which acquired over 500,000 signatures.

Third, she reveals how twelve-year-old Tamir Rice was fatally shot in under two seconds because officers allege his toy gun was an actual one. Although Ohio is an open-carry state, Rice's parents are blamed for his death, and not the police. Similarly, the author alludes to the cases of Aiyanna Stanley-Jones, Michael Brown, Eric Garner, and Akai Gurley. Each of these cases involve African Americans, both children (Stanley-Jones and Brown) and adults (Garner and Gurley). Moreover, the shooting of seven-year-old Aiyana Stanley-Jones in the head occurs because the officer says he feared for his life. Jones' parents are the targets of blame even though the police were exercising a no-knock raid and were looking for someone who was not in the house. Another example is the fatal shooting of the unarmed Michael Brown in Ferguson Missouri occurred when Darren Wilson, a police officer kills him. Eric Garner was unarmed and died while being choked by New York police department officer Daniel Pantaleo for allegedly selling loose cigarettes (but he was actually breaking up a fight) who applies a hold that has been outlawed by the department for over 20 years. NYPD Officer, Peter Liang, shoots and kills Akai Gurley in a dark stairwell after pushing a door open; however, when Liang's weapon (9 mm glock) discharges, the shot ricochets from the wall, and hits Gurley in the chest. Gurley then runs a few feet and falls in a pool of his own blood. Sadly, instead of assisting Gurley's girlfriend in administering CPR to a dying Gurley, Liang and his partner spent the next five minutes texting his Patrolman's Benevolent Association (PBA) delegate supposedly in an attempt to conjure up an acceptable explanation for the shooting, and never once called their supervisor or 911 for an ambulance. Despite receiving a conviction of manslaughter, upon the recommendation of New York District Attorney Peter Thompson to not receive jail time, Judge Danny Chun only sentenced Liang to 5 years' probation and 800 hours of community service.[68] To add further insult and injury to Gurley's family, the media publicized Gurley's criminal record, even though he was unarmed when he was shot and killed.

Although Gurley and Garner were not children, Stanley-Jones, Rice, and Brown were. Even though there are cases when a law enforcement officer points a gun at a Black child and a fatality does not occur,[69] the reality is that victims and their loved ones receive blame for their deaths. The aforementioned suggest several realities in regards to not allowing Black children to enjoy the innocence associated with childhood like children of other races. First, Black people are dehumanized and are not provided the privilege of being seen as human beings. When unarmed children are shot and killed and are then somehow blamed for their own deaths, we must question who is and is not valued in society.

Second, which relates to the first point, when they are forced to endure the negative media treatment of having their victimized children maligned and vilified in the public eye, the surviving family members do not receive the same empathy as murdered White children generally receive. In their article on the media coverage on the victims of the Sandy Hook massacre, Chaney and Robertson[70] clearly delineate the differential media treatment of Black and White child victims. Regardless of the circumstances in which they meet their demise, Black children never receive such glowing and affectionate terms as "angels." Chaney and Robertson emphasize the word "angels" is code for the superior physical characteristics, intellect, and character of White life and the inferior value of Black life. This assertion has intellectual grit when one considers the word "angels" never describes Black children who lose their lives. These scholars provide the following assertion:

> Clearly, the "angelic" status attributed to the White child victims of Sandy Hook Elementary School is a constant reminder of the societal (e.g., race, skin tone, and socioeconomic) privilege generally enjoyed by these children. However, Black life is just as important as White life, the untimely deaths of all children are tragic and the families, friends, and communities of all children suffer in unimaginable ways, and thus need support for the grief they have experienced (Malcolm, 2010). While the media has provided abundant support for the Sandy Hook Elementary School community, it is time for the media to minimize the grief and contribute to the healing of Black individuals, families,

and communities by creating a new narrative surrounding the death of poor, Black children in the inner-city. After learning about and showcasing the joys, pain, and lives of these children, their families, and communities, perhaps the day will soon come when the media will, like their Sandy Hook Elementary counterparts, also publicly refer to poor Black children in the inner city as "angels."[71]

Further victimization of Black children and their families occurs when the public actively seeks every negative or questionable occurrence in their life and broadcasts it. Case in point: While Trayvon Martin's school suspensions are open to the public, none of George Zimmerman's prior brushes with the law, which include an assault on a police officer, publicly vilifies him.[72] Hence, the perpetrator with a criminal record (Zimmerman) receives a certain amount of dignity that the Black child victim (Martin) did not.

Finally, Ellawala's[73] work comments on how dehumanization reveals secondary emotions (e.g., jealousy, sympathy, and hope), which are recognized as distinguishing humans from non-humans, are consistently denied to those who do not belong to one's social group (out group members) and preferentially attributed to one's group. This finding elucidates that regardless of the circumstances, there is no public recognition of Black children as "angels" when police tragically murder them. Essentially, this lack of regard after death sends a strong message to African Americans that their lives have no value.

Rattan et al.[74] tackles the fragility of the distinctions between juveniles and adults when race is considered. When comparing White and Black juvenile offenders, these authors find participants view Black juveniles as significantly more similar to adults than White juvenile offenders. Moreover, this distinction results in participant support for harsher juvenile sanctions, which invariably affects the treatment of Black juveniles in the criminal justice system. Consequently, the study also reveals the likelihood that when societal members are indoctrinated with less than favorable images of African Americans, along with racially coded language in reference to African Americans, such exposure can influence judges' and juries' perception of culpability and the punitive sentences they mete out. As a result, in the minds of many Americans, the lives of Black adults and Black children have no value, and thus, do not matter.

To deny Black children the innocence typically associated with childhood can have dire consequences for a presumably civilized society. Waytz and Schroeder[75] describe the subjugation of Black children as "dehumanization by omission." Basically, "dehumanization by omission" is a passive process whereby people fail to recognize others' fundamentally human mental capacities, as opposed to denying these capacities overtly. We believe this formulation of dehumanization is a good fit to describe the process whereby the public denigrates Black children murdered by law enforcement. Waytz and Schroeder also speak of "dehumanization by commission." Ultimately, "dehumanization by commission" emerges from desires to differentiate from among one's outgroups. Now, one could suggest that both forms of dehumanization, by omission and commission, are applicable to the dilemmas, which belie Black youths killed by law enforcement. However, dehumanization by omission fits best because when polled regarding race issues, White Americans claim to be colorblind yet do nothing to counter or even recognize the persistent belittling of Black child victims of police violence.[76] Further, Waytz and Schroeder posit both forms of dehumanization can occur consciously and unconsciously. However, they differ in regards to the manner in which they are rooted in one of two process: (1) the dynamic process of denying consideration of others' minds; (2) or a passive failure to consider others' minds. Essentially, this means that Whites can pretend to be oblivious to the dehumanization of Black children when law enforcement or those who act as law enforcement (i.e., George Zimmerman), assuage their conscience, and go on with their lives as normal.

In the article "Police Racial Violence: Lessons from Social Psychology" Richardson[77] provides compelling evidence regarding why the lives of Black children and adults is devalued when they are murdered by police. First, the author contends that the influence of implicit racial biases, stereotype threat, along with masculinity threat, are inevitable even in the absence of conscious racial bias. Second, officers are frequently not in situations where their interactions with non-White citizens are positive. Therefore, negative thoughts that officers may have of Black citizens may flourish which can manifest themselves in negative actions. Third, police departments often lean toward aggressive, proactive policing which emphasizes arrest and asset-forfeiture over forming relationships with community members. In addition, police training initiatives, which underscore forming a positive relationship with residents of marginalized communities, are eschewed as "social work" by officers and not "real" policing. Fourth, officers designated to patrol communities of color realize that residents view them as "illegitimate." Such assessments lead many officers to almost "demand" respect and place a premium on "taking charge of the situation" upon encountering citizens, especially Black youths. This can result in escalating instead of deescalating a potentially volatile encounter. Finally, despite the fact that fostering collegial relations with the Black community can reduce violent confrontations, officers tend to stigmatize these aspects of their professions that they view as "social work." As a result, there does not appear to be much optimism on the horizon regarding police allowing Black children to be "children."

BLACK PEOPLE IN AMERICA:
A LEGACY OF MALTREATMENT: A SUMMARY

The legacy of maltreatment of African Americans during their sojourn in America continues to manifest itself in the form of rampant police use of excessive force. In 1951, the The Civil Rights Congress (CRC) printed a 237-page petition to the United States titled "We Charge Genocide: The Crime of the Government against the Negro People." The document, signed by African American luminaries like Paul Robeson, W. E. B. Du Bois, Benjamin Davis Jr., and Clyde Jones, had a goal to explicate the government's complicit nature in regards to its genocidal treatment of its Black citizens. The text includes the following indignities as genocide: lynchings, poll taxes, healthcare disparities, and, most importantly, rampant unchecked police brutality. Ultimately, presentation of the paper occurs during the United Nations' meetings in Paris in December 1951. Not surprisingly, neither the American government nor White American journalists embrace the paper, accusing it of embellishing the amount of racism that actually exists in the United States. Moreover, consistent with both the social fabric and political tenor of the time, it was a subversive document inspired by communist elements.

The 1951 report is important for not only establishing a record of dissatisfaction by African Americans with their treatment in the United States, but also illustrating that the same problems have persisted for a substantial period. Specifically, when it comes to the use of excessive force by police against Black people, it proves that its occurrence has become firmly entrenched within American culture. It also reveals a reluctance to implement viable solutions to this problem.

In this introduction, we discussed the marginalization of African Americans. Likewise, we examined a history of Black devaluation that is as old as the existence of African Americans in America. Black Americans, from Sambos to Negroes to African Americans have existed outside of the realm of social acceptance, virtually a state of perpetual inertia when it comes to treatment similar to non-Black Americans. In all of society's institutions, particularly within schools and courts, such treatment systematically supports and justifies the disparate treatment of people of African descent.

In the same way, the American media has propagated the idea that "Black Lives Should Not Matter." Americans receive a daily dose of reality-based crime shows that disproportionately portray Blacks as deviants (i.e., robbers, drug-dealers, rapists, murders). The aforementioned is so great that it actually outpaces the genuine criminality of Black people in the larger society. Further, Black people are victims of high profile cases of police use of excessive force, such as Akai Gurley, Rekia Boyd, Philando Castile, Terrence Crutcher, Walter Scott, and countless others, and the media highlights any negative factor/incident in their backgrounds. Contrarily, the background records of "killer cops" largely remain anonymous to the public.[78]

Even when they are victims of bad policing, Black children do not enjoy the innocence that comes with childhood, and usually the Black child and his or her parents receive blame for their deaths. Case in point: When members of the Cleveland Police Department murder 12-year old Tamir Rice, who is playing with a toy gun in a park, he receives the description as an adult with a physical size that was large for his age. Not surprisingly, the heinous nature of Rice's killing by the Cleveland Police Department receives little attention.

The treatment of African Americans as second-class citizens has a long and disturbing history that does not appear to be close to subsiding anytime in the near future. On August 26, 2016, then San Francisco 49ers quarterback Colin Kaepernick refuses to stand for the national anthem before a preseason game against the Green Bay Packers. During an interview after the game, Kaepernick asserts he did not want to show pride in a flag that oppresses Black people and other people of color. He also intimates the oppression entails not holding police officers accountable for killing Black people by giving them "paid leave." However, instead of receiving praise for exercising his constitutional right to protest, some National Football League players and executives accused Kaepernick of being un-American, and he even loses some of his off-field endorsements. On the positive side, Kaepernick receives support from some current and former players and many veterans, and pledged to donate his first one million dollars along with profits from the skyrocketing sales of his jersey to community groups emphasizing social justice.[79]

Ultimately, Kaepernick modifies his protest from sitting to kneeling, which he did to respect veterans. Yet, what was the least discussed aspect of his protest was the fact that the majority of Americans do not seriously discuss police brutality against African Americans. Clearly, Americans did not express concern that Kaepernick did not stand for a national anthem written by a slave owner, Francis Scott Key, who was celebrating the killing of slaves in the song, than the larger problem of murders by African Americans at the hands of police. Hence, the legacy of maltreatment of Black people in America continues.

NOTES

1. Cleaver, Kathleen and George Katsiaficas C. *Liberation, imagination and The Black Panthers and their Legacy.* New York: Routledge, 2014. Spencer, Robyn Ceanne. "Engendering the Black Freedom Struggle: Revolutionary Black Womanhood and the Black Panther Party in the Bay Area, California." *Journal of Women's History* 20, no. 1 (2008): 90–113.

2. McDermott, Maeve."Rudy Guiliani calls Beyonce's Super Bowl Performance 'Attack' on Cops." *USA Today*, February 9, 2016, http://www.usatoday.com/story/life/people/2016/02/08/rudy-giuliani-criticizes-beyonce-super-bowl-formation-attack-on-cops/80018490/.

3. King, Shaun."King: Conservatives Ought to Direct Their Rage Toward Angry White Men-Not Beyonce," *New York Daily News*, February 22, 2016a, http://www.nydailynews.com/news/national/king-white-men-killed-7-8-cops-u-s-year-article-1.2539913.

4. Ibid.

5. Swaine, John, Oliver Laughland, James Lartey, and Ciara McCarthy. "Young Black Men Killed By Police at Highest Rate in Year of 1,134 Deaths," *The Guardian*, December 31, 2015, http://www.theguardian.com/us-news/2015/dec/31/the-counted-police-killings-2015-young-black-men?CMP=share_btn_fb.

6. Ibid.

7. Mbuba, Jospeter M. "Attitudes Toward the Police: The Significance of Race and Other Factors among College Students." *Journal of Ethnicity in Criminal Justice*, 8, no. 3 (2010): 201–215.

8. Kendi, Ibram. *The Black Campus Movement: Black Students and the Racial Reconstitution of Higher Education, 1965–1972.* New York: Palgrave MacMillan Publishers, 2012.

9. Ibid.

10. Landers, Amber J., Rollock, David, Rolfes, Charity B., and Demietrice L. Moore. "Police Contacts and Stress among African American College Students." *American Journal of Orthopsychiatry*, 81, no. 1 (2011): 72–81.

11. Wright, Ronda, Roberson, Kristina, Onsomus, Elijah O., Johnson, Yolanda, Dearman, Cathy, Blackman-Carr, Loneke T., Price, Amanda Alise, and Vanessa Duren-Winfied. "Examining the Relationship between Mindfulness, Perceived Stress, and Blood Pressure in African American College Students." *Journal of Best Practices in Health Professions Diversity: Education, Research, and Policy*, 11, no. 1 (2018): 13–30.

12. Feagin, Joe R. *Racist America: Roots, Current Realities, and Future Reparations.* 3rd edition. New York: Routledge, 2014.

13. Chaney, Cassandra, and Ray V. Robertson. "Can We All Get Along? Blacks' Historical and Contemporary (In)Justice with Law Enforcement." *Western Journal of Black Studies*, 38, no. 2 (2014): 108–122. Walker, April. "Racial Profiling-Separate and Unequal Keeping the Minorities in Line-the Role of Law Enforcement in America." *St. Thomas Law Review* 23, no. 4 (2011): 576–619.

14. Aymer, Samuel R. "'I can't breathe': A case study—Helping Black men cope with race-related trauma stemming from police killing and brutality." *Journal of Human Behavior in the Social Environment* 26, no. 3–4 (2016): 367–376. Brunson, Rod K. "Police don't like Black People": African-American Young Men's Accumulated Police Experiences." *Criminology and Public Policy* 6, no. 1 (2007): 71–101.

15. Bell, Derrick. *Faces at the Bottom of the Well: The Permanence of Racism.* New York, NY: Basic Books, 1992.

16. Crenshaw, Kimberle. "20 Years of Critical Race Theory: Looking Back to Move Forward." *Connecticut Law Review* 43, no. 5 (2011): 1253–1352. Solorzano, Daniel, Miguel Ceja, and Tara Yosso. "Critical Race Theory, Racial Microaggressions, and Campus Racial Climate: The Experiences of African American College Students." *Journal of Negro Education* 69, no. ½ (2000): 121–136.

17. Turner, Caroline S. "Incorporation and Marginalization in the Academy From Border Toward Center for Faculty of Color?." *Journal of Black Studies* 34, no. 1 (2003): 112–125. Villenas, Sofia. "The Colonizer/Colonized Chicana Ethnographer: Identity, Marginalization, and Co-Optation in The Field." *Harvard Educational Review* 66, no. 4 (1996): 711–732.

18. Pratt Harris, Natasha C., Michael M. Sinclair, Cynthia B. Bragg, Nicole R. Williams, Kalfani N. Ture, Belinda D. Smith, Isiah Marshall Jr., and Lawrence Brown. "Police-Involved Homicide of Unarmed Black Males: Observations By Black Scholars in The Midst of The April 2015 Baltimore Uprising." *Journal of Human Behavior in the Social Environment* 26, 3–4 (2016): 377–389.

19. Chaney, Cassandra, and Ray V. Robertson. "Racism and Police Brutality in America." *Journal of African American Studies*, 17, no. 4 (2013a): 480–505.

20. Tonry, Michael. *Punishing Race: A Continuing American Dilemma.* New York: Oxford University Press, 2012.

21. Charles, Christopher, and Yaba Blay. "Skin Bleaching and Global White Supremacy." *Journal of Pan African Studies* 4, no. 4 (2011): 4.

22. Loewen, James W. *Lies My Teacher Told Me: Everything Your History Textbooks Got Wrong*. New York: Touchstone, 2007.

23. Linter, Timothy. "Critical Race Theory and the Teaching of American History: Power, Perspective, and Practice." *Social Studies Research and Practice* 2, no. 1 (2007) 103–116.

24. Meiners, Erica R. *Right to Be Hostile: Schools, Prisons, and the Making of Public Enemies*. New York: Routledge, 2007.

25. Ibid.

26. Burrell, Tom. *Brainwashed Challenging the Myth of Black Inferiority*. New York, NY: SmileyBooks, 2010.

27. Dixon, Travis L. "Network News and Racial Beliefs: Exploring the Connection between National Television News Exposure and Stereotypical Perceptions of African Americans." *Journal of Communication* 58, no. 2 (2008): 321–337. Gabbidon, Shaun L. *Criminological Perspectives on Race and Crime*. 2nd Ed. New York: Routledge, 2010.

28. Loewen, James W. *Lies My Teacher Told Me: Everything Your History Textbooks Got Wrong*. New York: Touchstone, 2007.

29. Ibid.

30. Loewen, James W. *Lies My Teacher Told Me: Everything Your History Textbooks Got Wrong*. New York: Touchstone, 2007.

31. Dixon, Travis L. "Network News and Racial Beliefs: Exploring the Connection between National Television News Exposure and Stereotypical Perceptions of African Americans." *Journal of Communication* 58, no. 2 (2008): 321–337.

32. Rhames most notable film roles are Pulp Fiction (1994), Rosewood (1997), Baby Boy (2001), and Dark Blue (2002). He won a Golden Globe for his portrayal of Don King in Don King: Only in America (1997), has starred in all three of the Mission Impossible installment, and has received much critical-acclaim in film and television.

33. Fuhrman, Matthew and Wil Cruz. Ving Rhames says officers pulled their guns on him in his own home, July 28, 2018, Accessed on July 28, 2018, https://abcnews.go.com/US/ving-rhames-officers-pulled-guns-home/story?id=56890288

34. Ibid.

35. Armour, Jody David. *Negrophobia and Unreasonable Racism: The Hidden Costs of Being Black in America*. New York: University Press, 1997.

36. Bonilla-Silva, Eduardo. "The Invisible Weight of Whiteness: The Racial Grammar of Everyday Life in Contemporary America." *Ethnic and Racial Studies* 35, no. 2 (2012): 173–194.

37. Chaney, Cassandra, and Ray V. Robertson. "Media Reporting of the Sandy Hook Elementary School Angels." *The Journal of Pan African Studies*, 5, no. 6 (2013b): 74–114.

38. Cottman, Michael H. "Should the Parents of the Child Who Fell into Gorilla Enclosure Be Charged," BlackAmericaWeb.com, May 31, 2016. http://blackamericaweb.com/2016/05/31/should-the-parents-of-the-child-who-fell-into-gorilla-enclosure-be-charged/

39. Ibid.

40. Feagin, Joe R. *Racist America: Roots, Current Realities, and Future Reparations*. 3rd ed. New York: Routledge, 2014.

41. Ibid.

42. Bonilla-Silva, Eduardo. "The Invisible Weight of Whiteness: The Racial Grammar of Everyday Life in Contemporary America." *Ethnic and Racial Studies* 35, no. 2 (2012): 173–194.

43. Ibid.

44. *Hancock*. Directed by Peter Berg. Culver City, CA: Overbrook Entertainment, 2008.

45. Bonilla-Silva, Eduardo. "The Invisible Weight of Whiteness: The Racial Grammar of Everyday Life in Contemporary America." *Ethnic and Racial Studies* 35, no. 2 (2012): 173–194.

46. *The Blind Side*. Directed by John Lee Hancock. Los Angeles, CA: Alcon Entertainment, 2009.

47. Bonilla-Silva, Eduardo, 2012.

48. Feldmeyer, Ben and Darrell Steffensmeier. "Immigration Effects on Homicide Offending for Total and Race/Ethnicity-Disaggregated Populations (White, Black, and Latino)." *Homicide Studies* 13, no. 3 (2009): 211–226. Hall, Allison V., Perry, Jamie L., and Erika V. Hall. "Black and Blue: Exploring Racial Bias and Law Enforcement in the Killings of Unarmed Black Male Civilians." *American Psychologist* 71, no. 3 (2016): 175–186.

49. Tonry, Michael. *Punishing Race: A Continuing American Dilemma.* New York: Oxford University Press, 2012.

50. Becker, Sarah. "Race and Violent Offender Propensity: Does the Intraracial Nature of Violent Crime Persist On the Local Level?" *Justice Research and Policy* 9, no. 2 (2007): 53–86.

51. Bloom, Lisa. *Suspicion Nation: The Inside Story of the Trayvon Martin Injustice and Why We Continue to Repeat it.* Berkeley, CA: Counterpoint, 2014.

52. Blow, Charles M. "Crime, Bias, and Statistics," *The New York Times*, September 7, 2014.   http://www.nytimes.com/2014/09/08/opinion/charles-blow-crime-bias-and-statistics.html?_r=0.

53. Blow, Charles M. "Crime, Bias, and Statistics," *The New York Times*, September 7, 2014.   http://www.nytimes.com/2014/09/08/opinion/charles-blow-crime-bias-and-statistics.html?_r=0.

54. Chaney, Cassandra, and Ray V. Robertson. "Media Reporting of the Sandy Hook Elementary School Angels." *The Journal of Pan African Studies*, 5, no. 6 (2013b): 74–114.

55. Bloom, Lisa. *Suspicion Nation: The Inside Story of the Trayvon Martin Injustice and Why We Continue to Repeat it.* Berkeley, CA: Counterpoint, 2014.

56. Dixon, Travis L. "Network News and Racial Beliefs: Exploring the Connection between National Television News Exposure and Stereotypical Perceptions of African Americans." *Journal of Communication* 58, no. 2 (2008): 321–337.

57. Chaney, Cassandra, and Ray V. Robertson. "Media Reporting of the Sandy Hook Elementary School Angels." *The Journal of Pan African Studies*, 5, no. 6 (2013b): 74–114.

58. Kenney, Tanasia. "FBI Director Claims the 'Ferguson Effect' and Black Lives Matter Are To Blame For the Rise in Violent Crimes. . . . Again," *Atlanta Blackstar*, May 13, 2016. http://atlantablackstar.com/2016/05/13/fbi-director-claims-the-ferguson-effect-and-black-lives-matter-are-to-blame-for-the-rise-in-violent-crimes-again/.

59. Kenney, Tanasia. "FBI Director Claims the 'Ferguson Effect' and Black Lives Matter Are To Blame For the Rise in Violent Crimes. . . . Again," *Atlanta Blackstar*, May 13, 2016. http://atlantablackstar.com/2016/05/13/fbi-director-claims-the-ferguson-effect-and-black-lives-matter-are-to-blame-for-the-rise-in-violent-crimes-again/; Mac Donald, 2016.

60. King, Shaun."King: White Men Killed More American Police than any other Group, But Conservatives will not Address the Facts," *New York Daily News*, May 11, 2016b. http://www.nydailynews.com/news/national/king-cops-killed-white-men-conservatives-silent-article-1.2632965 . Balko, Radley. "Once again: There is no 'War on Cops' and those who claim otherwise are Playing a Dangerous Game," *The Washington Post*, September 10, 2015. https://www.washingtonpost.com/news/the-watch/wp/2015/09/10/once-again-there-is-no-war-on-cops-and-those-who-claim-otherwise-are-playing-a-dangerous-game/.

61. Woods, Baynard. "'Ferguson Effect' Did Not Impact Crime in Baltimore-But 'Gray Effect' May Have," *The Guardian*, March 15, 2016. http://www.theguardian.com/us-news/2016/mar/15/ferguson-effect-baltimore-freddie-gray-effect-crime.

62. Bonilla-Silva, Eduardo. *Racism without Racists: Color-Blind Racism and the Persistence of Racial Inequality in America.* 4th ed. Lanham, MD: Rowman & Littlefield, 2014. Feagin, Joe. R. *Racist America: Roots, Current Realities, and Future Reparations.* 3rd ed. New York: Routledge, 2014.

63. Poe-Yamagata, Eileen. *And justice for some: Differential treatment of minority youth in the justice system.* DIANE Publishing, 2009.

64. Park, Madison, and Holly Yan. "Gorilla Killing: 3 Year-Old Boy's Mother Won't be Charged," *CNN*, June 6, 2016. http://www.cnn.com/2016/06/06/us/harambe-gorilla-death-investigation/

65. Cottman, Michael H. "Should the Parents of the Child Who Fell into Gorilla Enclosure Be Charged," BlackAmericaWeb.com, May 31, 2016. http://blackamericaweb.com/2016/05/

31/should-the-parents-of-the-child-who-fell-into-gorilla-enclosure-be-charged/. Park, Madison, Grinberg, Emanuella, and Tiffany Ap. "'We'd Make the Same Decision,' Zoo Director Says of Gorilla Shooting," *CNN*, May 31, 2016. http://www.cnn.com/2016/05/30/us/gorilla-shot-harambe/

66. Cottman, Michael H. "Should the Parents of the Child Who Fell into Gorilla Enclosure Be Charged," BlackAmericaWeb.com, May 31, 2016. http://blackamericaweb.com/2016/05/31/should-the-parents-of-the-child-who-fell-into-gorilla-enclosure-be-charged/

67. Savali, Kirsten W. "Racists Prove That They Care More About Gorillas Than Black Children," *The Root*, June 1, 2016, http://www.theroot.com/articles/culture/2016/06/harambe-cincinnati-zoo-black-children/

68. Feuer, Alan. "Ex-New York Officer gets 5 years of Probation in Fatal Brooklyn Shooting," *The New York Times*, April 19, 2016. https://www.nytimes.com/2016/04/20/nyregion/peter-liang-ex-new-york-police-officer-sentenced-akai-gurley-shooting-death-brooklyn.html

69. The City of Chicago recently settled a multimillion-dollar suit with the family of Davianna Simmons because the Chicago Police Department pointed a loaded gun at the then three-year-old, during a raid on her grandparents' home on August 29, 2013.

70. Chaney, Cassandra, and Ray V. Robertson. "Media Reporting of the Sandy Hook Elementary School Angels." *The Journal of Pan African Studies*, 5, no. 6 (2013b): 74–114.

71. Ibid, 104.

72. Bloom, Lisa. *Suspicion Nation: The Inside Story of the Trayvon Martin Injustice and Why We Continue to Repeat it*. Berkeley, CA: Counterpoint, 2014.

73. Ellawala, Themal. "Pulling the Trigger: Dehumanization of African Americans and Police Violence." *Scholarly Undergraduate Research Journal at Clark University* 2, no. 1 (2016): 2–8.

74. Rattan, Aneeta, Levine, Cynthia S., Dweck, Carol S., and Jennifer L. Eberhardt. "Race and the Fragility of the Legal Distinctions between Juveniles and Adults." *PloS One* 7, no. 5 (2012): 1–5.

75. Waytz, Adam and Juliana Schroeder. "Overlooking Others: Dehumanization by Commission and Omission." *TPM: Testing, Psychometrics, Methodology in Applied Psychology* 21, no. 3 (2014):1–16.

76. Bonilla-Silva, Eduardo. *Racism without Racists: Color-Blind Racism and the Persistence of Racial Inequality in America*. 4th ed. Lanham, MD: Rowman & Littlefield, 2014.

77. Richardson, L. Song. "Police Racial Violence: Lessons from Social Psychology." *Fordham Law Review* 83, no. 6 (2015): 2961–2976.

78. Johnson, Adam. "5 Times the Media has Smeared Black Victims of Police Killings since Michael Brown," *Alternet.org*, August 6, 2015. http://www.alternet.org/media/5-times-media-has-smeared-black-victims-police-killings-michael-brown

79. Johnson, Martenzie. "Colin Kaepernick's Parents break Silence: We absolutely Support Him," *The Undefeated*, December 10, 2016. https://theundefeated.com/features/colin-kaepernicks-parents-break-silence-we-absolutely-do-support-him/

Chapter Two

Early Antecedents of Police Brutality against African Americans

In Chapter 1, we focused on the history and legacy of marginalization of peoples of African descent, particularly those in the United States. The topic of lynching is important, because it is foundational to understand the contemporary police use of excessive force against Black Americans and the reluctance of the United States as a nation to do anything substantive to prevent this from occurring.

Chapter 2 examines additional contemporary circumstances that brought America to where it stands vis-à-vis African Americans and police brutality. To discern the current state of policing, the chapter will specifically delineate eight areas. First, plantation overseers (laying a foundation for American police brutality). Second, lynchings and early American race riots (with an emphasis on some of the visceral ones: the Tulsa Race Riot, Rosewood, East St. Louis Riot, and Detroit 1943). Third, policing and brutality during the Jim Crow and Civil Rights Eras. Fourth, the Black Power movement and policing. Fifth, the Mollen Commission and its impact. Sixth, the notorious history of the Philadelphia Department and Chief Frank Rizzo. Seventh, the Los Angeles Police Department's Rampart Division. Finally, Jon Burge, Chicago Police Department, and forty years of police torture.

PLANTATION OVERSEERS: LAYING A FOUNDATION FOR AMERICAN POLICE BRUTALITY

The policing of Black people has always occurred in America.[1] Additionally, deaths of Black men at the hands of law enforcement, using conservative estimates, can be traced as far back in the United States to 1619, when the first slave ship, a Dutch Man-of-War, landed in Virginia.[2] Hence, as the trans-Atlantic slave trade grew, states adopted laws to govern enslaved Africans and protect the investments of those who owned them. The afore-mentioned statutes, known as Slave Codes, emerged from the highly effec-tive Barbadian Slave Law. British colonizers to control the enslaved and to justify and legitimize its practice implemented these statutes. Thus, African human cargo had the status of chattel, no human rights, and Whites inflicted any punishment upon a person of African descent, which he or she saw fit.[3] It is from the highly effective Slave Codes in the South from which the paddy rollers or police officers in this region evolved which we will discuss short-ly.[4] Finally, some assert enforcement of the second amendment to the Con-stitution (i.e., the right to bear arms) did not allow Congress to take away the state's ability to arm local militias and control newly freed Africans.[5]

In the North, the first established city police services were in Philadelphia (1751), Richmond, Virginia (1807), Boston (1838), and New York (1845). These city police departments came after systems of policing controlled by locally elected sheriffs in New York City and Albany County, in 1626 and the 1660s respectively. Further, these early modern United States police forces were highly decentralized, fragmented, and evolved from the early English system of policing that dates to the eleventh century, imported by early American colonists.[6] More specifically, the basis for them was the London model created by Sir Robert Peel in 1829. These British police forces began with approximately 3,000 officers who wore blue uniforms to distinguish themselves from military officers (who wore red uniforms) and ordinary civilians. However, Peel's force did possess a top-down administra-tive structure and titles similar to the contemporary military in the United States.[7] Finally, the early northern police departments were not bastions of liberalism because the impetus of enforced law in the Northern states was to control enslaved Africans who had escaped from the South.[8]

According to W. Marvin Dulaney[9] "by the middle of the eighteenth cen-tury, every southern colony had a slave patrol. Although in some commu-nities all white males were required to serve some time as patterollers, their ranks were usually poor whites. The patrols were authorized to stop, search, whip, maim, and even kill any African slave caught off the plantation with-out a pass, engaged in illegal activities, or running away."

The above quote is descriptive of the scope of power exhibited by eight-eenth century slave patrols and is eerily similar to the role and function of twenty-first century police officers and their treatment of African Americans. Primarily, White police officers today appear to be able to brutalize persons of African descent and, by extension, other poor persons of color, with impu-nity. Likewise, similar to those early slave patrols of the eighteenth century, police treatment of blacks becomes more repressive and punitive the greater the perceived presence of African Americans in any geographical area.[10] It is important to note that the previously mentioned assessment of a black threat does not have to pose an actual danger to White agency at all. The tipping point for Whites to believe that an African American presence is an intimidating menace can be as low as 12 percent in any city or neighborhood (Loewen 2004).

The first slave patrol was in the colony of Carolina in 1704, followed by patrols in Virginia 1727, North Carolina and Tennessee in 1753, Georgia 1757, and existed in some form in each state in the United States by the end of the 1700s.[11] Slave patrols served the following purposes: (1) maintain the status of the enslaved African as a piece of property; (2) maintain White supremacy; and (3) prevent possible insurrections (Robinson 2017). Put more succinctly, southern states depended on these early enforcers of the law as the first line of defense against the aforementioned insurrections, especially since their financial interests were always in jeopardy because of attacks by abolitionists, insurrections, and attempted insurrections like those by Denmark Vessey, Gabriel Prosser, and Nat Turner (Bogus 1998).

The threat of a plantation takeover by enslaved Africans was so real that we note two facts. First, the south instituted an informal policy referred to as "meritorious manumission." Meritorious manumission offered freedom to any enslaved person who notified plantation owners of an attempted escape and received freedom as their reward. This policy is partly responsible for the lack of successful revolts on American soil. An estimated 252 known attempted slave revolts were thwarted by another enslaved person notifying their enslavers of the pending threat crushed revolts/uprisings on American plantations.[12]

A lynching was essentially a public murder and the ultimate form of racialized social control of Black bodies.[13] In February 2015, the Equal Justice Initiative, founded by Civil Rights attorney Bryan Stevenson who also serves as the organization's executive director, issued a report on the history of lynchings in the United States, based on five years of research and visits to 160 sites around the South. The report documented approximately 3,959 lynchings of African Americans in twelve Southern states from 1877–1950.[14] It is important to mention that lynchings were not only a Southern racial control mechanism and the world may never know the true number of lynchings. However, hangings were often public spectacles, which involve severing the victims' limbs, as well as their castration, in which their genitals were souvenirs. Furthermore, law enforcement either did not prevent or assisted with these hangings and many include an alleged assault of a White woman.[15]

In a study of lynching in the deep South from 1882–1930, Beck and Tolnay[16] produce several findings that can aid in understanding how contemporary acts of police brutality against African Americans serve a similar social control function as lynchings. First, lynchings were more frequent in turbulent economic times, specifically, when the price of cotton was declining and inflationary pressure was increasing. Secondly, public murders, or lynchings of Blacks increased when the relative size of the Black population increased. Third, these authors find mob violence was greater against Blacks when economically marginalized whites perceived their economic status was more precarious. Not surprisingly, tolerance for and occurrence of acts of violence against Blacks by police undergo an uptick when contemporary White view their economic condition as threatened by the presence of Blacks. For instance, Holmes[17] reveals Whites are supportive of repressive police tactics against people of color, i.e., minorities, which ostensibly includes African Americans, when they believe Blacks and other marginalized societal groups are becoming a larger proportion of the population in a geographic region. The aforementioned phenomenon, referred to as minority threat or the minority threat hypothesis, suggests when the perceived threat of a marginalized group increases, policing practices are put in place to socially control the group in question. Additionally, Holmes contends that police brutality has a broad definition and does not always involve physical force. Excessive force is frequently inclusive of such non-physical acts as the use of profane language and unnecessary searches. Finally, the aforementioned can be surmised as police often distrust Blacks and view them as potential criminals who deserve more draconian police practices. The previously mentioned should not be surprising because law enforcement officers, within their subculture, see extralegal force as an essential instrument of control against individuals police perceive as threatening.

Higgins et al. (2011) conducted another contemporary study that connects past lynchings of Blacks to contemporary police practices toward this group. Their study sought to understand racial profiling in decisions to search suspected criminals. Using propensity score matching, the authors posit Whites are less likely than racial and ethnic minorities to experience an illegal search. Moreover, their study revealed several facts regarding racial profiling. First, even after equating Blacks and Whites on several co-variates, Blacks are more likely to experience an illegal search. Second, there is no significant difference between Whites and Hispanics regarding their likelihood of experiencing an illegal/unwarranted search. Third, police behavior may relate to existing negative and criminal stereotypes about Blacks in the media. Finally, and not surprising, Blacks and other marginalized groups have more negative attitudes towards police than Whites because they have a higher frequency of negative direct and indirect interactions with them than Whites. While the reader may wonder how these contemporary realities connect to past lynchings, we assert racial profiling, similar to lynching, increases in frequency and voracity when White hegemony perceives African Americans as a threat.

In his study titled "Racialized Policing: Residents' Perceptions in Three Neighborhoods," Ronald Weitzer investigates citizens' thoughts on racial bias by police in three neighborhoods in Washington, D.C. that vary by racial and class composition. The study looked at one middle-class Black neighborhood, a middle-class White neighborhood, and Black residential community of lower socioeconomic status. Relying on in-depth interviews of residents in each of the communities, Weitzer[18] reveals the following. First, there was agreement in each of the residential communities that police treat Blacks and Whites differently. However, Whites saw the disparate treatment as justifiable because of Blacks' greater involvement in criminality (as measured via official arrest statistics). Conversely, both Black neighborhoods believed their harsh treatment by police was because of the continued significance of racism.

Police, which includes their involvement in lynchings, can possibly surmise the unfair treatment of African Americans delineated in Weitzer, as the residual effect of earlier maltreatment of African Americans. Case in point: In his article titled "Exploring Relations among Forms of Social Control: The Lynching and Execution of Blacks in North Carolina, 1889–1918," Phillips[19] presents information regarding police malfeasance in situations involving lynchings of African Americans that can serve as a precursor to unfair treatment of Blacks by police today. Specifically, the author begins in the introduction with a brief overview of the lynchings of William Burnett and Duncan McPhatter in 1892. In the case of Burnett, fifty masked men took him from his jail cell and left his dead body hanging from a tree. Two days after Burnett's removal from the jailhouse and death by hanging from a tree, a mob pulls McPhatter from a Central Carolina train and lynches him for allegedly shooting a young deputy sheriff. Although at a later date it was determined McPhatter's brother was responsible for the killing of the deputy, law enforcement allowed mobs to murder both men before they could have their day in court. Thus, lynchings are a means of social control of Blacks and police officers and other law enforcement officials were at least partially responsible for not allowing each man to have his day in court.

To further cement the effectiveness and utility of lynching as a means of racial violence and social control, Ward (2012) also points out that more than 3,000 Blacks were hanged/lynched from 1882–1947 which included the consent and collaboration of White law enforcement officers and legal authorities. In addition, between the years of 1890–1917, Ward (2012) points out two to three Black southerners lost their lives each week due to various methods such as hanging, burning at the stake, or murder. Lastly, Ward (2012) illustrates law enforcement officers encouraged or permitted lynchings with the following examples: (1) police would often levy false charges against Blacks, namely, rape and sexual assault, when no rape or sexual intimacy occurred; (2) police would overlook acts of White criminality, which included, but was not limited to, lynchings. A couple egregious examples of the aforementioned happened in Texas and Maryland, respectively. In 1917, a group of adults in Texas compelled a young boy to castrate a lynched Black male. Similarly, in Maryland in 1931, adults picked up a young boy to throw a rope over a branch of a tree to aid in the lynching of a Black man.

In his book, *Beyond the Rope: The Impact of Lynching on Black Culture and Memory* Professor Karlos K. Hill[20] explores how society can make a perfunctory connection between contemporary police brutality and lynchings. Specifically, he delves into the reality of how the tragic shootings of unarmed Blacks by private citizens and law enforcement continues unchanged in the face of protests, town hall meetings, and pledges from law enforcement agencies and politicians to address the problem. Moreover, in a *Washington Post* article titled "Study Finds Police Fatally Shoot Unarmed Black Men at Disproportionate Rates," Lowery[21] produces evidence that police killings of unarmed Blacks is just as harmful to the Black community as the lynchings of the past. First, Black men make up only 6 percent of the population in 2015, but account for 40 percent of the unarmed persons shot by police in 2015.

Second, of the 990 fatal shootings by police in 2015, 93 percent involved persons who were unarmed. Third, the 40 percent of unarmed deaths by police, which Black men represent, was a rate seven times greater than that of White men. Fourth, the most significant factor determining whether police shot an unarmed person was Black skin. Fifth, when encountering Black males, police exhibit shooter bias because they perceive Blacks to be a greater threat to their safety than non-Blacks and are conditioned to view Black and Brown persons with added suspicion, regardless of training. Sixth, using newspaper reports and other sources, the *Washington Post* was able to document twice the number of fatal shootings by police in 2015 than actually reported by the FBI. The aforementioned should not come as a surprise since not all law enforcement agencies submit their shooting data to the FBI.[22] Finally, in the first three months of 2016, 12 percent of Blacks killed by police were unarmed compared to only 6 percent of Whites.

The connection between past lynchings and contemporary police brutality against Black citizens comes with some caveats. Particularly, Hill[23] notes a salient problem when attempting to make such a comparison. Chiefly, lynchings were public executions, often witnessed by hundreds and, at times, thousands of persons. However, police killings, at least technically speaking, are most often deemed legal even if they frequently occur under dubious circumstances. Nevertheless, journalist Monique Judge in the article titled "No Justice, No Peace, Just Crooked Police" which appeared in the publication the *Root*, makes some intriguing points. Judge[24] uses the shooting of unarmed African American male, Patrick Harmon, 50, in Salt Lake City, Utah on August 13, 2017, as a starting point to make her case that police killings and police brutality against unarmed African Americans is synonymous to lynchings. First, she illustrates the irrelevance of video evidence when the victim is Black. In other words, there were videos in the murders of Tamir Rice, Philando Castille, Eric Garner, Walter Scott, and Alton Sterling, but the murder of the police officer occurs in every case except Scott's. Secondly, one notes that despite the fact that American citizens have first amendment protections, whenever African Americans engage in peaceful protests there is the strong presence of militarized police forces who assault these peaceful protesters. Conversely, the police, when patrolling assemblies of the alt-right, particularly in Charlottesville, Virginia, rarely harass neo-Nazis. Third, the often-tenuous circumstances in which police stop and detain African Americans, often ends in a fatality for the unarmed citizen of African American descent. Case in point: Police stop Patrick Harmon for riding a bicycle at night erratically without a rear red light. Although Utah law does not require bicycles to have a rear red light, police ran Harmon's information and informed him that he had several outstanding warrants and informed him that he would be detained and placed under arrest and he was shot three times in the back and fell and died.[25] The detaining officers claimed that Harmon allegedly lunged at them with a knife. However, a grainy officer bodycam video appears to offer no credence to the story of the officers who eventually are later cleared. Sam Gill, the district attorney of Salt Lake County asserted that the shooting was legally justified because Harmon was armed and turned back to lunge at the officers while running away. Conversely, Harmon's niece unequivocally suggests he was murdered.[26]

Nevertheless, to cap off the current discussion perhaps we can provide greater insight regarding why contemporary forms of lynching (i.e., the improper murder of African Americans) still occur, and Bjorhus and Webster's[27] article, which was published in the *Minneapolis Tribune*, is important to this discussion. In their article titled, "Shielded by the Badge, Part 1" Bjorhus and Webster elucidate intriguing information regarding the criminal justice system's inability to hold law enforcement officers accountable for their actions. First, among forty-four states with comparable law enforcement licensing, Minnesota ranks thirty-eighth in revoking licenses. Comparatively, the national average is twelve times higher than Minnesota's. Secondly, the *Tribune's* review found more than 500 current or former licensed police officers/peace officers who have been convicted of crimes, such as: (1) drinking and driving; (2) assault; (3) trespassing and disorderly conduct. Lastly, three-fourths of the convicted officers were never subject to any discipline and more than 140 were still on the job.

In the section that follows, we discuss the following race riots: The East St. Louis Race Riot, The Tulsa Race Riot, Rosewood, and the Detroit Race Riot of 1943. The purpose of focusing on the aforementioned is to not only explicate the terrible set of circumstances that led to these events, but also to delineate the role of law enforcement, police officers, and affiliated agencies in allowing these events to occur or not doing enough to prevent them. Through devoting attention to these historical events, we illustrate how law enforcement has contributed, directly or indirectly, to brutal and treacherous acts against African Americans that persist to this day.

EAST ST. LOUIS, ILLINOIS RACE RIOT OF 1917

The East St. Louis, Illinois race riot that took place from July 2–5, 1917 was an appalling event in African American history and the reader must consider two important points related to this incident. First, although the major violent events began on July 2, one can infer that the events taking place days before set the wheels of disaster in motion. Secondly, despite the bravery of the woefully outnumbered Blacks to put forth substantial resistance, it deserves to be called a massacre than an actual riot. [28]

Although there is disagreement regarding the final numbers, officially, forty-eight persons died (thirty-nine blacks and eight whites). [29] Yet, a substantial number of historians estimate that more than 100 persons died. [30] Equally important, over a thousand working class Whites went through the city beating, shooting, and hanging African Americans in the city streets. [31] Analogous to the other major racial disturbances/massacres that have occurred in American history, three major factors facilitated the situation in East St. Louis. First, a perceived threat of Black economic progress, which served to turn the prevailing racial order of the day on its head. Specifically, a smaller skirmish transpires between Blacks and Whites on May 28. Reportedly, the encounter was the result of a White protest against Black migration and culminated in the injury of some Blacks. Additionally, White frustration over the use of Blacks as replacement workers for Whites who were seeking higher wages from the Aluminum Ore Company, which was the city's largest employer, was also a catalyst. Next, some unexpected, unconfirmed, or some unsubstantiated claim that some White person or person(s) were harmed intentionally was utilized as justification for terrorizing a group of people. [32] Particularly, the lynchpin, which started the melee, was the killing of two plainclothes White police officers by Blacks who mistakenly took them for Whites that were trying to kill them. [33] Not long before the officers drove through the African American neighborhood, a group of White men had driven through the area shooting at houses during the late night hours of June 1, 1917. Thus, it should not come as a surprise that the car filled with two White plains-clothes officers and two other occupants, driving through the same residential area, were assumed to be attackers, were then shot, and killed. [34]

In short, the major racialized events outlined in this chapter, the East St. Louis Race Riot of 1917, the Tulsa Race Riot of 1921, the Rosewood Massacre of 1923, the Detroit Race Riot of 1943, all deserve attention in a work regarding police brutality against African Americans. Initially, and most importantly, each event involved law enforcement either helping Whites to harm Blacks or literally doing nothing to protect Black residents from being victims of White violence. Further, although there were other events that could have been included (e.g., Red Summer of 1919) these events stood out because they provided a succinct example of the extent to which White Americans hold racial animus against African Americans. Lastly, each event can be compared to contemporary events (e.g., shooting of Mike Brown, the choking death of Eric Garner) in which law enforcement did little to not only protect the rights of Blacks but also seemed to be unwilling to even render the most basic type of aid and bring comfort to the Black community after the events.

THE TULSA RACE RIOT OF 1921

The Black citizens of Tulsa, Oklahoma will forever remember June 1, 1921 and peoples of African descent should remember it across the globe. On this day one of America's, if not the world's, most shining examples of African American economic independence and self-sufficiency ceased to exist.[35] The aforementioned section of Tulsa's Greenwood district, which went by the monikers "Black Wallstreet," and "Little Africa," was burned to the ground by White racial extremists (i.e., racists) due to jealousy and an unsubstantiated assault of a White woman named Sarah Page.[36]

Over the years, several stories circulated regarding how the riot started. Inconsistencies notwithstanding, we will do our best to delineate the most common narratives around this tragic event. Dick Rowland, a young African American "shoe-shine boy," entered the Drexel building in downtown Tulsa to use the segregated restroom. As he approached the elevator, he apparently had not stopped evenly with the floor, tripped, and fell on seventeen-year-old White elevator operator, Sarah Page.[37] Conflicting accounts range from Rowland mainly bumping into her, merely brushing her hand and, perhaps the most controversial of all accounts, the two were engaged in a romantic affair.[38] Additionally, some accounts assert that Page yelled "rape," while others suggest that other onlookers yelled "rape."[39] Moreover, soon after the arrest of Rowland amid accusations that he had sexually assaulted Page resulting in an armed standoff by a White mob who came to the jail to kill Rowland and a woefully outnumbered group of Black citizens who came to offer protection to Rowland.[40] Then, when shots were fired, this triggers days of looting, killing, and the ultimate burning of Black Wallstreet.[41]

Estimates of how many died during the approximately two days of racial warfare vary. Wilson and Wallace[42] posit that 300 Black residents died. Hirsch (2002) asserts that anywhere between thirty-nine and 300 people died with Blacks accounting for seventy-five to eighty percent of the total. Wilson and Wallace[43] assert that thousands of Blacks died and that Tulsa, Oklahoma, and America itself, would like to undercount the "official" numbers of Blacks murdered as much as possible. Madigan[44] stressed that Tulsa fire officials originally gave the death total as 185, but receives a later revision approximately ten days after the riot to ten Whites and twenty-six Black deaths.

In the aftermath, of June 2nd at least 6,000 Blacks had been taken to temporary internment camps at the Tulsa fairgrounds and angry Whites looted their homes and property.[45] Additionally, thirty-five square blocks were ruined, and five hotels, thirty-one restaurants, four drugstores, eight doctors' offices, one school, two dozen grocery stores, a Black hospital, the public library, and at least a dozen churches sustained damage.[46]

Nevertheless, the role of law enforcement in the massacre is interesting to say the least. Unfortunately, the full extent of police participation, or lack thereof when it comes to actually protecting and serving citizens, is not completely clear. Still, some things are valid. First, the police chief of the city of Tulsa deputized White citizens to do whatever they wanted to Black citizens and he ordered city gun shops to arm them.[47] Second, the police allowed a White mob to gather at the courthouse to attempt to take Dick Rowland from jail with a desire to lynch him without arresting anyone.[48] Third, White rioters were assisted by city government, police, and the National guard by placing Blacks in internment camps while Whites looted their homes and property and, by some accounts, assisting in dropping bombs on the community with airplanes.[49] To add, a grand jury blamed Blacks for the riot and Whites received no convictions for their participation in these crimes. Fourth, a Federal lawsuit dismissed the case and survivors received no reparations because the statute of limitations had expired. However, some suggest the dismissal of the lawsuit was due to fear it would open the door for lawsuits for reparations for slavery and other atrocities committed against Blacks across the diaspora.

Fifth, all the Black survivors and their descendants received was: (1) $50,000 for current and future scholarships in 2003; (2) the opening of the John Hope Franklin, the famous African American historian from Oklahoma, Reconciliation Park in 2010; (3) The Greenwood Cultural Center that opened in 1995, which represented the culmination of a fundraising campaign which began in 1970.[50] Finally, no Black citizen received compensation for lost property and we do know that there was over a million dollars damage to property in the Black community and Oklahoma schools did not teach the history of the race riot until ninety years after the incident.[51]

THE ROSEWOOD RACE RIOT OF 1923

One of the most tragic racial demolitions of an American town occured from January 1 through January 5, 1923 in Rosewood, Florida, leaving an indelible stain on the history of race relations in the sunshine state. This tragic event is included among the incidents, which connect race riots/uprisings, law enforcement action/inaction, Black suffering, and brutal treatment of African Americans for several reasons. First, Rosewood is an example of Whites attacking Blacks and inflicting substantial damage to a town/community that was approximately 40 percent African American.[52] Second, the actions of law enforcement are questionable/suspect at best and non-existent at worst in terms of not only attempting to stop the event, but in terms of arresting Whites who commited crimes (e.g., murdering innocent Blacks). Third, the impact of the event in terms of continuing a pattern of Whites and law enforcement being able to not harm Blacks with relative impunity.

Although many specific details remain sketchy, on January 1, an African American escaped convict named Jesse Hunter[53] allegedly assaults a White woman, Fannie Taylor. Not unlike other racial events (e.g., Tulsa Race Riots), there is considerable debate as to whether Fannie Taylor was sexually assaulted because many Black residents posit the alleged perpetrator could have been a local White man whom Taylor was said to be having an affair with. However, it was clear that she had been beaten and many suggest she accused a Black man of beating her (however that assault was interpreted as rape to local Whites) to avoid the wrath of her husband.[54] Adding to the controversy, Jones[55] posits, Philomena Goins, the granddaughter of Sarah Carrier (who did laundry for Taylor), accompanied her to Taylor's home on January 1, asserts she overheard Taylor trying to convince White residents of Sumner (a nearby town that was predominantly White and approximately three miles from Rosewood) she was attacked by a Black man. However, she and her grandmother witness a White man leave Taylor's home that morning.

Soon after Taylor's claim of assault, Whites began to look for Jesse Hunter and his alleged accomplices, Sam Carter and Aaron Carrier. While Hunter eludes capture, the capture and incarceration of Carrier maintains his protection, while January 2 saw the capture and lynching of Carter. Not unlike the lynching of other Blacks in the South, the perpetrators cut his fingers and ears from his body, and used them as souvenirs.[56] On January 3, a rumor circulates among Whites that Sylvester Carrier (Aaron's first cousin who not liked by Whites because he was an independent Black man with no fear of Whites), was providing refuge for Jesse Hunter.[57] Then, on January 4, a White mob consisting of between twenty and thirty persons, armed with guns, attacked the home of the Carrier family who were among the most respected members of the Black community in Rosewood.[58] The shoot-out lasts several hours and reports indicate two Whites lost their lives, along with

Sylvester and Sarah Carrier. Furthermore, in addition to the wounding of several Whites and Blacks, surviving Blacks hid in the nearby woods and swamps.[59] Florida Governor Cary Hardee receives notification of the events the following day and offers to send in the National Guard but Sheriff Elias Walker reportedly refuses his help. Then on January 6, Blacks who escaped into the woods and swamps, with the aid of White train conductors John and William Bryce evacuated by train to Gainesville, Florida. On January 7, approximately 200 to 300 additional Whites arrived via horseback and cars (Model T's) to Rosewood and burned down what remained of the town while the homes of two White residents were not touched.[60]

In the end, there was official documentation of the deaths of six Blacks and two Whites. Although we may never know the official numbers of those dead and wounded, on May 4, 1994, Florida Governor Lawton Chiles signed into law House Bill 591 which compensated fifty living survivors, albeit seventy years later, with a $150,000 each along with creating a scholarship fund.[61] Finally, we note four important points regarding law enforcement's response to the carnage. First, as stated earlier, Sheriff Walker put a name to the alleged assault (Jesse Hunter) when Fannie Taylor only mentions that a Negro was responsible. Second, despite accepting help from Alachua County law enforcement, he rejects aid from the National Guard to quelch the melee. Third, he deputizes at least two of the Whites who were part of the mob that attacked the Carrier house. Finally, a month after the incident, a grand jury was convened and no Whites were charged for anything, namely property damage or murder.[62]

THE DETROIT RACE RIOT OF 1943

Similar to other incidents where Whites attacked African-Americans, and to some extent police, the Detroit race riot deserves consideration. Just like several of the urban uprisings that we will later discuss at length, the Detroit Race Riot of 1943 was precipitated by such factors as inadequate housing and job opportunities, racial animus by Whites, and poor relations between Blacks and the police.[63]

The riot began the night of June 20, 1943, at roughly 10 PM, when 200 people, both Black and White, began fighting at Bell Isle Park. More specifically, White residents took it upon themselves to attack any person they see, even some African Americans who had just gotten off from work and were unaware of what was transpiring.[64] Further, over 100 participants in the riots receive some jail time.[65] Conversely, other sources assert that as many as 1,800 are arrested and approximately 85 percent of the arrests were of African Americans, with several of the murders were not solved.[66] The police shot Black rioters in the back, killing twenty-five. By contrast, only nine

Whites were killed and possibly none by police.[67] Thus, we can surmise that the problem of police victimizing Blacks instead of "protecting and serving" is one with a deep and rich history.

Conceivably, a deeper understanding of why the riot took place can be discerned by presenting some of the facilitating events in the years before the riot. To state it differently, one must comprehend the following events that allow the uprising. First, from 1940–1943 Detroit's population increases by an estimated 500,000 with a large proportion of the increase consisting of African Americans who were leaving the South for better social and economic opportunities. Second, prior to the massive population boom, African Americans in Detroit were relegated to two small residential sections of the city. Nonetheless, the population increase creates a concomitant need for more housing, which resulted in the federal government, in an effort to address the housing shortage, building the Sojourner Truth housing projects, which opened to residents in February of 1942. Unfortunately, Whites became resentful and began to feel disenfranchised at the construction of a housing project for the city's Black residents. Third, another fault line occurs when Blacks can join the United Auto Workers Union or earn promotions for their hard work, which results in strikes by White workers. Fourth, despite the fact that the government built housing for Blacks, it was common for Blacks to be required to pay twice the rent their White counterparts were charged. Further, due to the level of disgruntlement by the perceived social and economic advancement of African Americans, an estimated 25,000 White Packard plant employees walked out on the job. Lastly, the riots ended on July 22, 1943 when President Theodore Roosevelt, per a request from then Detroit Mayor Edward Jeffries, Jr., provides assistance from the federal government.

POLICING AND POLICE BRUTALITY DURING JIM CROW AND THE CIVIL RIGHTS AND BLACK POWER MOVEMENTS

African American men, women, and children endured brutal treatment at the hands of police/law enforcement during the Jim Crow era (1896–1965), which began with the Supreme Court decision in *Plessy v. Ferguson*.[68] The start of the Jim Crow era notwithstanding, the tradition of Blacks receiving disparate treatment at the hands of police continues unabated from the Jim Crow era to the present.

In his study of the lynching of Black and Brown bodies, police brutality, and racial control in post-racial America, Embrick[69] critically examines the connection between structural inequalities that privilege Whites over other groups, which has resulted in America moving toward two different, separate and unequal, nations. His study concludes that in contemporary American society, being a person of color in general, and a Black person in particular, involves informing one's children they must do more socially and economically to advance than Whites. Likewise, it entails helping them to navigate the terrain of a society in which they must constantly fear for their lives in ways not common to their White counterparts.

In his article titled "They Found out That We Are Men: Violence, Non-Violence and Black Manhood in the Civil Rights Era," Simon Wendt explicates the dilemma faced by peaceful protestors against racial injustice in Birmingham, Alabama in 1963. Particularly, Wendt[70] illuminates a paradox, which centered on how protestors were to exhibit true manhood while challenging racism and injustice non-violently at the same time as sprayed with high-powered streams of water and attacks by police dogs. The predicament is notable because it serves as an intellectual underpinning of sorts for this section of the chapter. Further, it serves as a starting point for a summary of police conduct during the Civil Rights and Black Power Movements, which in many ways was just an extension of the type of policing that Blacks have endured since the creation of the police.[71]

There are three major points that one can glean from Wendt which are pertinent to an understanding of police violence towards African Americans during the Civil Rights and Black Power movements. First, during the enslavement of peoples of African descent, White violence, and by extension police violence, was an attempt to emasculate Black males and maintain Whites' position at the top of the racial hierarchy. Second, lynchings, which became more prominent after the end of enslavement and continue today (often referred to as "suicides"), served as a form of racialized social control just as unchecked police brutality today, that are not foreign to most African Americans. Nevertheless, lynchings, analogous to contemporary police brutality, challenge Black masculinity in two ways. Foremost, White males lynched Black men with impunity. Next, the ability of White males to kill Black males on the basis of a mere accusation of disrespecting a White woman while simultaneously sexually disrespecting Black women (who could be raped by White men at their leisure) with virtually no threat of penalty, served as an expression of White male dominance over Black men. Lastly, Black seekers of justice did not easily accept non-violent resistance, which is the hallmark of the civil rights era. Leaders of the fight for Black justice from Ida B. Wells, to W. E. B. DuBois, to Booker T. Washington, at different times expressed disdain for the perceived passivity of non-violent resistance.

Joseph[72] provides information that supports the discussion of the civil rights and Black Power movements in the same manner. Particularly, there are three specific reasons the two movements merit a simultaneous discussion. First, the Black Power Era (1954–1975) coincided with the golden age of the Civil Rights movement, and, as a result, both movements can be perceived as supporting changes in the racial order of the day and acting as a catalyst for the emergence of socio-political leaders (e.g. Martin Luther King, Huey P. Newton, Fred Hampton). Second, the discussion of the two movements separately is rooted in the reality that one is undergirded in the American Democratic tradition and the other within a backdrop of anti-colonial and Third World liberation movements. Regardless, both movements took place in a backdrop of epic historic events. Finally, both events, the Black Power and Civil Rights movements, inspired new waves of organizational and community-activist activities.

Interestingly, despite its global impact for people of African descent across the diaspora, some regard the Black Power movement as the spiteful twin of the Civil Rights Movement.[73] One can assert this divergent view regarding the two movements may be because Whites have a greater visceral reaction to the Black Power movement than the Civil Rights movement. Additionally, the Black Power movement has been wrongly associated with thoughtless acts of violence, sexism, and self-destructive rage.

Contrary to the unflattering narrative of the Black Power movement that mainstream America promulgates, Karenga[74] presents a compelling counter narrative. Specifically, he contends the Black Power movement was inclusive of several items. First, it consisted of religious, political, cultural, and economic tendencies. For instance, its religious thrusts were both Islamic and Christian; the Islamic motivation was in the Honorable Elijah Muhammad and the Nation of Islam. Reverend Albert Cleage, founder of the Shrine of the Black Madonna, led the Christian focus. Despite the inherent differences in the two religions, they shared some similarities in terms of their importance for African American advancement. Both essentially viewed African Americans as the chosen people of God. Further, each saw Jesus and God as Black. Finally, each viewed Black people as divine and Whites as the opposite.

Numerous organizations attempted to galvanize Black people during the 1960s and early 1970s. Yet, no organization arguably had as much impact as the Black Panther Party for Self-Defense. Founded in 1966 in Oakland, California by Huey Newton and Bobby Seal, the group took its name from the Lowndes County Freedom organization in Lowndes County, Alabama (Jones 1998). The organization emerges as a response to unchecked police brutality against African Americans and only exists as a revolutionary organization from approximately 1966 to 1982.[75] The organization dropped the word "self-defense" from its name in 1968 and began working with Whites and other progressive groups of color in social justice programs and initiatives, such as drug education, health care clinics, and free breakfasts.[76]

The Black Panther Party reached its peak in 1969.[77] At this point, the panthers had an estimated 10,000 members and at least 45 chapters across America (The Socialist Alternative 2018). Perhaps not a surprise, the creation of the organization and its initial focus on arming its members, drew the ire of the government and law enforcement agencies across the country. Additionally, on December 4, 1969, Fred Hampton, deputy chairman of the Illinois chapter of the BPP was shot to death in his sleep at point blank range by the Chicago Police Department. Then, on December 6, 1969, the Los Angeles Police Department, more specifically its Special Weapons and Tactics team (S.W.A.T.) initiated a raid on the BPP headquarters. It was around this time that the Federal Bureau of Investigation (FBI) director J. Edgar Hoover named the BPP as a threat to the internal security of America. The aforementioned was buttressed by the fact the BPP had an approval rating of 90 percent by Blacks in some major cities in the United States. The raid on the BPP headquarters resulted in no deaths, but in a little over three years of existence, nine police officers and ten BPP members had died in confrontations across the country. Ultimately, during the first S.W.A.T. raid, six BPP members received charges and are jailed (Balko 2013; Karenga 2010; The Socialist Alternative 2018). Thus, the volatile relationship between law enforcement and Blacks during the Black Power and Civil Rights movements were nothing new, just a continuation of what has been going on since the existence of law enforcement.

The Counter-Intelligence program of the FBI, or more affectionately known as Cointelpro, was a major impediment to the Black Power, Civil Rights Movement, or any organization that had a goal of ushering in equality for all regardless of color (Cointelpro: The FBI's War on Black America 2012). Begun in 1956, the program initially had a purpose of identifying and exposing members of the Communist Party in the United States. By 1961, the program expanded to surveil and disrupt the activities of not only the BPP, but also the Civil Rights Movement, the Nation of Islam, Congress of Racial Equality, the American Indian Movement, and other movements and organizations designed to achieve justice for disenfranchised groups.[78]

In terms of surveilling the Civil Rights Movement, the FBI started keeping very close tabs on Reverend Martin Luther King, Jr. in 1962. Particularly, the FBI's goal was to prevent King from becoming a "messiah" who could transform the conditions of African Americans throughout America. Some of the tactics utilized by law enforcement, i.e., the FBI, to derail King involve photographic surveillance, wire tapping/bugging his hotel rooms, sending anonymous letters encouraging him to commit suicide, and attempting to break up his marriage by insinuating he was engaging in extra-marital affairs.[79]

Although the FBI is an intelligence organization, it is illegal for this agency to surveil its citizens to discredit them as political leaders.[80] The Watergate Scandal and the extensive surveillance activities and abuses of power by the FBI, Central Intelligence Agency (CIA), National Security Agency (NSA), and the Internal Revenue Service (IRS) led to the creation of the Church Committee in 1975, headed by Senator Frank Church who was a Democrat from Idaho (The Socialist Alternative 2018). The committee published fourteen reports in 1975 and 1976 (de-classifying 50,000 pages of the reports), which was the most extensive review of intelligence activities ever made available to the public.[81] Furthermore, intelligence agencies engage in domestic surveillance activities on American citizens (such as MLK and the BPP), and the reports also highlighted the government's efforts to assassinate foreign leaders, like Patrice Lumumba of the Congo, Fidel Castro of Cuba, and Rafael Trujillo of the Dominican Republic to name a few. Several national civil rights organization, the antiwar movement, Students for a Democratic Society, the Puerto Rican Young Lords, and the American Indian Movement (AIM) were subject to intense spying.[82] Ultimately, the committee's efforts led to the creation of executive order 11905 to ban U.S. sanctioned assassinations of foreign leaders.

THE MOLLEN COMMISSION

A predecessor to the Mollen Commission was the Knapp Commission. Led by Judge Whitman Knapp in 1972, the commission examined two general categories of corrupt officers, *grass eaters* and *meat eaters*. *Grass eaters* characterizes officers who engage in relatively less fraudulent dealings, essentially those who accept any type of freebee that came their way. On the other hand, *meat eaters* characterizes officers involved in major corruption, such as offering protection to drug dealers as well as buying and selling drugs.[83]

The Mollen Commission, analogous to the Knapp Commission, elucidated that pockets of police brutality and dishonesty exist within the New York City police department because the police culture supports it (Pursuing Corrupt Cops 1993). Specifically, the commission found law enforcement officers engage in behaviors ranging from drug dealing to beatings of citizens to illegal searches and seizures, which were most prominent in the most blighted communities. Further, the commission, convened by New York City Mayor David Dinkins and chaired by Judge Milton Mollen, had a purpose of further looking into department malfeasance and police brutality.[84] The commission found, similar to the Knapp Commission, which preceded it, that NYPD officers provide protection to drug dealers, sold drugs, beat up citizens, gave false testimony to protect each other, and had a relatively ineffective Internal Affairs department.[85] Additionally, the commission found in the 30,000-member department a reluctance by officers to report corrupt fellow officers for fear of reprisals by other officers or that their advancement up the ranks would decrease.[86]

Perhaps most disturbing are officer transgressions uncovered by the commission, which are known as "testilying." This practice entails officers providing false testimony to facilitate a conviction or to cover for each other. This practice is particularly unsettling because it takes place in open court where the officer is under oath and goes against the very foundation of law enforcement. Hunt and Manning[87] provide additional insight into why police lie. First, they suggest that lies can be either of little issue or troublesome. Secondly, the officers analyze, in an eighteen-month ethnographic study, two types of troublesome lies: case lies and cover lies. The former refers to lies that an officer tells on paper or in court to bring about a conviction. The latter refers to untruths told to superiors, colleagues, or in court to provide a shield against discipline. Thirdly, lying, within the social context of policing, is an endorsed practice, differentially compensated and executed, and judged by the culture of the profession. Finally, the researchers find that despite pervasive lying within the police profession, when done in a courtroom; the officer risks legal/moral sanctions, which may result in a loss of standing.

Lastly, Ivkovic[88] examines the extent and nature of police venality by delving into existing data to bring forth a reliable analysis of the methodologies (e.g., interviews, surveys) used when studying police corruption. She discerns that although both quantitative and qualitative approaches to studying police dishonesty have weaknesses, a mixed methods approach is most effective when examining this not often studied topic. Further, she delineates that it is during the process of learning the culture of the profession that officers ignore dishonesty within their ranks to earn the trust and acceptance of their comrades. To conclude, she discovers, many frequently resist asking officers about their own misconduct.

FRANK RIZZO AND THE
PHILADELPHIA POLICE DEPARTMENT

Francis "Frank" Lizarro Rizzo, Sr. (November 26, 1921–July 16, 1991) was the former police commissioner (1967–1971) and mayor for two terms (1972–1980) of the city of Philadelphia, Pennsylvania. A high school dropout, Rizzo joined the Navy and received a discharge due to his diabetes. It was soon after, in 1943, he joined Philadelphia Police department where he quickly earned a reputation as a brave officer.[89] In terms of his tenure as police commissioner, he was considered one of the most notorious, racist, and brutal cops in the history of the city. In addition, many regard him as a hulking figure who after ordering raids on the offices of the Black Panthers throughout the city.[90] After the raid of their offices, members of the BPP were reportedly humiliated when forced to strip to their underwear and parade in front of newspaper cameras.[91] Additionally, he had a reputation of ordering his officers to raid gay hangouts, organize four squads of officers to pilfer the local offices of the Student Non-Violent Coordinating Committee (SNCC) in the city, and capitalized on White working-class fears of the city's rising crime rate to endear himself to many Whites in the city. Finally, in 1967, he allegedly ordered some of his officers to beat up a group of 3,500 African American students who were protesting for a Black history curriculum in front of a school administration building, which caused a gulf in his perception by Blacks and Whites.[92] Some describe the situation as a "police riot," and 22 people were seriously injured and 57 arrested.[93]

Upon becoming mayor in 1972, Rizzo was wildly popular among his mostly White supporters. Elected to two terms, he tried to earn a third term in 1986 but lost his bid to be mayor again. Then, he switched to the Republican Party and ran again against Ed Rendell at the time of his death from a heart attack at the age of 70 in 1991.[94] Regardless, the following issues marred his time of mayor of the city of brotherly love. First, the city's police officers received frequent accusations of being too quick to use force against African Americans. Second, the city lost 140,000 jobs during his time as mayor and the city's population decreased by 260,000. Third, the city faced lawsuits from accusations of discriminatory hiring practices against African American police and fire department applicants. Fourth, he granted pay increases and exceedingly generous retirement pensions for officers, which financially crippled the city. Essentially, the city owes the retired officers and their beneficiaries between 1.2 and 1.7 million dollars each. Fifth, in 1979, the Department of Justice charged Rizzo and city officials with allowing rampant police abuse. To put the aforementioned into perspective, from 1970 to 1978, the police shot and killed no fewer than 162 persons. Finally, in a bit of irony, Philadelphia, during his tenure as mayor became the first city to fund and build an African American history museum which opened in 1976.[95]

In 1998, the donation of a 2,000 pound, ten feet tall, bronze statue of Rizzo was given to the city in his honor, placed in the Thomas Paine Plaza in front of the Municipal Services building. Not surprisingly, the city has made plans to move the statue because of the polarizing relationship that Rizzo had with minority residents of the city of Philadelphia and the more than 20,000 signatures on a petition calling for the statue's removal.[96]

LOS ANGELES RAMPART DIVISION SCANDAL

The Los Angeles Police Department (LAPD) is one of many in the United States with a torrid history regarding its treatment of African Americans. One permanent stain on the city and its police department is the Rampart Division scandal of the 1990s. More specifically, a few years after the notorious beating of unarmed Rodney King, the LAPD was once again embroiled in controversy centered on its Community Resources against Street Hoodlums (CRASH) anti-gang unit that operated in the Rampart Division of the city.[97] The scandal associated with the CRASH unit resulted in over 70 officers accused of planting evidence, unprovoked beatings and shootings, dealing and stealing drugs, and perjury.[98]

The key figure in the CRASH unit scandal was Officer Rafael Antonio Perez aka Ray Lopez (Date of Birth: August 22, 1967–). The apprehension of the 32-year-old LAPD Officer, Perez, occured on September 8, 1999, due to Perez stealing approximately one million dollars' worth of cocaine from an evidence locker. Perez received a plea bargain that required him to give information on any other types of corruption that had been taking place within the department. Then, over a course of several months, Perez shared accounts of LAPD officers making unlawful arrests, lying in court, planting evidence, and bogus arrests, which would become the worst scandal in the history of the LAPD.[99]

Many suggest the seeds for what would become the CRASH scandal occur when undercover LAPD officer, Frank Lyga, shoots and kills African American officer, Kevin Gaines, who was wearing plainclothes and suspected of an affiliation with one of the Los Angeles street gangs. However, the authors of this book suggest the spark, which ignited the controversy, was when Javier Francisco Ovando, who was a member of the 18th street gang, received a charge of assaulting LAPD officers Rafael Perez and Nino Durden.

For the most part, the CRASH unit operated independently from the rest of the LAPD. They were a 12 to 20-man unit, tight knit, who often rewarded fellow unit members when they shot gang members. Furthermore, Cannon surmises three major events were responsible for the misdeeds of the CRASH unit. First, CRASH unit officer and close friend to Perez, David Mack, stole $722,000 from a Bank of America in South Central Los Angeles. The heist was an inside job orchestrated by Mack and his girlfriend, who was a teller at the bank, Errolyn Romero. Mack received a conviction for federal bank robbery charges and was given a 14-year prison sentence on March 17, 1999. There was speculation that Perez played a role in the robbery but there was no concrete evidence to substantiate that premise. Second, on February 26, 1998, a suspect who was being detained and about to be interrogated. Officer Brian Hewitt, entered the interrogation room, beat, and choked the suspect until he vomited blood. The suspected gang member received treatment at a local hospital and reported the incident upon his release. Furthermore, the firing of Officer Hewitt and one other officers occured after Chief Bernard Parks brings them up on administrative charges.

Lastly, in March of 1998, the L.A.P.D's property division, where seized drugs are stored, discovered six pounds of cocaine were missing and the name on the sign out sheet was Rafael Perez. The internal affairs unit launched a secret investigation of Perez soon after because the case he reportedly signed the cocaine out for had been resolved before he signed for the cocaine. On the morning of August 25, 1998, L.A.P.D. officers arrest Perez at his home and he was encouraged to flip/snitch when prosecutors threaten to charge his wife (who worked with the department, but was not an officer). Two additional nails in Perez's coffin were results from a forensic examination of his finances, which uncover unexplained deposits into his bank account in addition to substantial remodeling of his home that went beyond what was normal for a police officer's salary. Thus, in cutting a deal. Perez agrees to tell the full story about all of the corrupt activities that were taking place in the unit. Perez provided more than 50 hours of information, revealing that he had been dealing cocaine since 1997, that he and Durden both shot Ovando, that the unit would routinely set up gang members on guns and weapons charges, and that their commanding officer, Sgt. Edward Ortiz approved of everything, in exchange for a five-year prison sentence.

JON BURGE, EX-CHICAGO COP

Jon Graham Burge (Date of Birth: December 20, 1947–September 19, 2018) is a convicted felon and former Chicago Police Department Detective Commander. Burge spent nearly four years of a four and one-half year sentence in a Federal prison for being the ringleader of a torture ring that used burnings, beatings, and electric shock to force confessions from more than 200 suspects from 1972–1991. Miller[100] delineates the steps Burge would take with defendants when he needed a confession. First, he would enter the interrogation room. Second, he would set a little black box down with a crank that produced a high-voltage electric shock. Third, he would attach one of the wires protruding from the box to the suspect's handcuffed ankles and he would attach the other to their chained hands. Fourth, he would place a plastic bag over the accused person's head, crank the box, and listen to suspects' blood-curdling screams as they passed out and confessed upon regaining consciousness or confessed on the spot. Of note, all torture victims were Black men and all the cops were White[101] Unfortunately, the statute of limitations had expired on the crimes of which Burge was accused and he ultimately was convicted on June 28, 2010 of perjury and obstruction of justice charges that stemmed from the 1989 civil suit for damages against him for alleged torture.[102] Notably, more than 30 Black men remain behind bars based on Burge's investigations/claims.[103]

Before becoming a police officer in 1970, Burge served a relatively brief stint in Vietnam. Amid speculation, he perfects his torture techniques, he receives an honorable discharge in 1969.[104] It was not long after a promotion to detective, two years after being hired, that his reign of terror began. In any event, during his trial Burge refused to testify but broke his silence upon being released early in 2014 for good behavior. Although Burge has no remorse for his crimes, describing some of his victims as human vermin, animals, and vicious criminals,[105] he received a $4,000 per month pension from the City of Chicago until his death in 2018.

The entire Burge ordeal left an indelible stain on the city of Chicago and its police department. As of 2014, the city doled out an estimated $67 million in payments to victims and more than $20 million to the lawyers that defended Burge. Overall, Burge has cost the city, i.e., taxpayers, more than $120 million, including $15 million investigating Burge, and $22 million in pension costs to Burge and his cohorts.[106]

On May 6, 2015, the Chicago City Council voted unanimously (42–0) to pass the Reparations Ordinance which approved $5.5 million dollars to build the Chicago Torture Justice Center. The center serves as a safe space to provide trauma-services and other resources to Burge's victims (20 of which have been released from prison as of 2016, and 4 were released from death row) and to reconnect the city and the African American community (Chicago Torture Justice 2018; Miller 2015). Finally, the Reparations Ordinance mandates that Chicago Public Schools make Burge's torturing of Black men a focus of discussion. The ordeal will be part of the curriculum for every eighth and tenth grader in the city of Chicago.[107]

EARLY ANTECEDENTS OF POLICE BRUTALITY AGAINST AFRICAN AMERICANS

In this chapter, we discussed contemporary circumstances that have brought American society to its current situation regarding police brutality against African Americans. We began by explicating some of the foundational events that established a precedent for the rampant malfeasance that we see today. First, we discussed the plantation overseer as the first police officers in the South and delineated how could mete out whatever form of justice that he saw fit. Second, we discussed some of the early American racial riots. We use the term "riot" loosely, because in each of the events that we previously discussed, African Americans were primarily attempting to defend themselves from attacks by Whites. Sadly, in most of these cases, the police either assisted White perpetrators or stand by idly and do nothing. Third, we examined the role of law enforcement during the Civil Rights and Black Power movements, with a particular emphasis on the efforts to de-stabilize groups (e.g., the Black Panthers) and derail the positive momentum for societal change. Lastly, we delved into some of the nationwide controversies and scandals involving police officers and departments. The purpose of the aforementioned focus was to illustrate that in order for large-scale abuses of police power to occur, institutional deviance must be embedded and receive support. In other words, these horrific events involved more than just "a few bad apples." In chapter 3, we will present a summation of the 30 in-depth qualitative interviews with collegiate students. Our rationale for interviewing Black college students was that they represent our future as a nation, and as African Americans, they simultaneously represent our best prospects for meaningful reforms in the future.

NOTES

1. Dulaney, W. Marvin. *Black Police in America*. Bloomington: Indiana University Press, 1996.

2. Robinson, Michael A. "Black Bodies in the Ground: Policing Disparities in the African American Community-An Analysis of Newsprint from January 1, 2015 through December 31, 2015." *Journal of Black Studies* 48, no. 6 (2017): 551–571.

3. Wadman, Robert C. and William Allison. *To Protect and to Serve: A History of Policing in America*. Upper Saddle River, NJ: Pearson College Division, 2004.

4. Hadden, Sally E. *Slave Patrols: Law and Violence in Virginia and the Carolinas*. Cambridge, Massachusetts: Harvard University Press, 2001.

5. Bogus, Carl T. "The Hidden History of the Second Amendment," *U. C. Davis Law Review* 31, no. 80 (1998): 309–411.

6. Berger, Ronald J., Free Jr., Marvin D., Deller, Melissa, and Patrick K. O'Brien. *Crime, Justice, and Society: An Introduction to Criminology*. 4th ed. Boulder, Co: Rienner, 2015.

7. Balko, Radley. *Rise of the Warrior Cop: The Militarization of America's Police Forces*. New York: Public Affairs, 2013.

8. Dulaney, W. Marvin. *Black Police in America*. Bloomington: Indiana University Press, 1996. Robinson, Michael A. "Black Bodies in the Ground: Policing Disparities in the African American Community-An Analysis of Newsprint from January 1, 2015 through December 31, 2015." *Journal of Black Studies* 48, no. 6 (2017): 551–571.

9. Dulaney, W. Marvin. *Black Police in America*. Bloomington: Indiana University Press, 1996.

10. Balko, Radley. *Rise of the Warrior Cop: The Militarization of America's Police Forces*. New York: Public Affairs, 2013. Holmes, Malcolm D. "Minority Threat and Police Brutality: Determinants of Civil Rights Criminal Complaints in US Municipalities." *Criminology* 38, no. 2 (2000): 343–368.

11. Hadden, Sally E. *Slave Patrols: Law and Violence in Virginia and the Carolinas*. Cambridge, Massachusetts: Harvard University Press, 2001.

12. Anderson, Claud. *Powernomics: The National Plan to Empower Black America*. Bethesda, Maryland: Powernomics Corporation of America, 2001.

13. Loewen, James W. *Sundown Towns: A Hidden Dimension of American Racism*. New York: The New Press, 2005.

14. Robertson, Campbell. "History of Lynchings in the South Documents Nearly 4,000 Names," *The New York Times*, February 10, 2015. https://www.nytimes.com/2015/02/10/us/history-of-lynchings-in-the-south-documents-nearly-4000-names.html

15. Loewen, James W. *Sundown Towns: A Hidden Dimension of American Racism*. New York: The New Press, 2005. Robertson, Campbell. "History of Lynchings in the South Documents Nearly 4,000 Names," *The New York Times*, February 10, 2015. https://www.nytimes.com/2015/02/10/us/history-of-lynchings-in-the-south-documents-nearly-4000-names.html; Stevenson, 2015.

16. Beck, Elwood M., and Stewart E. Tolnay. "The killing fields of the deep south: the market for cotton and the lynching of blacks, 1882–1930." *American Sociological Review* (1990): 526–539.

17. Holmes, Malcolm D. "Minority Threat and Police Brutality: Determinants of Civil Rights Criminal Complaints in US Municipalities." *Criminology* 38, no. 2 (2000): 343–368.

18. Weitzer, Ronald. "Racialized Policing: Residents' Perceptions in Three Neighborhoods." *Law & Society Review* 34, no. 1 (2000): 129–155.

19. Phillips, Charles D. "Exploring Relations among Forms of Social Control: The Lynching and Execution of Blacks in North Carolina, 1889–1918," *Law and Society Review* 21, no. 3 (1987): 361–374.

20. Hill, Karlos K. *Beyond the Rope: The Impact of Lynching on Black Culture and Memory.* London: Cambridge University Press, 2016.

21. Lowery, Wesley J. "Study Finds Police Fatally Shoot Unarmed Black Men at Disproportionate Rates," *The Washington Post*, April 7, 2016, https://www.washingtonpost.com/national/study-finds-police-fatally-shoot-unarmed-black-men-at-disproportionate-rates/2016/04/06/e494563e-fa74-11e5-80e4-c381214de1a3_story.html?noredirect=on&utm_term=.df5b4eeaf252

22. Chaney, Cassandra, and Ray V. Robertson. "Armed and Dangerous? An Examination of Fatal Shootings of Unarmed Black People by Police." *The Journal of Pan African Studies* 8, no. 4 (2015): 45–78.

23. Hill, Karlos K. *Beyond the Rope: The Impact of Lynching on Black Culture and Memory.* London: Cambridge University Press, 2016.

24. Judge, Monique."No Justice, No Peace, Just Crooked Police," *The Root*, October 6, 2017, http://www.theroot.com/no-justice-no-peace-just-crooked-police-1819237633

25. Rosenberg, Eli. "Police Bodycam Shows Officer Fatally Shoot a Man Who Ran. Prosecutors Say it was Justified," *The Washington Post*, October 7, 2017. https://www.washingtonpost.com/news/post-nation/wp/2017/10/07/police-bodycam-shows-officer-fatally-shoot-a-man-who-ran-prosecutors-say-it-was-justified/?utm_term=.f7efc4eba6c9.

26. Lee, Trymaine. "A Video Again Casts Doubt on Police Shooting of a Black Man," *NBCNEWS*.com, October 7, 2017, https://www.nbcnews.com/news/nbcblk/video-again-casts-doubt-police-shooting-black-man-n808506. Rosenberg, Eli. "Police Bodycam Shows Officer Fatally Shoot a Man Who Ran. Prosecutors Say it was Justified," *The Washington Post*, October 7, 2017. https://www.washingtonpost.com/news/post-nation/wp/2017/10/07/police-bodycam-shows-officer-fatally-shoot-a-man-who-ran-prosecutors-say-it-was-justified/?utm_term=.f7efc4eba6c9

27. Bjorhus, Jennifer and Mary Jo Webster. (2017). "Shielded by the Badge, Part 1," *Minneapolis Star Tribune*, October 1, 2017, http://www.startribune.com/minnesota-police-officers-convicted-of-serious-crimes-still-on-the-job/437687453/

28. McLaughlin, Malcolm. "Ghetto Formation and Armed Resistance in East St. Louis, Illinois." *Journal of American Studies* 41, no. 2 (2007): 435–467.

29. Leonard, Mary Delach. "Legacy of 1917 East St. Louis Race Riot is Etched in Family Trees," *St. Louis Public Radio*, June 30, 2017, http://news.stlpublicradio.org/post/legacy-1917-east-st-louis-race-riot-etched-family-trees#stream/0

30. Wicentowski, Danny. "First Hand Accounts Show the Horror of East St. Louis' 1917 Race Riot," *RiverFrontTimes*, June 28, 2017, https://www.riverfronttimes.com/newsblog/2017/06/28/first-hand-accounts-show-the-horror-of-east-louis-1917-race-riot

31. McLaughlin, Malcolm. "Ghetto Formation and Armed Resistance in East St. Louis, Illinois." *Journal of American Studies* 41, no. 2 (2007): 435–467.

32. Feagin, Joe. R. *Racist America: Roots, Current Realities, and Future Reparations.* 3rd ed. New York: Routledge, 2014.

33. Leonard, Mary Delach. "Legacy of 1917 East St. Louis Race Riot is Etched in Family Trees," *St. Louis Public Radio*, June 30, 2017, http://news.stlpublicradio.org/post/legacy-1917-east-st-louis-race-riot-etched-family-trees#stream/0

34. Ibid.

35. Hirsch, James S. *Riot and Remembrance: The Tulsa Race War and Its Legacy.* Boston: Houghton Mifflin Company, 2002.

36. Wilson, John Jay and Ron Wallace. *Black Wallstreet.* New York: Seaburn Publishing Group, 2004.

37. Workneh, Lilly. "The Unforgettable Images Expose the Horror of the Tulsa Race Riots," *Huffington Post: Black Voices*, June 2, 2016. https://www.huffingtonpost.com/entry/tulsa-race-riots_us_574fc3aae4b0ed593f134a92

38. Greenwood, Ronni Michelle. "Remembrance, Responsibility, and Reparations: The Use of Emotions in Talk about the Tulsa Race Riots," *Journal of Social Issues* 71, no. 2 (2015): 338–355. Workneh, Lilly. "The Unforgettable Images Expose the Horror of the Tulsa Race Riots," *Huffington Post: Black Voices*, June 2, 2016. https://www.huffingtonpost.com/entry/tulsa-race-riots_us_574fc3aae4b0ed593f134a92

39. Hirsch, James S. *Riot and Remembrance: The Tulsa Race War and Its Legacy*. Boston: Houghton Mifflin Company, 2002. Michelle, 2015.

40. Workneh, Lilly. "The Unforgettable Images Expose the Horror of the Tulsa Race Riots," *Huffington Post: Black Voices*, June 2, 2016. https://www.huffingtonpost.com/entry/tulsa-race-riots_us_574fc3aae4b0ed593f134a92

41. Wilson, John Jay and Ron Wallace. *Black Wallstreet*. New York: Seaburn Publishing Group, 2004.

42. Ibid.

43. Wilson, John Jay and Ron Wallace. *Black Wallstreet*. New York: Seaburn Publishing Group, 2004.

44. Madigan, Tim. *The Burning: Massacre, Destruction, and the Tulsa Race Riot of 1921*. New York: Thomas Dunne's Books, 2003.

45. Wilson, John Jay and Ron Wallace. *Black Wallstreet*. New York: Seaburn Publishing Group, 2004.

46. Madigan, Tim. *The Burning: Massacre, Destruction, and the Tulsa Race Riot of 1921*. New York: Thomas Dunne's Books, 2003. Wilson, John Jay and Ron Wallace. *Black Wallstreet*. New York: Seaburn Publishing Group, 2004.

47. Sulzberger, A. G. "As Survivors Dwindle, Tulsa Confronts Its Past," *The New York Times*, June 19, 2011. http://www.nytimes.com/2011/06/20/us/20tulsa.html.

48. Wilson, John Jay and Ron Wallace. *Black Wallstreet*. New York: Seaburn Publishing Group, 2004.

49. Rao, Sammeer. "Its Been 96 Years Since White Mobs Destroyed Black Wallstreet," *Colorlines,* May 31, 2017. https://www.colorlines.com/articles/its-been-96-years-white-mobs-destroyed-tulsas-black-wall-street.

50. Sulzberger, A. G. "As Survivors Dwindle, Tulsa Confronts Its Past," *The New York Times*, June 19, 2011. http://www.nytimes.com/2011/06/20/us/20tulsa.html. Wilson, John Jay and Ron Wallace. *Black Wallstreet*. New York: Seaburn Publishing Group, 2004.

51. Madigan, Tim. *The Burning: Massacre, Destruction, and the Tulsa Race Riot of 1921*. New York: Thomas Dunne's Books, 2003. Sulzberger, A. G. "As Survivors Dwindle, Tulsa Confronts Its Past," *The New York Times*, June 19, 2011. http://www.nytimes.com/2011/06/20/us/20tulsa.html.

52. Jones, Maxine D. "The Rosewood Massacre and the Women Who Survived It." *The Florida Historical Quarterly* 76, no. 2 (1997): 193–208.

53. Dye, Thomas R. "The Rosewood Massacre: History and the Making of Public Policy." *The Public Historian* 19, no. 3 (1997): 25–39.

54. Bentley, Rosalind. "The Rosewood Massacre: How a Lie Destroyed a Black Town," *The Atlanta Journal Constitution*, February 17, 2017, https://www.myajc.com/news/national/the-rosewood-massacre-how-lie-destroyed-black-town/wTcKjELkGskePsWiwutQuO/

55. Jones, Maxine D. "The Rosewood Massacre and the Women Who Survived It." *The Florida Historical Quarterly* 76, no. 2 (1997): 193–208.

56. Dye, Thomas R. "The Rosewood Massacre: History and the Making of Public Policy." *The Public Historian* 19, no. 3 (1997): 25–39. Glenza, Jessica. "Rosewood Massacre a Harrowing Tale of Racism and the Road Toward Reparations," *The Guardian*, January 3, 2016, https://www.theguardian.com/us-news/2016/jan/03/rosewood-florida-massacre-racial-violence-reparations

57. Dye, Thomas R. "The Rosewood Massacre: History and the Making of Public Policy." *The Public Historian* 19, no. 3 (1997): 25–39.

58. Glenza, Jessica. "Rosewood Massacre a Harrowing Tale of Racism and the Road To-ward Reparations," *The Guardian*, January 3, 2016, https://www.theguardian.com/us-news/2016/jan/03/rosewood-florida-massacre-racial-violence-reparations

59. Bassett, C. Jeanne. "House Bill 591: Florida Compensates Rosewood Victims and Their Families for a Seventy-One-Year-Old Injury." *Florida State University Law Review* 22, no. 10 (1995): 503–523. Jones, Maxine D. "The Rosewood Massacre and the Women Who Survived It." *The Florida Historical Quarterly* 76, no. 2 (1997): 193–208.

60. Ibid.

61. Bassett, C. Jeanne. "House Bill 591: Florida Compensates Rosewood Victims and Their Families for a Seventy-One-Year-Old Injury." *Florida State University Law Review* 22, no. 10 (1995): 503–523. Dye, Thomas R. "The Rosewood Massacre: History and the Making of Public Policy." *The Public Historian* 19, no. 3 (1997): 25–39. Glenza, Jessica. "Rosewood Massacre a Harrowing Tale of Racism and the Road Toward Reparations," *The Guardian*, January 3, 2016, https://www.theguardian.com/us-news/2016/jan/03/rosewood-florida-massa-cre-racial-violence-reparations

62. Glenza, Jessica. "Rosewood Massacre a Harrowing Tale of Racism and the Road To-ward Reparations," *The Guardian*, January 3, 2016, https://www.theguardian.com/us-news/2016/jan/03/rosewood-florida-massacre-racial-violence-reparations; Bassett, C. Jeanne. "House Bill 591: Florida Compensates Rosewood Victims and Their Families for a Seventy-One-Year-Old Injury." *Florida State University Law Review* 22, no. 10 (1995): 503–523. Jones, Maxine D. "The Rosewood Massacre and the Women Who Survived It." *The Florida Historical Quarterly* 76, no. 2 (1997): 193–208.

63. Chandler, D. L. "Detroit Race Riots Began on this Day in 1943," *Newsone*, June 20, 2013, https://newsone.com/2605677/detroit-race-riot-1943/

64. Ibid.

65. Lieberson, Stanley and Arnold Silverman. "The Precipitants and Underlying Conditions of Race Riots." *American Sociological Review* 30, no. 6 (1965): 887–898.

66. Chandler, D. L. "Detroit Race Riots Began on this Day in 1943," *Newsone*, June 20, 2013, https://newsone.com/2605677/detroit-race-riot-1943/

67. Ibid. Russ, J. "The 1943 Detroit Race Riot," *Walter P. Reuther Library Wayne State University*, June 12, 2012. https://reuther.wayne.edu/node/8738

68. Karenga, Mualana. *Introduction to Black Studies*. 4th edition. Los Angeles, CA: University of Sankore Press, 2010.

69. Embrick, David. (2015). "Two Nations, Revisited: The Lynching of Black and Brown Bodies, Police Brutality, and Racial Control in 'Post-Racial' Amerikka." *Critical Sociology* 41, no. 6 (2015): 835–843.

70. Wendt, Simon. "They Finally Found Out that We Really Are Men: Violence, Non-Violence and Black Manhood in the Civil Rights Era," *Gender and History* 19, no. 3 (2007): 543-564.

71. Robertson, Ray V. ed. *Blacks Behind Bars: African Americans, Policing, and the Prison Boom.* San Diego, CA: Cognella Publishing, 2014.

72. Joseph, Peniel. "The Black Power Movement, Democracy, and America in the King Years." *American Historical Review* 114, no. 4 (2009): 1001–1016. Joseph, Peniel. "Black Liberation without Apology: Reconceptualizing the Black Power Movement." *The Black Scholar* 31, no. ¾ (2001): 2–19.

73. Joseph, Peniel. "The Black Power Movement, Democracy, and America in the King Years." *American Historical Review* 114, no. 4 (2009): 1001–1016.

74. Karenga, Mualana. *Introduction to Black Studies*. 4th edition. Los Angeles, CA: University of Sankore Press, 2010.

75. Umoja, Akinyele Omowale. "Repression Breeds Resistance: The Black Liberation Army and the Radical Legacy of the Black Panther Party." *New Political Science* 21, no. 2 (1999): 131–155.

76. Karenga, Mualana. *Introduction to Black Stu* dies. 4th edition. Los Angeles, CA: University of Sankore Press, 2010 .

77. Balko, Radley. *Rise of the Warrior Cop: The Militarization of America's Police Forces.* New York: Public Affairs, 2013.

78. Kayyali, Dia. "The History of Surveillance and the Black Community," *Electronic Frontier Foundation*, February 13, 2014. https://www.eff.org/deeplinks/2014/02/history-surveillance-and-black-community

79. Ibid.

80. Berger, Ronald J., Free Jr., Marvin D., Deller, Melissa, and Patrick K. O'Brien. *Crime, Justice, and Society: An Introduction to Criminology*. 4th ed. Boulder, Co: Rienner, 2015.

81. Young, Thomas. "40 Years Ago, Church Committee Investigated Americans Spying on Americans," *Brookings Now*, May 6, 2015. https://www.brookings.edu/blog/brookings-now/2015/05/06/40-years-ago-church-committee-investigated-americans-spying-on-americans/

82. Wolfe-Rocca, Ursula. "Cointelpro: Teaching the FBI's War on the Black Freedom Movement," *Rethinking Schools*, Vol. 30, no. 3, 2016. https://www.rethinkingschools.org/articles/cointelpro-teaching-the-fbi-s-war-on-the-black-freedom-movement

83. Berger, Ronald J., Free Jr., Marvin D., Deller, Melissa, and Patrick K. O'Brien. *Crime, Justice, and Society: An Introduction to Criminology*. 4th ed. Boulder, Co: Rienner, 2015.

84. Walker, Samuel, Spohn, Cassia, and Miriam DeLone. *The Color of Justice: Race, Ethnicity, and Crime in America*. 4th ed. Belmont, CA: Wadsworth, 2007.

85. " Pursuing Corrupt Cops," *The New York Times*, December 30, 1993, https://search-proquest-com.famuproxy.fcla.edu/docview/429388982?OpenUrlRefId=info:xri/sid:primo&accountid=10913

86. Rabb, Selwyn. "Policing the Police: Report Says Police Tolerate Corruption," *The New York Times*, January 2, 1994, https://search-proquest-com.famuproxy.fcla.edu/docview/429440041?OpenUrlRefId=info:xri/sid:primo&accountid=10913

87. Hunt, Jennifer and Peter K. Manning. "The Social Context of Police Lying," *Symbolic Interaction* 14, no. 1 (1991): 51–70.

88. Ivkovic, Sanja Kutnak. "To Serve and Collect: Measuring Police Corruption." *Journal of Criminal Law and Criminology* 93, no. 2-3: (2003): 593–650.

89. Gambacorta, David, Brennan, Chris, and Valerie Russ. "Was Frank Rizzo Racist, or Just a Product of His Time?," *Philly*.com, August 22, 2017, http://www.philly.com/philly/news/philadelphia-statue-legacy-was-frank-rizzo-racist-20170822.html

90. Blumgart, Jake. "The Brutal Legacy of Frank Rizzo, the Most Notorious Cop in Philadelphia History," *Vice*.com, October 22, 2015, https://www.vice.com/en_us/article/kwxp3m/remembering-frank-rizzo-the-most-notorious-cop-in-philadelphia-history-1022

91. Morris, John W. "Why is the Rizzo Statue Controversial?" *6abc* .com, August 18, 2017, http://6abc.com/politics/why-is-the-rizzo-statue-controversial/2321718/.

92. Ibid.

93. Gambacorta, David, Brennan, Chris, and Valerie Russ. "Was Frank Rizzo Racist, or Just a Product of His Time?," *Philly*.com, August 22, 2017, http://www.philly.com/philly/news/philadelphia-statue-legacy-was-frank-rizzo-racist-20170822.html

94. Ibid.

95. Blumgart, Jake. "The Brutal Legacy of Frank Rizzo, the Most Notorious Cop in Philadelphia History," *Vice*.com, October 22, 2015, https://www.vice.com/en_us/article/kwxp3m/remembering-frank-rizzo-the-most-notorious-cop-in-philadelphia-history-1022; Gambacorta, David, Brennan, Chris, and Valerie Russ. "Was Frank Rizzo Racist, or Just a Product of His Time?," *Philly*.com, August 22, 2017, http://www.philly.com/philly/news/philadelphia-statue-legacy-was-frank-rizzo-racist-20170822.html; Morris, John W. "Why is the Rizzo Statue Controversial?" *6abc* .com, August 18, 2017, http://6abc.com/politics/why-is-the-rizzo-statue-controversial/2321718/

96. Morris, John W. "Why is the Rizzo Statue Controversial?" *6abc* .com, August 18, 2017, http://6abc.com/politics/why-is-the-rizzo-statue-controversial/2321718/; Whack, Erin Haines. "Philadelphia Moving Statue of Controversial Ex-Mayor Frank Rizzo," *USA Today*, November 4, 2017. https://www.usatoday.com/story/news/nation-now/2017/11/04/philadelphia-moving-statue-controversial-ex-mayor-frank-rizzo/832309001/

97. Berger, Ronald J., Free Jr., Marvin D., Deller, Melissa, and Patrick K. O'Brien. *Crime, Justice, and Society: An Introduction to Criminology*. 4th ed. Boulder, Co: Rienner, 2015. Boyer, Peter J. "Bad Cops: Rafael Perez's Testimony on Police Misconduct Ignited the Biggest

Scandal in the History of the L.A.P.D. Is it the Real Story?" The New Yorker, May 21, 2001, http://www.asu.edu/courses/fms440mg/total-readings/badcops.pdf

98. Kahn, Carrie. "After Riots, Scandal Sparked Reform in LAPD," *National Public Radio*, April 25, 2012, https://www.npr.org/2012/04/25/151354376/after-riots-scandal-sparked-reform-in-lapd

99. Boyer, Peter J. "Bad Cops: Rafael Perez's Testimony on Police Misconduct Ignited the Biggest Scandal in the History of the L.A.P.D. Is it the Real Story?" *The New Yorker*, May 21, 2001, http://www.asu.edu/courses/fms440mg/total-readings/badcops.pdf

100. Miller, Michael E. "Cop Accused of Brutally Torturing Black Suspects Costs Chicago 5.5 Million," *The Washington Post*, April 15, 2015, https://www.washingtonpost.com/news/morning-mix/wp/2015/04/15/closing-the-book-on-jon-burge-chicago-cop-accused-of-brutally-torturing-african-american-suspects/?noredirect=on&utm_term=.1f373fedc58e

101. Friedman, Brandis. "Survivors of Torture Under Jon Burge Find a Place of Respite," WTTW.com, May 25, 2017, https://chicagotonight.wttw.com/2017/05/25/survivors-torture-under-jon-burge-find-place-respite

102. Lee, Trymaine. "Jon Burge, Ex-Chicago Cop Who Ran Torture Ring, Released from Prison," *MSNBC* .com, October 3, 2014, http://www.msnbc.com/msnbc/jon-burge-ex-chicago-cop-who-ran-torture-ring-released-prison

103. Friedman, Brandis. "Survivors of Torture Under Jon Burge Find a Place of Respite.," WTTW.com, May 25, 2017, https://chicagotonight.wttw.com/2017/05/25/survivors-torture-under-jon-burge-find-place-respite

104. Miller, Michael E. "Cop Accused of Brutally Torturing Black Suspects Costs Chicago 5.5 Million," *The Washington Post*, April 15, 2015, https://www.washingtonpost.com/news/morning-mix/wp/2015/04/15/closing-the-book-on-jon-burge-chicago-cop-accused-of-brutally-torturing-african-american-suspects/?noredirect=on&utm_term=.1f373fedc58e

105. Spielman, Fran. "Disgraced Chicago Cop Jon Burge Breaks Silence, Condemns $5.5 million Reparations Fund," Chicago Sun Times, April 17, 2015. https://chicago.suntimes.com/news/disgraced-chicago-cop-jon-burge-breaks-silence-condemns-5-5-million-reparations-fund/

106. Lee, Trymaine. "Jon Burge, Ex-Chicago Cop Who Ran Torture Ring, Released from Prison," *MSNBC* .com, October 3, 2014, http://www.msnbc.com/msnbc/jon-burge-ex-chicago-cop-who-ran-torture-ring-released-prison

107. Davis, Kelly. 2017. "CPS Adding Jon Burge Torture Scandal to Curriculum," *WGNTV*.com http://wgntv.com/2017/08/28/cps-adding-jon-burge-police-torture-scandal-to-curriculum/

Chapter Three

Methodology

Extant scholarship reveals Blacks and Whites generally perceive police differently; however, there is limited research information available regarding how *race and education* may influence these perceptions. The design of the current exploratory study is to identify how African American college students perceive police via a phenomenological framework. Phenomenology recognizes how reality relates to people's *perception* of reality. Phenomenologists or "interpretivists"[1] study human behavior in terms of how people define their world based on what they say and do, and are strongly committed to understanding how individuals perceive their world, from the "actor's" point of view. Phenomenology's use of everyday knowledge,[2] "practical reasoning,"[3] language and subjectivity, will be particularly useful in this study. African Americans do not perceive nor have the same experience with members of law enforcement as Whites.[4] Thus, focusing on the qualitative perspectives of Black college students allows us to determine whether race, gender, and education create different realities among a demographic, who only comprise 13 percent of the United States population.[5] Hence, by focusing on the phenomenological responses of Black college students who saw the start of the Black Lives Matter (BLM) Movement this will reveal the factors that shape perceptions of police. Thus, consistent with the aims of phenomenology, this study will examine the narratives of 30 college students as it relates to this question: *What if any differences exist between how Black male and female college students perceive members of law enforcement?*

SAMPLE

Thirty individuals participated in this study, and of this number, there were 18 females (60 percent) and 12 males (40 percent). Twenty-six participants

(87 percent) were African American/Black; one participant (.03 percent) was Black/Hispanic; one participant (.03 percent) was Black/Native American; and one participant (.03 percent) did not disclose their race. The participants range from 19–36 years; the mean age was 22.93 years; and the average amount of education was 13.5 years. Participant grade point averages (GPAs) range from 2.4–4.0, with an average of 3.14. Fourteen participants (47 percent) were from Florida; fourteen participants (47 percent) did not disclose their residential state; one participant was from California (.03 percent); one participant was from Maryland (.03 percent). The median income for participants ranged from less than $20,000 to over $660,000 annually; the median income of the participants was $40,000.

The participants represent various classifications. Fifteen (15) participants were juniors (50 percent), three participants were seniors (.10 percent), two participants were sophomores (.07 percent), four participants were graduate students (.13 percent), one participant was a freshman (.10 percent), and one participant (.10 percent) did not disclose their classification. The participants represented various disciplines. Ten participants (33 percent) were Criminal Justice majors, four participants (11 percent) were Sociology majors, and four participants (11 percent) were Psychology majors. In addition, three participants (.10 percent) were Public Administration majors, three participants (.10 percent) were Health Science majors, and two participants (1 percent) were Pre-Physical Therapy majors. Moreover, there was one English major (.03 percent), one Interdisciplinary Studies major (.03 percent), one Physical Therapy major (.03 percent), and one Political Science major (.03 percent).

PROCEDURES

Because this was an exploratory study, we implemented a purposive sampling procedure. Selection criteria include individuals who self-identify as African American, and are current undergraduate or graduate students. To incentivize participation, participants received a $40 gift certificate. An African American researcher who has extensive experience coding qualitative data conducted the interviews. The semi-structured interviews were audio recorded, last approximately 60 minutes, and were later transcribed. Participants completed a brief demographic questionnaire at the beginning of the interview. The design of the interview shed light on a variety of aspects in the participants' general view of police including recommendations regarding how law enforcement agencies and universities can address issues related to police brutality.

The current study specifically focuses on perceptions of police. Questions on the interview schedule inquire: (1) When you hear the word "police" what words immediately come to mind? (2) In general, how do you view the police? (3) On a scale of 1–10, with 1 being lowest and 10 being highest, how much do you trust the police? (4) When you hear of incidents of police brutality, does it influence how you feel about the police? If not, why not? If so, how so? (5) Do you believe the police treat Black people *better than, equal to,* or *worse than* White people? (6) When you become aware of an incident where a police officer used excessive force and he/she said, "I feared for my life!" *what do you think*? (7) When you become aware of an incident where a police officer used excessive force and he/she said, "I feared for my life!" *what do you feel*? (8) Has a police officer ever used an excessive amount of force on *you*? (9) Has a police officer ever used an excessive amount of force on *someone that you know*? (10) What steps, if any, do you believe law enforcement agencies should take to deal with issues related to police brutality? (11) What steps, if any, do you believe *universities and colleges* should take to deal with issues related to police brutality? (12) Is there anything else that you would like to share? Although we asked the participants 12 questions, the interviewer probed for more in-depth responses or probed for clarity in responses when necessary. Responses to the above items were included in the analysis so review of the full transcripts sought pertinent information to answer the research question.

ANALYSIS

We selected a qualitative analysis approach described by Bogdan and Bi-klen.[6] To begin, a researcher with extensive expertise in coding and analyzing qualitative data immersed herself in the data to gain a sense of the totality of the data.[7] The first step involved determining responses to the following four *quantitative* questions: (3) On a scale of 1–10, with 1 being lowest and 10 being highest, how much do you trust the police? (5) Do you believe the police treat Black people *better than, equal to,* or *worse than* White people? (8) Has a police officer ever used an excessive amount of force on *you*? (9) Has a police officer ever used an excessive amount of force on *someone that you know*? Frequencies were conducted on these questions.

The second step involved determining responses to the following eight *qualitative* questions: (1) When you hear the word "police" what words immediately come to mind? (2) In general, how do you view the police? (4) When you hear of incidents of police brutality, does it influence how you feel about the police? If not, why not? If so, how so? (6) When you become aware of an incident where a police officer used excessive force and he/she said, "I feared for my life!" *what do you think*? (7) When you become aware of an incident where a police officer used excessive force and he/she said, "I feared for my life!" *what do you feel*? (10) What steps, if any, do you believe law enforcement agencies should take to deal with issues related to police brutality? (11) What steps, if any, do you believe *universities and colleges* should take to deal with issues related to police brutality? (12) Is there anything else that you would like to share?

To identify the themes present, all narrative responses were content analyzed using grounded theory and an open-coding process[8] to identify themes from the narratives. To clearly abstract themes from the written responses, words and phrases were the units of analysis. Specifically, coding involved examining all responses, keeping track of emerging themes, determining commonalities in the patterns present, assigning words and symbols to each coding category, and examining how the themes present specifically relate to perceptions of law enforcement. The themes develop as the expert qualitative methodologist independently read and re-read the transcripts to identify words and phrases to represent topics, which might ultimately become themes. They then met together to discuss these topics and further refine the topics into potential themes. As the two researchers communicated about the topics or potential themes they each identify, they merge themes with the same meaning and sometimes eliminated themes that, in fact, were not pervasive in the data. Once the researchers had agreed on the themes, they each independently went back to the data to see if the themes represented the findings. The two researchers met again together, came to a consensus on themes, always going back to the data to refine the themes. The two researchers then coded the data independently (97 percent agreement). When coding disagreements arose, through returning to the original data and through discussion we achieve consensus. The results section represents the three major themes identified in the analysis process.

NOTES

1. Denzin, Norman K., and Yvonna S. Lincoln. "Major paradigms and perspectives." *Strategies of Qualitative Inquiry*, NYK Denzin and YS Lincoln, (eds.) Sage Publication, Thousand Oaks (1998).

2. Garfinkel, Harold. "Studies in ethnomethodology." Prentice Hall, 1967.

3. Pollner, Melvin. *Mundane reason: Reality in everyday and sociological discourse.* Cambridge University Press, 2010.

4. Dottolo, Andrea L., and Abigail J. Stewart. "Don't ever forget now, you're a Black man in America": Intersections of race, class and gender in encounters with the police." *Sex Roles* 59, no. 5–6 (2008): 350–364. Smith, Brad W., and Malcolm D. Holmes. "Community accountability, minority threat, and police brutality: An examination of civil rights criminal complaints." *Criminology* 41, no. 4 (2003): 1035–1064. Walker, April. "Racial Profiling-Separate and Unequal Keeping the Minorities in Line-The Role of Law Enforcement in America." *Thomas L. Rev.* 23 (2010): 576–619.

5. Pew Research Center (2018). *5 Facts about Blacks in the United States.* Retrieved from http://www.pewresearch.org/fact-tank/2018/02/22/5-facts-about-blacks-in-the-u-s/

6. Bogdan, Robert, and Sari Biklen. "Qualitative research for education: An introduction to theory and practice." Needham Heights, MA: Allyn and Bacon (2007).

7. Ibid.

8. Holsti, Ole R. *Content analysis for the social sciences and humanities*. Addison-Wesley Pub. Co, 1969. Strauss, Anselm, and Juliet M. Corbin. *Basics of qualitative research: Grounded theory procedures and techniques*. Sage Publications, Inc, 1990. Taylor, Steven J., Robert Bogdan, and Marjorie DeVault. *Introduction to qualitative research methods: A guidebook and resource*. John Wiley & Sons, 2015.

Chapter Four

College Students' Perceptions of Members of Law Enforcement

In this chapter, we present quantitative and qualitative findings from the study. Quantitative analysis was conducted on the following questions: (3) On a scale of 1–10, with 1 being lowest and 10 being highest, how much do you trust the police? (5) Do you believe the police treat Black people *better than, equal to,* or *worse than* White people? (8) Has a police officer ever used an excessive amount of force on *you*? (9) Has a police officer ever used an excessive amount of force on *someone that you know*?

QUANTITATIVE FINDINGS

In regards to Question 3 (On a scale of 1–10, with 1 being lowest and 10 being highest, how much do you trust the police?), results reveal a range of trust in police with rankings from two (lowest ranking) to seven (highest ranking). Three participants ($n = 3$) provide a rank of two (2). Three participants ($n = 3$) provide a rank of three (3). Three participants ($n = 3$) provide a rank of four (4). One participant provides a rank of 4.5. Nine participants ($n = 9$) provide a rank of five (5). Five participants ($n = 5$) provide a rank of six (6). Three individuals ($n = 3$) provide a rank of 6.5. One participant ($n = 1$) provides a rank of seven (7). The average ranking was 1.26. Furthermore, all participants (100 percent) believe police treat Black people worse than they treat White people. In addition, while the majority of participants have never personally experienced excessive force (77 percent), they are aware of the police using excessive force on someone they know (23 percent).

In regards to Question 5 (Do you believe the police treat Black people *better than, equal to,* or *worse than* White people?), participants unanimously believe the police treat Black people worse than they treat White people. More specifically, this was the view of 100 percent of all participants. In regards to Question 8 (Has a police officer ever used an excessive amount of force on *you*?), 23 participants (77 percent) did not personally experience police use of excessive force, while 7 individuals or 23 percent of participants experienced excessive force by police. In regards to Question 9 (Has a police officer ever used an excessive amount of force on *someone that you know*?), 23 participants (77 percent) had not had a police officer inflict excessive force on someone they knew, while 7 individuals or 23 percent of participants report a police officer using excessive force on someone they personally know. [See Table 4.1 – Participant Perceptions of Law Enforcement – Results from Quantitative Thematic Analysis]

QUALITATIVE FINDINGS

Qualitative analysis was conducted on the following four questions: (3) On a scale of 1–10, with 1 being lowest and 10 being highest, how much do you trust the police? (5) Do you believe the police treat Black people *better than, equal to,* or *worse than* White people? (8) Has a police officer ever used an excessive amount of force on *you*? (9) Has a police officer ever used an excessive amount of force on *someone that you know*?

Table 4.1. *Participant Perceptions of Law Enforcement* (N = 30): *Results from Quantitative Thematic Analysis*

Research Question	n	% of participants	Category
On a scale of 1-10, with 1	1	.03%	7
being lowest and 10 being	3	10%	6.5
highest, how much do you	5	17%	6
trust the police?	9	30%	5
Do you believe the police	1	.03%	4.5
treat Black people <u>better</u>	3	10%	4
than, <u>equal to</u>, or <u>worse than</u>	3	10%	3
White people?	3	10%	2
	0	0%	Better
	0	0%	Equal
	30	100%	Worse
Has a police officer ever	23	77%	No
used an excessive amount	7	23%	Yes
of force on <u>you</u>?			
Has a police officer ever	23	77%	Yes
used an excessive amount	7	23%	No
of force on <u>someone that</u>			
<u>you know</u>?			

Question 8: Has a police officer used an excessive amount of force on *you*?

Qualitative analysis of the narrative responses to Question 8 (Has a police officer used an excessive amount of force on *you*?) reveal the following two themes: (a) Personal Experience with Excessive Force; (2) Personal Experience with Aggressive Behavior. The *Personal Experience with Excessive Force* theme relates to the participant recounting an incident in which he/she was a victim of excessive force by a member of law enforcement. *The Personal Experience with Aggressive Behavior* theme relates to the participant recounting an incident in which a member of law enforcement verbally assaulted them.

Theme 1: Personal Experience with Excessive Force

Five participants (17 percent of participants) recount an incident in which he/ she was a victim of excessive force by a member of law enforcement. One participant recounts an incident where a police officer slams him to the ground during a party because the officer believes he started the fight. Malcolm (23-year old Black male; Criminal Justice Major) says:

> Yes. A police officer once slammed me on the ground at a party. I was in the wrong place at the wrong time. The officer thought that I was fighting even though I was with my girlfriend.

Another participant was waiting for a ride home when a police officer became aggressive with him. Cassie, a 21-year old Black female; Public Administration Graduate Student, expresses:

> I was about 13. I was at the movie theater on Christmas night with a few friends. A violent fight broke out outside of the theater and 3 police officers were clearing up the incident. I was standing waiting on my friends and a White female police officer approached me and told me to leave. I explained to her that I was waiting on my friends for a ride home. She grabbed my arm, squeezed it, and lifted it up and told me to leave before she flipped me and would make everything fall out of my pocket. After that, she let me go and I left.

Another individual shared a speeding incident quickly turned into a situation where his face was pushed to the ground and he was detained. Samuel (23-year old Black male; Criminal Justice Major) explains:

> Three years ago, I was speeding down the street and I was turning off and I was approached by 4 police cars. One in front of me, two on the side, and one in back. They said I was speeding and thought I was trying to run away. It was

three white officers and one black. One of them asked for my information. He asked step out of the car and I asked "why?" Then, he just opened my door, grabbed my arm and pulled me out and pushed my face in the ground. He said I was being detained because he smelled an odor in my car. He then picked me up off the ground and put me in the back seat (white officer). They then searched my car and did not find anything and they let me go.

Another participant, while on his way to recreate with his friends, were detained by police because they were Black males in "a drug-infested neighborhood." Lorenz (22-year old Black male; Psychology Major; Senior) remarks:

Myself and three other friends were riding in a car to go and play basketball. They (the cops), stopped us at a red light and pulled us over. They told us to get of the vehicle and had us sit down on the curve while they searched our car. When we asked them "why are you search us" they said because this is a drug-infested neighborhood. I told them, "We live here." They said, move. Like move to another neighborhood.

Theme 2: Personal Experience with Aggressive Behavior

While the aforementioned five participants were certain they were victims of excessive force, another, three individuals (10 percent of participants) were not victims of excessive force, per se, but recount the verbally aggressive nature by which members of law enforcement treated them. Chadwick (21-year old Black male; Psychology Major; Junior) states: "No, nothing physically. Now verbally, they have said, "Pull your fucking hands up! Get against the wall!" or they would shine their lights and drive." In support of the perspective provided by Chadwick, Angela (21-year old Black female; Pre-Physical Therapy Major) simply states: "Well, I would not say 'force,' but they were really demanding and aggressive." Similar to the experiences offered by the previous participants, Jewel (21-year old African American and Native American female; Criminal Justice Major) provides this extended narrative:

Maybe. An incident it affected me more emotionally than physically. My boyfriend and I were on our way to the CVS to get snacks and it was like 1:00AM. We get out of the car and we were play fighting. Then, a White lady who was outside saw us play fighting and it looked like a domestic case to her. She calls the cops and reports a possible altercation. We are unaware, walk into the CVS, and are looking at food and all of a sudden, two cops come then. Then several pairs of cops come in the store. In the end, six or seven cops surround us. They ask me if I was okay and I said "yes." I said, "What's going on?" He did not answer my question; they then separated us and asked us questions separately. They (cops) did not believe anything that I told them. They were questioning whether we were in a relationship. After all of those questions, they did not tell us why they stopped us until the end. They asked me "my name, where I went to school, where we met, all kinds of crazy stuff." They ended up just letting us go. They were all White cops, too.

Question 9: Has a police officer used an excessive amount of force on *someone that you know*?

Qualitative analysis of the narrative responses to Question 9 (Has a police officer used an excessive amount of force on *someone that you know*?) reveals the following two themes: (a) *Personal Experience with Excessive Force*; (2) *Non-Personal Experience with Excessive Force*. The *Personal Knowledge of Excessive Force* theme relates to the participant recounting an incident in which a person he/she knows was a victim of excessive force by a member of law enforcement. *The Non-Personal Knowledge of Excessive Force* theme relates to the participant recounting an incident in which he/she was personally told or learned about an incident in which a minority person was a victim of excessive force by a member of law enforcement.

Theme 1: Personal Knowledge of Excessive Force

Twenty-eight participants (93 percent of participants) recount an incident in which he/she knows someone who was a victim of excessive force by a member of law enforcement. In some cases, it is because the individual did not comply with the officer's direction. Michelle (21-year old; Black female; Public Administration; Graduate Student) states: "Yes, it was actually influenced because the individual ran. The police just beat him up." In other cases, an argument with police escalated to violence. Malcolm (23-year old Black male; Criminal Justice Major) admits: "Yes. A police officer slammed one of my friends. He and the police officer were arguing and then he slammed him." Others share having police officers slam the body of an individual. Chadwick (21-year old Black male; Psychology Major; Junior) shares: "Yes, but I did not see it, I just heard stories. My cousin says he was coming from the train station at night and he was stopped and searched and then slammed on the ground." In another case, a simple traffic stop resulted in the driver taken away in handcuffs. Brendon (24-year old Black male; Criminal Justice; Senior) says:

> Yes. *Could you briefly describe the incident?* We got pulled over for a traffic stop and the cop claimed that my friend kept having his hands in his pocket. So, he grabbed him, put his hands behind his back, threw him on the hood of the car, and handcuffed him.

The friend of Idris (19-year old Black male; Criminal Justice Sophomore) was also a victim of excessive force. This participant states: "Yes. My friend was fighting. The fight was over for an hour and we were still at the park chilling. Then, the police grabbed him and slammed him and they were twisting his arms behind his back and he was yelling in pain." Samuel (23-year old Black male; Criminal Justice Major) shares, "Yes, but I do not know all of the details. My friend just told me that he got slammed by an officer." Lorenz (22-year old Black male; Psychology Major; Senior) says: "Yes. They slammed one of my friends on the ground after chasing him because he had some drugs on him. But, they punched him after he had been hand-cuffed."

Another participant, Rachel (28-year old Black female; Sociology Major; Junior) tells of an incident where her friend, who was a convicted felon, was thrown to the floor of his home after calling the police because he was robbed. She says:

> Yes. A friend of mine. He was robbed and shot and when the police came to his house they threw him on the floor. He was the one who called the police. He believed this was done to him because he was a convicted felon.

In another case, the victim of abuse is not aware there is a warrant out for his arrest, and when the police come to his home, he is slammed to the ground and taken to jail. Anita (18-year old Black female; Criminal Justice; Junior) shares:

> Yes, it was at a barbecue. It was my cousin. He did not know he had a warrant so when the police came and tried to arrest him he just wanted to hug his daughter. The Black officer even told the White officers that what they were doing was unnecessary and then our family began to argue with police, but they slammed him on the ground and took him to jail.

In other cases, the victim was not resisting. Karen (23-year old Black female; Health Science; Pre-Physical Therapy; Senior) shares: "Yes, one of my cousins. I do not feel it was necessary. He was not running or resisting so I did not feel was necessary to go with force." Cassie (21-year old Black female; Public Administration Graduate Student) shares, "Yes. My older cousin got into a fight at a friend's house. When the police came to settle the situation. Instead of talking to him or trying to negotiate, he shot him." D'Andre (21-year old Black male; Interdisciplinary Studies; Junior) says, "Yes, I had a cousin who was shot by the police 16 times for a disturbance call."

In another case, the victim was mentally ill. Denise (20-year old Black female; English Major; Junior) expresses, "A cousin of mine. He is autistic and ADHD, schizophrenia, and they were trying to restrain him. But I felt they were using excessive force since he does have a mental illness." Faye (21-year old Black female; Criminal Justice; Junior) says: "Yes, my brother.

My brother was racially profiled by a Caucasian officer due to his dreads, the way he dresses, and the way he spoke. They actually pulled him from a social setting to question him about the usage of drugs and gang paraphernalia." Another participant recounted an incident when her cousin was physically assaulted in a way similar to what is frequently seen on a television show. Sarah (19-year old Black female; Sociology Major; freshman) shares:

> Yes. A cousin of mine. He has been in and out of jail. He had a warrant out so when they caught him, they were really rough with him. They choked him, slammed him on the ground. But this is stuff that they usually do to people, like on the show Cops.

Still others tell of situations where they believe the police did not handle the situation in an appropriate manner and escalated the situation. Elijah (19-year old Black male; Political Science Major; Senior) says:

> One of my friends was pulled over because they were driving too close to a car. The police officer made them get out of the side of the car, handcuffed them, and put them on the side of the road. I feel that was excessive for that particular situation.

Whitney (20-year old African American female; Pre-Physical Therapy Major) declares:

> No, but a police officer has abused their power with someone I know. My friend was telling me that he got pulled over for super-speeding (15 miles over the speed limit, which is an additionally $300) when he was only going 5 miles over. Mind you, he is dark-skinned, 6 '4, and close to 300 pounds. When he got pulled over the police officer was blunt and disrespectful. He also had his other friends (who were all black) in the car. He just started jumping to conclusions and asking had they been smoking and asked everyone to get out the car to be searched. In the end, he ended up letting them go with just a super-speeding ticket, but all of that was not necessary.

Paul (36-year old Black male; Public Administration; Graduate Student) shares:

> Yes, my cousin and my father. *Would you mind explaining your recollection of what happened in one of those incidents?* My Dad—He was selling narcotics and the police came to our house and they asked to speak to him and he said he did not have any narcotics. The police asked him to come outside and he said "no." They asked him again, he said no, they grabbed him, and forcefully brought him out of the house. They searched him outside of the house. He had nothing on him, so they just told him to go back into the house.

Makala (23-year old Black female; Criminal Justice; Graduate Student) shares this narrative:

> It happened in the South and he was 22. Basically, the officer pulled him over and told him to get out the car. They searched car, another officer came and he (victim) was told to "put his hands up," and when he did it the second officer said "Boy, you think you are slick, we are going to find what is in this car." The victim replied, "yes sir" and started laughing. The officer threw him to the ground and put his knee in his back and busted up his face really bad. They (the officers) did not find anything. Both of the officers were White.

Curtis (21-year old Black male; Criminal Justice; Junior) provides this extended comment:

> Yes, one of my friends in high school. Basically we were near the mall and an officer pulled over and asked for our names. We gave him our names and the officer told my friend that he looked familiar. And then he told him to empty out his pockets. My friend said no. After that, the officer got out of the car and called for backup. The officer told me to stay on the side while he patted my friend down. He found a black and mild (small cigar) that he thought was a blunt (marijuana), he told him to get on the wall, he patted him down again. I told the officer that "we do not do that type of stuff." The officer did not necessarily excessive force, but he pushed my friend on the wall pretty hard so it was basically racial profiling.

Angela (21-year old Black female; Pre-Physical Therapy Major) provides this extended narrative:

> Yes. So during my sophomore year in college, this incident occurred outside the on-campus apartments. It was me, my roommate, and one of my close friends from home, who was a guy. In this incident, they (police) were targeting him more than us, just because we were accessories. We were in the car on the way to get something to eat. Upon getting into his car, it really smelled like marijuana. So, the police rode by and stopped us and asked us "where are you headed?" Then, my rolled down the window and said, "We are going to get something to eat." The officer smelled marijuana and asked us to get out the car. He then asked us, "do you have anything else in your possession?" He made us get out of the car and sit on the curb. He then called for backup. A black and another white police officer came for a total of three officers on the scene. The (cops) just automatically assumed that there were more drugs and weapons in the car. They got our names and student id numbers. They told us that we would have to go to a counseling session. The (cops) were really being aggressive with him.

In some cases, the excessive force used by police has a fatal outcome for the victim. James (24-year old Black male; Criminal Justice Major; Senior) proclaims:

A relative of mine did. He and his girlfriend were driving a car and he was supposedly swerving a bit because he was sleepy. So, he got pulled over by a police officer but something happened and he asked him to step out of the car. I do not know what happened after that, he detained him. He had him sitting on the curb. Then the police officer started yelling at his girlfriend. My uncle got mad and started yelling at the officer and he stood up (while in handcuffs) and the officer shot him twice, once in the neck. Then the ambulance took too long and he bled to death.

Qualitative Findings. Qualitative analysis was conducted on the following eight questions: (1) When you hear the word "police" what words immediately come to mind? (2) In general, how do you view the police? (4) When you hear of incidents of police brutality, does it influence how you feel about the police? If not, why not? If so, how so? (6) When you become aware of an incident where a police officer used excessive force and he/she said, "I feared for my life!" *what do you think*? (7) When you become aware of an incident where a police officer used excessive force and he/she said, "I feared for my life!" *what do you feel*? (10) What steps, if any, do you believe law enforcement agencies should take to deal with issues related to police brutality? (11) What steps, if any, do you believe *universities and colleges* should take to deal with issues related to police brutality? (12) Is there anything else that you would like to share?

Question #1: When you hear the word "police," what words immediately come to mind?

Grounded theory analysis of Question 1 (When you hear the word "police," what words immediately come to mind?) reveals five emergent themes: (a) Police Brutality; (b) Conflicting; (c) Racist; (d) Law Enforcers; (e) Negative. The *Police Brutality* theme relates to the participant using words and/or phrases related to the police using excessive force or being physically brutal with African Americans. The *Conflicting* theme relates to the participant using words and/or phrases that describe the police as possessing positive and negative qualities. In particular, this theme relates to the participant using words or phrases that describe the police as protectors and aggressors. The *Racist* theme relates to the participant using words and/or phrases that describe the police as racist, or immediately having negative perceptions of African American people. The *Law Enforcers* theme relates to the participant using words and/or phrases that describe the police as those who ensure that members of society follow the law. *The Negative* theme relates to the participant using words and/or phrases that describe the police in negative ways. In particular, this theme relates to police using their authority to make citizens feel inferior.

Theme 1: Police Brutality

Eight individuals (27 percent of participants) use words and/or phrases relat-ed to the police using excessive force or being physically brutal with African Americans. Denise (20-year old Black female; English Major; Junior) feels, "Brutality and distrust. What's been happening recently with all of these unarmed people who have been killed by police and the distrust that many African Americans and myself have toward policemen." Brendon (24-year old Black male; Criminal Justice; Senior) provides this comment, "Breaking the law. Police Brutality. Why those words? Usually when you hear the word police, a law is being broken or someone is breaking the law. With that being said, the police are called to come in an enforcement." Asia (22-year old African/Native American female; Psychology Major; Junior) shares,

> I think brutality. I think law. Umm, I think community service. Why do you think brutality?? In my head that is usually coupled together. And you know, Kendrick Lamar's album just came out and he talks a lot about police brutality. Why do you think law???? Because essentially, their job is to enforce laws.

Anita (18-year old Black female; Criminal Justice; Junior) replies, "Brutality. They are always late. *Why do you feel this way?* Because when they have to come to White communities, they are there in 5 minutes or less. But, when we (African Americans) call them to come to the Black community, it takes forever. By the time they come, the people have already ran away or we have handled it ourselves." Jewel (21-year old African American and Native American female; Criminal Justice Major) proclaims, "Brutality, violence, hypocrites, biased. *Why those words?* Law enforcement is supposed to pro-tect and serve, but I feel like they pick and choose who they want to protect."

Chadwick (21-year old Black male; Psychology Major; Junior) shares, "Brutality. Gangs. *Why?* It is more so Los Angeles culture and how we are brought up, people see the police as the biggest gang in America." Angela (21-year old Black female; Pre-Physical Therapy Major) explains, "I think of someone who is there to protect us and to ensure our safety, but also when thinking of police, I think of the whole Black Lives Matter movement. And, the police brutality cases that occur frequently." Zoe (21-year old African American/Black; Female; Physical Therapy Major; Junior) says, "Brutality. *Why?* Because I am African American and historically African Americans have not had a great relationship with police officers or law enforcement throughout the lower income communities, which I come from."

Theme 2: Conflicting

Eight individuals (27 percent of participants) use words and/or phrases that describe the police as possessing positive and negative qualities. In particular, this theme relates to the participant using words or phrases that describe the police as protectors and aggressors. Leah (21-year old Black female; Health Science; Pre-occupational Therapy Senior) provides this extended view:

> Serve, Aggression, abuse of power, tickets. *What does serve mean?* They are supposed to serve the community. They took an oath to serve and protect. It does not mean that they actually do. *What does the word aggression mean to you?* I think that they exhibit aggressive behavior. I do not think that all of them are bad. I just think they are when they interact with certain races. I think they come to you like they have a chip on their shoulder. Like they already have preconceived notions based on what you look like. I guess they have a prejudice.

Elijah (19-year old Black male; Political Science Major; Senior) says:

> Fear and that is a new feeling. Because my father is a retired police officer. That is because I originally saw the police, I saw them as protectors. But when I see what they do to other Blacks I do not see them as protectors. I say other Black friends because they (police) see my other Black friends as threatening and they do not see me as threatening. I am not threatening because I am 5'3, so I do not think they will look at me as the threatening type. However, the idea of someone looking threatening is an illusion. Because I feel that it (someone looking threatening) is an excuse because some of the biggest people I know are some of the nicest people that I know.

Keri (22-year old African American/Black female; Psychology Major; Junior) thinks of the following:

> White supremacy. Authority. Jail. *Why those words?* Statistics and experience from what I have seen growing up. Growing up, whenever we see the police around, we think authority. Someone above us. Be on your best behavior. Nothing really comes to mind when I think of police. Just police, authority.

Michelle (21-year old; Black female; Public Administration; Graduate Student) voices:

> Safety, White people, and discrimination. *Why those words?* Because it is a lot going on with police and African Americans as far as how they treat them. And white people, it is usually the White people that treat African Americans differently because they feel that we are lower than them. *What exactly do you mean by lower?* They basically belittle us. They feel that they deserve more input in terms of what goes on in the community.

Malcolm (23-year old Black male; Criminal Justice Major) shares:

Protection, corruption, and majority. *Why those words?* I guess because what I have experienced in my past dealing with police. One time I was 13 or 14, myself and my friends were playing games at Game Stop. We left and began walking to subway in a predominantly White area and were stopped by police. One trooper looked in subway and 3 other officers came into the subway and kicked some tables, threw us on the floor, and searched us. When they found out we did not have anything, they told us they thought we were older.

Idris (19-year old Black male; Criminal Justice; Sophomore) says, "White. *Why?* I think that the majority of the policemen that I see/run into are Caucasian, except for campus police." Makala (23-year old Black female; Criminal Justice; Graduate Student) asserts, "Trouble and corruption. *Why those words?* Because I feel that now social media captures the majority of the incidents that have taken place and it reveals the officers' true colors." Whitney (20-year old African American female; Pre-Physical Therapy Major) shares, "There's a lot of negative and positive thoughts that come to mind when I think of the police. Prior to coming of age, to understand today's society, I viewed the police as positive figures, like super heroes. Now, I view the police, not all policemen, but the majority, as cowards with guns."

Theme 3: Racist

Seven individuals (23 percent of participants) use words and/or phrases that describe the police as racist, or immediately having negative perceptions of African American people. Sarah (19-year old Black female; Sociology Major; Freshman) proclaims, "Racist. Because they prejudge Black people in general, but especially Black males. They just assume Black men are 'thugs' or 'gangsters' even if they are dressed nicely. They just assume Black men are bad like they have something against them." Karen (23-year old Black female; Health Science; Pre-Physical Therapy; Senior) proclaims, "Racist, pigs." *Why?* Because you hear so many stories about them killing innocent African Americans. Then you hear stories about how they racially profile African Americans in nice cars. They will pull you over because you are African American."

Another participant also believes the police assume the worst when dealing with Blacks. Eduardo (29-year old African American/Hispanic; Male; Pre-Physical Therapy Major; Junior) shares, "I usually think, oh fuck, here we go!" *Why?* I have lived in great places, but history shows otherwise when it comes to police interactions with skin color. When you are black or brown, I feel like police think we are more of a threat." Aaliyah (20-year old Black Female; Sociology Major; Sophomore) says, "Social institution. Enforcement. Unjust. Biased. *Why those words?* The history of police in America. Them being a part of the problem in terms of racism in general. Me, being an

African American, I grew up having a fear of police." Lorenz (22-year old Black male; Psychology Major; Senior) says, "Fear. Death. *Why those two words?* Due to what I see on social media and television when it comes to the interaction between African Americans and police officers." Celeste (22-year old Black female; Sociology; Junior) shares:

> Suspicion. Anxiety. Distrust. *So why do these words come to mind?* Because growing up I was taught not to trust the police. And in recent times, due to video footage of police killings it has led to more distrust of police officers. Particularly, White police officers. *Why White police officers?* Because it seems like the typical arrest, stop and frisk, escalates to the point of death for the Black victim because the officer does not identify with the victim. *Why do you feel the officer does not identify with the Black victim?* Because in most cases, it seems like the officer goes into the situation assuming the worst from the Black victim. They just assume a Black man is carrying a weapon or poses a threat to his life. It almost seems like they are carrying out some sort of racist agenda.

Paul (36-year old Black male; Public Administration; Graduate Student) offers this view:

> Racism, prejudice, and untruth. Because when I think about police you feel negative. The past experiences of my family and my own past experience. *Could you share one of those experiences?* When I was 24, I was driving in an upscale community and I was stopped by a police officer. I asked them "why do you need my license?" He just asked for it again. I told him to wait because I had to look forward. After he checked my license, he said it was suspended. He asked me "Why are you driving with a suspended license?" I told him that I did not know it was suspended. I asked him "why was it suspended?" He told me that I was lying. He gave me a $300 ticket and told me to leave my car there and find my way home. I got stopped because I was in a nice community. I called one of my fraternity brothers to pick me up.

Theme 4: Law Enforcers

Four individuals (13 percent of participants) immediately think of the police as enforcers of the law. Samuel (23-year old Black male; Criminal Justice Major) simply states, "Twelve. Because police always have a 12-gauge shotgun." James (24-year old Black male; Criminal Justice Major; Senior) says the following, "Gatekeeper. *Why does the word come to mind? Because they are supposed to be the gatekeepers of the criminal justice system.* Like, I guess they are the front men to the criminal justice system. They are the ones out front that you always see." Faye (21-year old Black female; Criminal Justice; Junior) expresses, "Law enforcement, crime. *Why those two words?* Because I know that police officers enforce the law and they also either hinder or help when it comes to crime." Cassie (21-year old Black female;

Public Administration Graduate Student) says, "Authority. Because they are looked as someone with a higher power in society."

Theme 5: Negative

Three participants (10 percent of the total number of participants) had a less than favorable view of police. Rachel (28-year old Black female; Sociology Major; Junior) asserts, "Protect. I do not want to say 'superior,' but that is how they feel." *What do you mean by "superior"?* "Some police officers come off as if they are above the citizens. They have like a God complex. They feel like they are above everyone in terms of their ranking." D'Andre, (21-year old Black male; Interdisciplinary Studies; Junior) provides this perspective, "I view police as people who are supposed to help but basically they are harmful to my community." Curtis (21-year old Black male; Criminal Justice; Junior) feels,

> When I think of police, I think of words such as "watch out," "be cautious," and "controlling." *Why those words?* Basically, with all of the things that I have seen in reality and movies. I feel the police is almost like a gang. I know that it (police brutality) has been going on a long time, but it is now becoming a viral thing because of technology. It is being caught on phones, social media, and everything else.

Question #2: In general, how do you view the police?

Grounded theory analysis of Question 2 (In general, how do you view the police?) reveals four emergent themes: (a) Negative; (b) Conflicting; (c) Law Enforcers; (d) Racist. *The Negative* theme relates to the participant using words and/or phrases that describe the police in negative ways. In particular, this theme relates to police using their authority to make citizens feel inferior. The *Conflicting* theme relates to the participant using words and/or phrases that describe the police as possessing positive and negative qualities. In particular, this theme relates to the participant using words or phrases that describe the police as protectors and aggressors.

The *Law Enforcers* theme relates to the participant using words and/or phrases that describe the police as those who ensure that members of society follow the law. The *Racist* theme relates to the participant using words and/or phrases that describe the police as racist, or immediately having negative perceptions of African American people.

Theme 1: Negative

Thirteen participants (43 percent of the total number of participants) use words and/or phrases that describe the police in negative ways. In particular, this theme relates to police using their authority to make citizens feel inferior. Paul (36-year old Black male; Public Administration; Graduate Student) shares: "Nine times out of ten, negative. Because of my own experiences." Lorenz (22-year old Black male; Psychology Major; Senior) states: "I have a negative view of police. Due to my own interactions with police." Malcolm (23-year old Black male; Criminal Justice Major) believes: "There are some good ones, but I have mostly seen bad ones. Every experience that I have had with police growing up has been bad." D'Andre (21-year old Black male; Interdisciplinary Studies; Junior) shares, "I view police as people who are supposed to help but they basically they are harmful to my community." Brendon (24-year old Black male; Criminal Justice; Senior) states:

> In general, I view the police as service workers just doing their job. But, at the same time, I do not really trust them that much. *Why do you not trust them that much?* Because there have been times that they have not explained their reasoning for doing things. *What times or could you provide me an example?* When we one of my friends were handcuffed during a routine traffic stop and detained.

Several participants use the term "abuse of power" to describe the police. Celeste (22-year old Black female; Sociology; Junior) states: "I view them as arrogant. It often seems like an abuse of power on their end. It seems like some police officers go into the field just so they can carry a gun and badge and police others." Karen (23-year old Black female; Health Science; Pre-Physical Therapy; Senior) shares:

> I do not want to say "all" police officers' abuse their power. However, it is a majority of police officers abuse their power. They tend not to think before they retaliate and end up hurting innocent individuals. Or, stereotyping individuals.

Cassie (21-year old Black female; Public Administration Graduate Student) remarks:

> Honestly, I do not really see them as a positive figure within society today because they abuse their authority. However, I feel as though there are police officers out there who have good cause and intentions, but they're given a stereotype because of other officers' doings.

Zoe (21-year old African American/Black; Female; Physical Therapy Major; Junior) says:

> I feel as if they are here to protect and serve us, however, a lot of them abuse their power. *How do you believe that they abuse their power?* Because when you are skilled at something that someone else is not skilled at or they are not

an expert at, you tend to think of them as being beneath you or inferior. *In your opinion, how does this apply to police officers?* Because they're physically trained and everyone is not trained like police. Once they know that they have that type of training (with firearms), they have the advantage over us regular people.

Denise (20-year old Black female; English Major; Junior) remarks: "Umm, I do not really trust them because who they target. They target Black and Brown bodies and they really do not do right by the people." Chadwick (21-year old Black male; Psychology Major) says:

> In my opinion, I do not like the police. They have been harassing me from a young age. *What exactly do you mean by harassment?* For instance, when I was around 11 or 12, I would be walking to the park with a basketball or a football in my hand, and they would just pull me over and ask me where am I going? They would just assume that I am doing something.

Leah (21-year old Black female; Health Science; Pre-occupational Therapy Senior) remarks:

> Umm, not in a good light. I think that the bad apples really spoil the bunch. It is hard to see beyond the bad apples. The ones that abuse their authority and are brutal and step over the line for what their job entails. Taking advantage of their authority. Not upholding their oath to protect and serve.

Keri (22-year old African American/Black female; Psychology Major; Junior) says:

> I do not like the police, but I know that we need them. *Why do you feel that way?* I feel this way because I have a lot of family members behind bars that I believe should be out. I feel like the police department does not benefit the African American community. I feel like it benefits Caucasians. *Why do you feel that way?* For example, drug use is pretty much equal between the races. But the drug war targets inner-cities.

Theme 2: Conflicting

Eleven participants (37 percent of the total number of participants) use words and/or phrases that describe the police as possessing positive and negative qualities. In particular, this theme relates to the participant using words or phrases that describe the police as protectors and aggressors. Elijah (19-year old Black male; Political Science Major; Senior) says, "I believe it is a good organization that has flawed tactics. Generally speaking I believe that the job of the police is a good job, but it is often tainted by people's bias and ignorance." Samuel (23-year old Black male; Criminal Justice Major) proclaims:

I see them as good and bad. Good because it is actually people doing their job and not just being there for a paycheck or for the abuse of power. The bad, corruption. The justice system is not equal.

Jewel (21-year old African American and Native American female; Criminal Justice Major) believes:

A double-edged sword. On one hand, you want to trust them. They are the ones you call if you have an emergency. But, then when you see hundreds, perhaps thousands of reports of them beating and killing people it is hard to really trust and believe in them.

Curtis (21-year old Black male; Criminal Justice; Junior) surmises:

That is a tough question. From when I was younger until 10th grade of high school, I saw the police as a great unit that protects and serves and actually do their jobs. From 11th grade until now, not all, but certain ones, I see them as bad people.

Anita (18-year old Black female; Criminal Justice; Junior) considers:

Some police are good and some are bad. *Why do you feel this way?* Because I have been pulled over for really stupid things. I think they do not expect a Black person to have nice things, so they will just pull you over for anything.

James (24-year old Black male; Criminal Justice Major; Senior) shares:

I think that at least half of them are pretty good. But like the old saying goes, "one bad apple spoils the entire bunch." When you hear about all these cop killings in the media, it makes people in the Black community have a distrust of police officers.

Another participant used the metaphor of "bad apples" to describe police that are abusive when performing their duties. Asia (22-year old African/Native American female; Psychology Major; Junior) says:

Umm, I think that there are some bad apples in the bunch. Overall, I do not have a bad view of police. When I see them I do not cringe. If something bad happens, I still call them. But, I definitely do take precautions to avoid them. *Like what?* If a police officer is driving behind me, I will turn. If I see a police officer, I will keep my distance. Because you do not want to be around where the police are. I do not want to be involved with anything that has to do with the police. If I am at an event where the police are, it is their job to be focused on what is going in and not for me to be bothering them.

Rachel (28-year old Black female; Sociology major; Junior) articulates:

I do not have any negative feelings and I do not have any positive feelings. I am sort of in the middle. I have had positive experiences but you do have those bad cops that engage in racial profiling and shoot unarmed citizens. I have actually had a police officer assist me with changing my tire. I have had them let me out of tickets with a warning. I have had a police officer follow me home when I thought a guy was following me home from the club.

Faye (21-year old Black female; Criminal Justice; Junior) declares:

I view them in two ways. First, from a helpful standpoint whereas they assist and help with justice and what is right and wrong. Second, I also look at them as a threat. Because of the way they go about situations. For example, I cannot allow myself to forget certain cases like Trayvon Martin and many others where innocent African American, mostly males, were either beaten, shot down, or racially profiled for reasons that still cannot be explained today.

Makala (23-year old Black female; Criminal Justice; Graduate Student) views the police as:

Untrained and uneducated men who have more authority over your life than you actually do. *Why do you feel this way?* Because the police academy is only 5–6 months. So, in 5–6 months they (police officers) pretty much think they know when a human being is being defiant. For example, if an African American male has a mental illness the officer is often unable to diagnose it and treat him properly. Instead, they often use excessive force.

Eduardo (29-year old; African American/Hispanic; Male; Pre-Physical Therapy Major; Junior) says:

Police have an honorable job, but the people behind the job give policing a bad stigma. *Why do you feel this way?* If you look at Rodney King, there were five or six officers beating up Rodney King. That is like a group of people (the cops) that did something bad. But if you look up an officer named Tommy Norman, he goes out in the community and helps his community. So, a couple of bad apples spoil the bunch.

Theme 3: Law Enforcers

While one participant, Angela, a 21-year old Black female; Pre-Physical Therapy major proclaims: "Well, I perceive the police differently because personally, I have never had any bad encounters with them," the majority of participants saw the police as "a necessary evil" who sometimes abuse their authority and unfairly target Blacks and other people of color.

Three participants (10 percent of the total number of participants) used words and/or phrases that describe the police as those who ensure that members of society follow the law. Michelle (21-year old; Black female; Public

Administration; Graduate Student) says: "I view them as certain individuals who take on the role of patrolling our communities and making sure that we are safe." Aaliyah (20-year old Black Female; Sociology Major; Sophomore) shares:

> I view them as a necessary evil. We need police to enforce laws, protect, and serve. On the other hand, those laws are not all inclusive in regards to their enforcement and content. Some of them are targeted toward people of color.

Theme 4: Racist

Three participants (10 percent of the total number of participants) used words and/or phrases that describe the police as racist, or immediately having negative perceptions of African American people. Whitney (20-year old African American female; Pre-Physical Therapy Major) remarks:

> It is hard to answer, but the majority of policemen that I have encountered are male Caucasians who are racist. *Why would you describe them as racist?* I think what makes them racists is their mannerisms, their tone, their demeanor all changes once they see the color of my skin. When I have been pulled over, I have had all bad encounters. I will ask questions, they will not answer them, and I respectfully. I am not a disrespectful person and that seems to be all that I get (disrespect) and high tickets when I am pulled over for something small.

Sarah (19-year old Black female; Sociology Major; Freshman) states:

> As prejudiced. Because you have even your own Black cops who will treat their fellow brothers the same as white cop would or sometimes even worse. *Why do you feel that is the case?* Even in healthcare, home buying, white people always come first and they get treated better than a minority will get treated. *Why do you feel that White people always come first?* Because people view Black people different than the view White people. For instance, if you "Google" a White girl you will see a happy smiling face and if you "Google" Black girl you will get a nappy-headed savage-looking person.

Idris (19-year old Black male; Criminal Justice; Sophomore) discloses:

> I feel as though the job is necessary, but the treatment of African Americans is unfair. They are not really in our favor. They kind of have their own agenda. *What do you mean by their own agenda?* I mean the way in which they approach similar situations, but the difference is the race. Like, it can be a White man walking down the street with a gun. And a black man walking down the street with a gun. Both of them can be in an open carry state and both situations would be approached differently.

Question #4: When you hear of incidents of police brutality, does it influence how you feel about the police? If not, why not? If so, how so?

Grounded theory analysis of Question 4 (When you hear of incidents of police brutality, does it influence how you feel about the police? If not, why not? If so, how so?) reveals two emergent themes (a) Affirmative; (b) Negative. The *Affirmative* theme refers to words and/or phrases that relate to negative personal, familial, or communal actions of police causing participants to have a less than favorable perception of law enforcement as a whole. The *Negative* theme refers to words and/or phrases that relate to participants not allowing the actions of some police to cause them to have a less than favorable perception of law enforcement as a whole.

Theme 1: Affirmative

Twenty-eight participants (90 percent of the total number of participants) share negative personal, family, or communal experiences with police that have caused them to have a less than favorable view of law enforcement. Keri (22-year old African American/Black female; Psychology Major; Junior) replies, "Yes. It makes me think less of them. Why? Because I am all for justice and equality." Paul (36-year old Black male; Public Administration; Graduate Student) admits: "Yes, because it reinforces what I already think about police. Stuff that I see and stuff that I do not see." Michelle (21-year old; Black female; Public Administration; Graduate Student) states: "Yes, because I feel like that I cannot trust them to protect us and our community." Malcolm (23-year old Black male; Criminal Justice Major) conveys, "Yes. I just think here it goes again. I wonder if anything is going to be done." Whitney (20-year old African American female; Pre-Physical Therapy Major) proclaims, "Of course. It is psychologically detrimental to the Black community just to know that our lives still are not valued." Karen (23-year old Black female; Health Science; Pre-Physical Therapy; Senior) states: "Yes, it does. *Why?* Because it is just to hear stories about them killing individuals because they are Black. You do not trust them, just shoot kill first." Denise (20-year old Black female; English Major; Junior) says:

> Yes. Umm, it is sad because when I hear about police brutality it does not surprise me. I kind of expect it from police because of their history with brutalizing people. It has affected to the point that I cannot trust them the way that I would like to, but I can't.

Faye (21-year old Black female; Criminal Justice; Junior) believes:

> To some extent, it does because seeing people like me being discriminated against, beaten and killed over the color of their skin solidifies for me that

racism still exists and it confuses me because we normally seek the police for help.

Elijah (19-year old Black male; Political Science Major; Senior) shares: "Most definitely. *Why so?* It takes me a minute to have respect for them. I do not really have too much to say. My respect for them leaves a lot." Rachel (28-year old female; Sociology Major) says, "Most definitely. Because when you think of the police, you think of people who are supposed to protect and serve. I feel that there has been more profiling than protecting that has been taking place lately." Leah (21-year old Black female; Health Science; Pre-occupational Therapy; Senior) remarks:

> Definitely. It would be hard not to. The videos you see are traumatic. For the most part, you are seeing what happened. They are murdering people for simple infractions. The guy who got shot in the car with his daughter. I mean, he did not even do anything. You could see his daughter crying in the background.

Sarah (19-year old Black female; Sociology Major; freshman) admits:

> Yes. You wake up every day and there is a different case of any innocent Black man being shot for being Black who is unarmed. Like the case of Philandro Castille whose girlfriend filmed the entire thing.

Celeste (22-year old Black female; Sociology; Junior) states:

> Yes. *Why?* Because it further adds to the notion that many Black people have that police officers are not to be trusted. Many of us, we were raised to view officers as Pigs. So, when we see a video of police brutality it reinforces our negative view of police officers.

James (24-year old Black male; Criminal Justice Major; Senior) shares:

> Yes. I try not associate it with all cops, but it is so prevalent now it is hard not to. *Why do you say it so prevalent now?* I mean, it's everywhere. That and racism are the hot-button issues. You can turn on the news literally every night and you will see something about.

Idris (19-year old Black male; Criminal Justice; Sophomore) admits: "Yes. It's because it happens too often. It was not a rare thing to hear. Now, when it happens, I am just like "again." Aaliyah (20-year old Black Female; Sociology Major; sophomore) remarks: "Yes. It reinforces my strong feelings that the system victimizes people of color. Modern police brutality give off the essence of Jim Crow type punishments." Cassie (21-year old Black female; Public Administration Graduate Student) states, "Yes. *How?* It gives me a negative outlook about them. Because of their actions, it makes me feel that I am unsafe around them. If those incidents never happened, I would not have a negative influence about them."

Several participants did not believe they or their family members were safe. Makala (23-year old Black female; Criminal Justice; Graduate Student) simply states, "Yes, because I look at the situation and I think, 'that could have been me.'" Lorenz (22-year old Black male; Psychology Major; Senior) states: "Yes, it does influence the way I feel about them. *Why does it influence the way you feel about them?* Because I can picture the individuals being brutalized as myself. In other words, that could be me being brutalized." D'Andre (21-year old Black male; Interdisciplinary Studies; Junior) shares, "Yes. I feel as if police can do it to another black man in the same situation, they can do it to me as well." Brendon (24-year old Black male; Criminal Justice; Senior) states, "Yes, it does. Because I can identify with many of the victims of police brutality. *How can you identify with them?* Umm, by me being a young African American male." Angela (21-year old Black female; Pre-Physical Therapy Major) explains,

> Yes, it does affect the way I feel about police. For example, when Koryn Gaines incident occurred it made me think, what if this was my mother in this situation? Or, like the cases in which black males are affected. It makes me realize that it could have been my brother.

Samuel (23-year old Black male; Criminal Justice Major) says:

> Yes, it does. Because they say the justice system is supposed to be fairly equal, but blacks and minorities get treated fairly different. *How?* So, if you were to get pulled over and approached by a White officer, the talk is very different. I got pulled over by the university police, the officer was Black, and he did not make me fearful of being pulled over.

Curtis (21-year old Black male; Criminal Justice; Junior) asserts:

> Of course. *Why?* Because when you think of police, you should think of people who are out there to get the bad guys that deserve to be in jail. But, in reality, the police are those bad guys who deserve to be in prison or jail.

Eduardo (29-year old; African American/Hispanic; Male; Pre-Physical Therapy Major; Junior) articulates,

> My background was in the military. We do a little bit of police officer training, detaining suspects, and stuff like that. I feel like when police officers cross the line they burn that trust. Then, the community you are serving can no longer trust you. For instance, when a police officer roughs up someone, the commu-

nity basically turns its back on the police force itself. So now, the police officers have even more problems.

Jewel (21-year old African American and Native American female; Criminal Justice Major) states:

> Yes, it does. *How so?* The more I hear about these types of incidents (brutality/ shootings), I feel like it is becoming the norm and people are getting complacent. I would say, "I am just tired of hearing about this type of violence." I am just "over" the police. That is where the distrust comes in.

Zoe (21-year old African American/Black; Female; Physical Therapy Major; Junior) communicates:

> Yes, it does influence how I feel about police. It just fuels the fire. *Why do you feel this way?* Because police brutality has always been evident and there are not laws in place enforcing that. So, they do what they please and get off on administrative leave with no consequences.

Chadwick (21-year old Black male; Psychology Major; Junior) expresses:

> Yes, especially when there is video proof that there was no type of harm done. I mean, there was no harm to the police. The victim could have his hands in the air, presenting no harm, and still get killed.

Theme 2: Negative

Two females (10 percent of the total number of participants) did not perceive the police in a negative way. However, these females found it difficult to make a distinction between the person wearing the uniform and the duties that they perform. Case in point: Anita (18-year old Black female; Criminal Justice; Junior) states: "No. It makes me think of people differently, not the police per se. I know what the police are here to do; it is just the people in the uniform that I do not trust." Asia (22-year old African/Native American female; Psychology Major; Junior) shares this perspective:

> No, because that particular police officer may be rotten. I do not judge all police on the actions of one. But I do get disappointed in the other officers that are around because they do not do anything. All it takes is for one person to stand up and do the right thing. *Do you feel officers stand up for the right thing frequently enough?* No. There is so much that goes into why they do not stand up. Like what comes next. Desk duty, peer pressure, pay cuts, the values of your entire department. Too many influences to make someone do the right thing all the time.

Question #6: When you become aware of an incident where a police officer used excessive force and he/she said, "I feared for my life!" *what do you think?*

Grounded theory analysis of Question 6 (When you become aware of an incident where a police officer used excessive force and he/she said, "I feared for my life!" *what do you think?)* reveals three emergent themes: (a) Racism; (b) Disbelief; (c) Fabrication. The *Racism* theme refers to words and/or phrases that relate to participants' belief that race, being a racial minority, or African American as the reason why the police fear for their life. The *Disbelief* theme refers to words and/or phrases that relate to the participant having doubt that the member of law enforcement is being truthful regarding fearing for their life. The *Fabrication* theme refers to words and/or phrases that relate to the participant believing that fear is an excuse, justification, and/or cover-up for wrongdoing.

Theme 1: Racism

Six individuals (20 percent of the total number of participants) used words and/or phrases that relate to participants' belief that race, being a racial minority, or African American as the reason why the police fear for their life. Leah (21-year old Black female; Health Science; Pre-occupational Therapy; Senior) says, "I think, come on, really. You chose this job. You know what this job entails. Why did you not use another tactic? When you subdue the individual, the first idea is to shoot if you are a person of color. It is like there is no other option. There is no scale to judge their level of fear, I mean they (the cops) can be fabricating. That is where it gets sticky." Sarah (19-year old Black female; Sociology Major; Freshman) alleges, "I think they felt like the person was bad because they were Black person. They just assume and then they shoot first." Samuel (23-year old Black male; Criminal Justice Major) feels, "It is possible, but when White officers shoot Black people it is always justifiable and it should not be like that." Elijah (19-year old Black male; Political Science Major; Senior) asserts, "I think that it is false. Simply put, I feel police officers are liars and the only threatening thing is a Black person's skin tone. When you look at the things that go on in the live videos (of police shootings), their stories never add up." Whitney (20-year old African American female; Pre-Physical Therapy Major) feels, "Frustrated. I feel depressed and imprisoned. I have darker siblings and darker skinned, my boyfriend is dark skinned." Celeste (22-year old Black female; Sociology; Junior) reveals, "I do not understand how you fearing for your life leads to an unarmed civilian getting killed. It makes no sense; you are a trained officer. That is how a lot of America sees Black people as super predators, so they believe that excuse. Why not reach for your Taser or pepper spray? Why shoot to kill?"

Theme 2: Disbelief

Seven individuals (23 percent of the total number of participants) use words and/or phrases that relate to the participant having doubt that the member of law enforcement is being truthful regarding fearing for their life. Rachel (28-year old Black female; Sociology Major; Junior) says, "Why are you a police officer, if you fear for your life? I mean how can you protect someone who you are afraid of?" Curtis (21-year old Black male; Criminal Justice; Junior) shares, "I understand they are trained to fight those type of situations. Basically, you put your life on the line every day for those type of situations. You should not fear anything because that is your job." Eduardo, (29-year old; African American/Hispanic; Male; Pre-Physical Therapy Major; Junior) feels: "It is what you signed up for. So basically, the job description is to protect and serve the people. If you did not want the fear of your life being in danger then you do not sign up for it." James (24-year old Black male; Criminal Justice Major; Senior) asserts:

> I do not believe it is true, mainly because the person is unarmed but you have a gun, a Taser, some pepper spray, a baton, and all this equipment on. You have all these things to protect yourself against this person and one could argue with all of the police shootings going on, that the suspect should be fearing for their life.

Brendon (24-year old Black male; Criminal Justice; Senior) believes: "First thing I start to think of is did the person who he used deadly force on have a weapon. And, if not, then I do not think he should have feared for his life because he has weapons other than a gun himself." Makala states, "I think if you feared for your life, "How did the situation start and what events led up to you deciding to take your gun?" Lorenz (22-year old Black male; Psychology Major; Senior) says: "I think, so did the person they killed (feared for their life). The individuals who feared for their life did not get to live to tell their story."

Theme 3: Fabrication

Seventeen individuals (57 percent of the total number of participants) use words and/or phrases that relate to the participant believing that fear is an excuse, justification, and/or cover-up for wrongdoing.

Asia (22-year old African/Native American female; Psychology Major; Junior) feels, "It is an excuse. It is a justification to react the way that they did. But I feel like it can be true. Black people are naturally bigger, stronger, and faster than White people. That paired with environmental influences, can cause people to actually have a fear of White people. But when they use the fear to kill someone, that is a justification and an excuse. You did not have to kill them because you were fearful." Michelle (21-year old; Black female; Public Administration; Graduate Student) proclaims, "I do not really feel that they fear for their life because they are trained to handle these situations." Malcolm (23-year old Black male; Criminal Justice Major) says, "I feel they are making up a justifiable reason for them to shoot someone." Keri (22-year old African American/Black female; Psychology Major; Junior) explains, "Justification. They are just using a justification for whatever they did. When they take the oath, it is something like 'I will risk my own life to save someone else's' or something like that. It's something they say to get out of the situation that they are in."

Several participants use the word "lie" or "lying" to describe members of law enforcement that blame fear for why they murdered a Black person. Paul (36-year old Black male; Public Administration; Graduate Student) says, "They are lying. *Why do you think they are lying?* I think they (police) already have preconceived notions about other cultures and races. I think the 'I feared for my life,' is just a generic answer. I mean, how can you fear for your life when you are a police officer? You are the law and 9 times out of 10 the courts will believe the law enforcement officer." Karen (23-year old Black female; Health Science; Pre-Physical Therapy; Senior) asserts, "I feel like he is lying. He is trying to cover up. I feel as though they are just making excuses." Chadwick (21-year old Black male; Psychology Major; Junior) feels, "I think of a lie and a cover up, to cover up his mistake or actions. Especially when it has been proven that his life was not in any danger." Jewel (21-year old African American and Native American female; Criminal Justice Major) asserts, "I think they are lying. They are liars! It is a copout. An excuse." Anita (18-year old Black female; Criminal Justice; Junior) states, "I think that they are lying. *Why do you feel this way?* I just think the media portrays us as negative people. So, whenever you look at a dark-skinned person, you think something bad is going to happen."

Other participants use the term "bull" and "bullshit" to describe the actions of police. Idris (19-year old Black male; Criminal Justice; Sophomore) exclaims, "I think it is bull because you are the one with a gun in the situation. You are the one with the vest on in the situation. You are the one with training on how to defuse the situation. So you are the one fearing for your life when this is the primary thing that you do." Zoe (21-year old African American/Black; Female; Physical Therapy Major; Junior) states, "I think it is bullshit because you are trained and equipped for situations that get out of hand and you vow to protect and serve, not to take innocent lives away. So, that is just an abuse of power to me. And, if they fear for their lives in situations like that, then they do not need to be police officers because they are not serving or protecting anyone."

Two participants use the term "scapegoat" to describe the actions of police. Faye (21-year old Black female; Criminal Justice; Junior) feels, "They are using the phrase as a scapegoat. It is just an excuse to forcefully attack the victim and because of their position they always escape, so they continue to use it." Aaliyah, (20-year old Black Female; Sociology Major; Sophomore) provides this view, "I think that if they did fear for their life, I think it is a scapegoat. I think by saying that, if the person is of color, they are acknowledging stereotypes about Black people and that would also suggest within their line of work they are trained to fear a person of color. Which means the criminal justice system is racist."

Several individuals use the word "excuse" to describe the actions of law enforcement who claim they fear for their life when fatalities occur. Cassie (21-year old Black female; Public Administration; Graduate Student) feels, "I think that the police uses that excuse to protect themselves from their wrong doing." D'Andre (21-year old Black male; Interdisciplinary Studies; Junior) feels, "I view it as an excuse to try and cover-up the wrong that they have done." Denise (20-year old Black female; English Major; Junior) asserts, "I take that as an excuse to brutalize people. For instance, Tamir Rice. They shot twelve-year-old boy in 2 seconds. They say it to excuse their actions. The stand your ground law protects them from consequences when they shoot them." Angela (21-year old Black female; Pre-Physical Therapy Major) states, "I believe that it is an excuse. I think that they are more scared of us (African Americans) than we are scared of them. They feel like when they approach us that we may appear intimidating which leads to them feeling as though they have to protect themselves."

Question #7: When you become aware of an incident where a police officer used excessive force and he/she said, "I feared for my life!" *what do you feel?*

Grounded theory analysis of Question 7 (When you become aware of an incident where a police officer used excessive force and he/she said, "I feared for my life!" *what do you feel?)* reveals two emergent themes: (a) Fabrication; (b) Frustration and Anger. The *Fabrication* theme refers to words and/ or phrases that relate to the participant believing that fear is an excuse, justification, and/or cover-up for wrongdoing of law enforcement. The *Frustration and Anger* theme refers to words and/or phrases that relate to participants' resentment of police who use excessive force yet claim they fear for their life. This theme also refers to words and/or phrases that relate to the participant believing police use "fear for their life" as a way to obstruct justice.

Theme 1: Fabrication

One person, Samuel (23-year old Black male; Criminal Justice Major) shares: "I really do not have any feeling because I do not know what the officer was fearful of," this was not the consensus of most participants.[1] In particular, sixteen individuals (53 percent of participants; one person did not provide a response to this question) used words and/or phrases that relate to the participant believing that fear is an excuse, justification, and/or cover-up for wrongdoing of law enforcement." Rachel (28-year old Black female; Sociology Major; Junior) relates, "I feel like sometimes that is an excuse for the excessive force. I feel like them saying that their life is danger will make it justifiable to the public to kill someone." Michelle (21-year old; Black female; Public Administration; Graduate Student) shares, "I feel disappointed because they are trying to switch the situation around to make it seem like they are a victim." Karen (23-year old Black female; Health Science; Pre-Physical Therapy; Senior) shares: "I feel like he is lying. He is trying to cover up. I feel as though they are just making excuses." Cassie (21-year old Black female; Public Administration; Graduate Student) remarks: "I feel as though it is an excuse they use to protect themselves. I also feel as though they are not really threatened by the suspect." Denise (20-year old Black female; English Major; Junior) says, "Tired. Because how many more officers are going to use that excuse. It is exhausting. They say that one thing and they are let off the hook. Just tired and angry." Brendon (24-year old Black male; Criminal Justice; Senior) says: "I feel upset. Because I feel as though the officer is just using that as an excuse for the amount force he used because it may have not been necessary."

Anita (18-year old Black female; Criminal Justice; Junior) states: "I feel numb because when they (police) say that you know that they are going to get away." Faye (21-year old Black female; Criminal Justice; Junior) articulates:

> I feel as though it is unjust. And it is just about as bad as pleading insanity. Because when you plead insanity, you have to remain insane for the rest of your life. Because the minute they realize you are sane, you will be in jail the rest of your life. So, when I say it is just as bad as pleading insanity, I am saying that you would allow this obnoxious behavior and this form of excuse to exist forever.

Curtis (21-year old Black male; Criminal Justice; Junior) says:

> I understand they are trained to fight those type of situations. Basically, you put your life on the line every day for those type of situations. You should not fear anything because that is your job.

Eduardo (29-year old; African American/Hispanic; Male; Pre-Physical Therapy Major; Junior) shares this view:

> It's upsetting to me, because it is no longer, "Hey, I am in fear for my life." It is a copout. Because after the shooting and after the investigation, they go to court and say, "I was in fear for my life," then the police officer gets away with murder. But, if as an African American I do the same thing, I get put away for murder.

Jewel (21-year old African American and Native American female; Criminal Justice Major) says:

> I roll my eyes or laugh. I feel disgusted that they think that is acceptable. Now that I think about it. They think it (acts of brutality) are acceptable because they continue to get away with it.

Zoe (21-year old African American/Black; Female; Physical Therapy Major; Junior) admits:

> I feel hurt, because of the fact that these are innocent lives being taken away from families. People are devastated and children are growing up without their parents because of the situation that got out of hand and my trust for officers continues to diminish.

Angela (21-year old Black female; Pre-Physical Therapy Major) relates:

> I feel, maybe scared. I think, "What if I was placed in this predicament?" They may mistake any of my sudden movements as me trying to target them instead, and that may not be the situation.

Theme 2: Frustration and Anger

Thirteen individuals (43 percent of participants) use words and/or phrases that relate to participants' resentment of police who use excessive force yet claim they fear for their life. This theme also refers to words and/or phrases that relate to the participant believing fear for their life as a means to obstruct justice.

Lorenz (22-year old Black male; Psychology Major; Senior) says: "I feel sad. Sometimes anger." Paul (36-year old Black male; Public Administration; Graduate Student) says: "I feel anger, frustration, and a sense of disbelief." Malcolm (23-year old Black male; Criminal Justice Major) admits: "I feel a little angry because of the simple fact that I know he is going to get off for it." Elijah (19-year old Black male; Political Science Major; Senior) admits: "Angry. Initially, I become angry. Because I feel is they are so easily scared, then maybe it is not the job for them." Chadwick (21-year old Black male; Psychology Major; Junior) states: "It makes me very angry and causes me to think of the steps I could take to prevent this from happening in the future." Makala (23-year old Black female; Criminal Justice; Graduate Student) shares: "I feel anger, especially when they (the victim) are unarmed and you (the officer) have a deadly weapon. So, how can you (the officer) say you fear for your life when they (the victim) is unarmed?" Idris (19-year old Black male; Criminal Justice; Sophomore) says: "I feel disgusted and angry. *Why?* Because, I feel like that is the get out of jail free card. That is all they have to say for them to not get in trouble for what they did."

Aaliyah (20-year old Black Female; Sociology Major; sophomore) remarks:

> Towards the police officers, I feel unsympathetic. I feel angry, but not surprised. Towards those people that have been brutalized, I feel a hurt for them and their families. I know that regardless of what happens, this was going to happen to them or to someone else. It did not need to happen, but because of the way the system is set up, it continues to happen.

Keri (22-year old African American/Black female; Psychology Major; Junior) states, "I feel pissed, especially when they (the victim) is unarmed. If that person being harmed is not trying to harm someone else, I feel even more pissed." Sarah (19-year old Black female; Sociology Major; Freshman) articulates:

> I feel insulted. Because it is just like me saying: "There is a white man walking my way so I have to shoot him." That would be me assuming that he is a bad person because he is White. But that is what they (cops and White people) assume that he is bad because he is Black, when it is White people doing all of the mass shootings in society.

Celeste (22-year old Black female; Sociology; Junior) shares:

> Anger. Because as a Black person, I understand that could have been my brother or uncle. I can see the pain what the families go through. And for these killings to not result in at least a conviction, even when they are caught on film, is insulting. White people care more about animal abuse than Black people. They care more about dog fighting than they do police brutality against Black people.

James (24-year old Black male; Criminal Justice Major; Senior) expresses:

> It frustrates and angers me. Because I feel like, I am hearing more and more police officers use the phrase and it seems like it is all that they have to say to get away with killing an unarmed Black person.

Asia (22-year old African/Native American female; Psychology Major; Junior) states:

> Angry. Disappointed. *Why?* Anger because it should not happen. It is wrong. Disappointment because the person did not choose or try to choose another option. Sometimes it is circumstantial. At other times I am embarrassed, if the Black person that was killed was being irate and ignorant and all of those things. It just makes black people look bad.

Question #10: What steps, if any, do you believe law enforcement agencies should take to deal with issues related to police brutality?

Grounded theory analysis of Question 10 (What steps, if any, do you believe law enforcement agencies should take to deal with issues related to police brutality?) reveals four emergent themes: (a) Stricter Hiring and Training Practices; (b) Reevaluate Current Laws and Policies; (c) Required Body Cameras; (d) Nothing Will Change. The *Stricter Hiring and Training Practices* theme refers to words and/or phrases that relate to participants' assertion that stricter hiring and training practices will help prevent police brutality. The *Reevaluate Current Laws and Policies* theme refers to words and/or phrases that relate to participants' belief that laws and policies should make police accountable when they use excessive force and/or murder a Black person. The *Required Body Cameras* theme refers to words and/or phrases that relate to the participant believing that if members of law enforcement were required to wear body cameras and/or dash cameras, this would minimize police brutality. The *Nothing Will Change* theme refers to words and/or phrases that relate to participants' belief that racism in society and members of law enforcement is so deep that will nothing will eradicate police brutality.

Theme 1: Stricter Hiring and Training Practices

Nineteen participants (63 percent of the total number of participants) use words and/or phrases that relate to participants' assertion that stricter hiring and training practices will help prevent police brutality. Samuel (23-year old Black male; Criminal Justice Major) states, "Yes, practice more tactics so they can be more trained." Leah, (21-year old Black female; Health Science; Pre-occupational Therapy; Senior) opines, "I think more thorough training should be given. Some type of audit. Look at their records or files and any citations for brutality or doing something awful. Then they should be fired. The hiring process should be standardized. They should have more thorough background checks. I also think they should have rigorous sensitivity training." Karen (23-year old Black female; Health Science; Pre-Physical Therapy; Senior) says, "I feel like they should do some type of training on how to handle certain situations. The police officer is taking his power and running with it. They should do some sort of mental training to see if something is wrong with them." Malcolm (23-year old Black male; Criminal Justice Major) says, "They need to develop better communication skills and properly train officers to use force." Denise (20-year old Black female; English Major; Junior) shares, "I feel like they should go through in-depth background screenings. Also, the way they are trained."

Eduardo (29-year old; African American/Hispanic; Male; Pre-Physical Therapy Major; Junior) says, "Police officers need to realize that they are not the judge, jury, and executioner. If you cannot put someone down with two shots from your pistol, then you do not need to be on the force." Sarah (19-year old Black female; Sociology Major; Freshman) asserts, "They should question someone before they put their hands on them. They should make sure the person knows what they are getting in trouble for before they get violent. They should be certain that they have probable cause before they take their gun and shoot it. They should have to call back up before they shoot someone who is unarmed, so they will have someone there to validate why they shot an unarmed man or woman."

Some individuals recommend that members of law enforcement have a better understanding of the African American culture. Paul (36-year old Black male; Public Administration; Graduate Student) feels, "I think they should take more classes on cultural awareness. It will make them more aware of the cultures of other groups. The course should not last a day or two; it should last about a week." Faye (21-year old Black female; Criminal Justice; Junior) expresses, "The steps I feel that law enforcement should take, starts with getting feedback about the way they make African Americans feel. Do not look at it like it is a form of bashing or making their name look bad, but really consider how their approach affects others." Idris (19-year old Black male; Criminal Justice; Sophomore) feels, "First, they have to address the fact that there is a difference in how they treat white people compared to Black people. Secondly, if you can see the difference, treat them equally."

Faye (21-year old Black female; Criminal Justice; Junior) says, "The steps I feel that law enforcement should take, starts with getting feedback about the way they make African Americans feel. Do not look at it like it is a form of bashing or making their name look bad, but really consider how their approach affects others." Idris (19-year old Black male; Criminal Justice; Sophomore) feels, "First, they have to address the fact that there is a difference in how they treat white people compared to Black people. Secondly, if you can see the difference, treat them equally." Lorenz (22-year old Black male; Psychology Major; Senior) simply says, "I feel like that they should psychologically test officers for racial biases." Curtis, (21-year old Black male; Criminal Justice; Junior) feels, "First, they must provide counseling for officers regarding anger management and racial profiling. They should have something before they go out and patrol."

One participant asserts law enforcement create a new training course. Chadwick (21-year old Black male; Psychology Major; Junior) says, "I feel like they should create a new training course. And, I feel the placement of cops should be taken into consideration. For example, cops that grew up in the 'hood,' or the 'inner city,' should service those areas because they would know how to deal with those areas." Anita (18-year old Black female; Criminal Justice; Junior) strongly believes, "They (police) should take psychology courses to teach them how to deal with people. They need to follow the lead of Starbucks and provide police with extensive diversity training."

Rachel (28-year old Black female; Sociology Major; Junior) asserts, "I feel like a police officer should not police a neighborhood that he or she is unfamiliar with. I feel like police should do more community service to get to know people and build trust. They should actually go out to different neighborhood and introduce themselves to build a better rapport with the citizens in the community. I believe those community service hours should be done before they are sworn."

Keri (22-year old African American/Black female; Psychology Major; Junior) expresses, "Actually take the integrity training seriously. They should interact with the neighborhood so that they can have a better relationship, better trust. I think they should learn and understand Black culture more. *Why?* So they can better understand what causes certain negative deviant behavior. If they can better understand it, they will be less violent or brutal when addressing it."

Jewel (21-year old African American and Native American female; Criminal Justice Major) provides this extended comment:

> I think that college needs to be a requirement, not a bonus (in terms of pay). The screening process needs to be more in depth in terms of finding out what types of experiences these guys have had, mental health issues. The training needs to be much more extensive and consistent. For example, officers need to be trained on how to deal with all types of people from all different walks of life. And, there needs to be a much greater focus on de-escalated situations as opposed to resorting to using force. Finally, it needs to be a crime for officers to shoot and kill someone. It should not be justified by their badge. There are hundreds of dangerous jobs in the world and they are held accountable.

Theme 2: Reevaluate Current Laws and Policies

Five individuals (17 percent of the total number of participants) use words and/or phrases that relate to participants' belief that laws and policies should make police accountable when they use excessive force and/or murder a

Black person. D'Andre, (21-year old Black male; Interdisciplinary Studies; Junior) feels, "Umm, pass laws to where policemen's gun not show up with loaded guns." Whitney (20-year old African American female; Pre-Physical Therapy Major) says, "Umm, have their officers suffer consequences when they do not follow proper protocol, not make excuses." Cassie (21-year old Black female; Public Administration; Graduate Student) relates, "I honestly think they should take the same route that they would with any other citizen. If you are in a position of authority or not, there should always be consequences for your actions."

Celeste (22-year old Black female; Sociology; Junior) feels, "They should re-evaluate stop and frisk because it disproportionately impacts Black communities. They should know how to defend themselves besides using their gun." James (24-year old Black male; Criminal Justice Major; Senior) conveys, "There should be some classes taken regularly by officers with video footage illustrating what to do and what not to do and potentially volatile situations. Stiffer and harsher punishments should be used against police officers who have used excessive force. If they feel there are harsh punishments, they will not do that again."

Theme 3: Required Body Cameras

Four individuals (13 percent of the total number of participants) use words and/or phrases that relate to the participant believing that if members of law enforcement were required to wear body cameras and/or dash cameras, this would minimize police brutality. Elijah (19-year old Black male; Political Science Major; Senior) asserts, "I think every police officer should have a body camera in use at all times. I also feel that the attorneys and prosecutors should have more checks and balances. *What do you mean by this?* I feel like each party should be held accountable by all of the evidence. I feel that when the attorneys see the evidence they should seek to serve the citizens and find them justice instead of working with their friends (the police)."

Angela (21-year old Black female; Pre-Physical Therapy Major) exclaims, "I do not know what steps can be taken for law enforcement agencies to deal with issues related to police brutality. *Why do you feel this way?* I feel this way because there have been steps taken to calm to resolve this issue. *What steps are you referring to?* Such as, body cameras." Brendon (24-year old Black male; Criminal Justice; Senior) feels, "They should either have body cams or having a journalist or a ride along person with a camera to document things. Because they do that in the army when soldiers are deployed." Makala (23-year old Black female; Criminal Justice; Graduate Student) feels, "They should go through training. Specifically, a psychological examination. A White cop should not view a Black person any differently than they view a White person. Taxpayers spend money on this equipment (dash cams, body cams) and it should be used without any exceptions. Your vehicle should not go out into the field if the dash cam is not working."

Theme 4: Nothing Will Change

Three individuals (10 percent of the total number of participants) used words and/or phrases that relate to participants' belief that racism in society and members of law enforcement is so deep that will nothing will eradicate police brutality. Zoe (21-year old African American/Black; Female; Physical Therapy Major; Junior) says, "Honestly, law enforcement agencies they won't take any steps." Michelle (21-year old; Black female; Public Adminis-tration; Graduate Student) states, "I do not feel like they can really do any-thing. *Why?* I feel that each individual has their own thoughts and that indi-vidual is going to do what they think is right." Aaliyah (20-year old Black Female; Sociology Major; Sophomore) opines, "Well, the issue related to police brutality is racism. I feel like it is so deeply interwoven into the system that there is really no true rectification that will happen in my lifetime."

Question #11: What steps, if any, do you believe universities and colleges should take to deal with issues related to police brutality?

Grounded theory analysis of Question 11 (What steps, if any, do you believe *universities and colleges* should take to deal with issues related to police brutality?) reveals four emergent themes: (a) University-Led Education on Interacting with Law Enforcement; (b) University-Led Law Enforcement Community Efforts; (c) University-Advocating Attitudinal and Policy Changes in Law Enforcement; (d) University Accountability of Law Enforcement.

The *University-Led Education on Interacting with Law Enforcement* re-fers to words and/or phrases that relate to participants' belief that universities and colleges should initiate seminars, workshops, and courses that advise students of their legal rights as well as how to interact with members of law enforcement. The *University-Led Law Enforcement Community Efforts* theme refers to words and/or phrases that relate to participants' belief that universities should bridge the acrimonious relationship between minority communities and members of law enforcement. The *University-Advocating Attitudinal and Policy Changes in Law Enforcement* theme refers to words and/or phrases that relate to participants' belief that universities should en-sure that members of law enforcement change how they perceive African Americans and abide by laws and policies that protect all citizens. The *Uni-versity Accountability of Law Enforcement* theme refers to words and/or phrases that relate to participants' belief that universities and colleges should be at the forefront of making law enforcement accountable for police brutality. Included within this theme is the view that universities should take the lead in organizing protests against law enforcement in the wake of police brutality.

Theme 1: University-Led Education on Interacting With Law Enforcement

Fourteen individuals (47 percent of the total number of participants) used words and/or phrases that relate to participants' belief that universities and colleges should initiate seminars, workshops, and courses that advise students of their legal rights as well as how to interact with members of law enforcement. For example, Curtis (21-year old Black male; Criminal Justice; Junior) believes, "Colleges should teach students how to de-escalate a situation." Lorenz feels, "Colleges should teach students how to de-escalate a situation." Samuel (23-year old Black male; Criminal Justice Major) replies, "Just provide seminars and trainings to prevent police brutality within the community." Malcolm (23-year old Black male; Criminal Justice Major) says, "Have seminars on how to interact with police. Or teach about the steps to take to avoid conflict with police." Michelle (21-year old; Black female; Public Administration; Graduate Student) proclaims, "I feel that they should educate the students and faculty more. *Why do you feel this way?* Because it would change the way they view officers and also when it comes to being in contact with them." Cassie (21-year old Black female; Public Administration Graduate Student) states, "I feel like they should take the same steps that they would for any other citizens. It does not matter if you are on campus or outside in the regular world, there should always be consequences for your actions. I also believe more awareness for police brutality should be given on campuses because students and police officers interact with one another on a daily basis."

Several participants believe individuals should know their rights. Keri exclaims, "Umm, I guess classes like Sociology of law in which students can learn more about their rights and which laws are what." Anita (18-year old Black female; Criminal Justice; Junior) believes, "Students need to be cooperative and taught their rights. A lot of Black people do not know their rights." Elijah (19-year old Black male; Political Science Major; Senior) remarks, "They should make students aware of their rights and let them know what they have and have not to do when they are pulled over by police." Karen (23-year old Black female; Health Science; Pre-Physical Therapy; Senior) expresses, "All you can do is inform the students of the situations and teaching what not to do. So that they will not end up dead. Honestly, there is not anything that you can do."

Idris (19-year old Black male; Criminal Justice; Sophomore) expresses, "I guess educate more people on their rights and in law related majors try to put out more educated people in the law enforcement field. I feel the more educated you are the more level headed and work oriented you will be. You will be able to focus on the job on hand and make you less biased." Aaliyah (20-year old Black Female; Sociology Major; Sophomore) states, "I feel like the college should educate the people interested in changing the system in a way that is inclusive and recognizes the faults in the system of law enforcement. Attempt to not perpetuate the same tropes about people of color that exist in law enforcement."

Another participant believes education on interacting with police would be beneficial. Chadwick (21-year old Black male; Psychology Major; Junior) says, "Possibly more seminars that explain police brutality and the steps you should take to prevent things like altercations when you get pulled over or like being searched." James (24-year old Black male; Criminal Justice Major; Senior) shares this view: "They should educate some students with how to engage with police officers on one traffic stops. They should teach students to do whatever they have to do to get out of that one on one encounter, so they can deal with that on the other side (the legal end)." Still another participant stressed the importance of education. D'Andre (21-year old Black male; Interdisciplinary Studies; Junior) shares, "They should educate students on how to act when they encounter policemen. Have policemen come to the classrooms to educate student how to act in certain situations."

Theme 2: University-Led Law Enforcement Community Efforts

Five individuals (17 percent of the total number of participants) used words and/or phrases that relate to participants' belief that universities should bridge the acrimonious relationship between minority communities and members of law enforcement. Faye (21-year old Black female; Criminal Justice; Junior) says, "We should have more positive interactions with them. We need to interact with them positively." Leah (21-year old Black female; Health Science; Pre-occupational Therapy; Senior) expresses, "Umm, I guess all they really can do is have seminars and panel discussions about. The university officers should take a step to reach out to students and explain what they do from their perspective." Paul (36-year old Black male; Public Administration; Graduate Student) discloses, "They should have police officers come to the university and give courses so that students will know about them and their purpose in the community." Jewel (21-year old African American and Native American female; Criminal Justice Major) states, "I think they (police) should be more transparent. Like community policing. I mean, on campus I see 15 cop cars, but I have no idea what they are doing. So, in that sense, it seems like they are harassing students as opposed to fighting crime and protecting us." Brendon (24-year old Black male; Criminal Justice; Senior) opines, "I think that the universities should reach out to the local police departments in their cities, so that officers could come and talk to the students and hold seminars so they and the students can build a positive relationship."

Theme 3: University-Advocating Attitudinal and Policy Changes in Law Enforcement

Five individuals (17 percent of the total number of participants) used words and/or phrases that relate to participants' belief that universities should ensure that members of law enforcement change how they perceive African Americans and abide by laws and policies that protect all citizens.

Two participants believe police must change what they think of African Americans. Denise (20-year old Black female; English Major; Junior) says, "I feel like the problem is that this dislike/trust of police officers starts at an early age. Not having so many schools on high school campuses. I feel that when teachers are having a hard time with a student they call police." Makala (23-year old Black female; Criminal Justice; Graduate Student) shares, "I feel the first step any law enforcement officer should take is to not view any African American male as the same. In other words, they should not stereotype them. They should treat them with respect."

In addition to attitudinal changes, three participants believe university policy should take a firm stance and not condone police violence. Eduardo (29-year old; African American/Hispanic; Male; Pre-Physical Therapy Major; Junior) states, "Make sure that their police force knows what excessive force is and to make sure that they (the university) will not stand by you (the brutal officer), you are going to be on your own." Celeste (22-year old Black female; Sociology; Junior) believes, "Maybe just more research that can lead to policy changes. I mean, the protesting is not effective. *Why do you feel protesting is not effective?* For the past few years we have been protesting, we have Black Lives Matter, and none of it has proven to be effective. I mean, we marched after Trayvon Martin was killed and nothing happened? *What do you think should be done then?* The people who are being targeted the most by police brutality, which is Black people; we need to organize ourselves like we did in the 50's and 60's that brought forth the Civil Rights Acts." Another female reiterated the desire for positive change for the future. Zoe (21-year old African American/Black; Female; Physical Therapy Major; Junior) reveals, "Umm, the younger generation are our future. So, we should focus more on bettering ourselves since we are next in line. Sooner or later, these people will be out of office and we will be the ones making the decisions. So, if we do not like what we are experiencing or what we see, it is up to us to make that change."

Theme 4: University Accountability of Law Enforcement

Four participants (13 percent of the total number of participants) used words and/or phrases that relate to participants' belief that universities and colleges should be at the forefront of making law enforcement accountable for police brutality. Included within this theme is the view that universities should take the lead in organizing protests against law enforcement in the wake of police brutality. One participant (Angela, a 21-year old Black female; Pre-Physical Therapy Major) states, "There is not a lot of incidents of police brutality that I know of on University campuses," however this view was not shared by the majority of individuals. In particular, participants believe PWIs and HBCUs have a responsibility to eradicate police brutality. Whitney (20-year old African American female; Pre-Physical Therapy Major) feels, "Mainly PWIs (Predominantly White Institutions) need to break psychologically chains of having white people 'scared.' Rachel (28-year old Black female; Sociology Major; Junior) says, "HBCUs especially should be at the forefront of leading the movement to have police officers be held accountable. They can do it by. Well, I have not really thought about it. I mean protesting does not help. I do not feel any really changing of laws come out of protesting. Sometimes a lot of community damage comes from protesting and that is not conducive to the movement to bring about change."

While Rachel (28-year old Black female; Sociology Major; Junior) believes "protesting does not help," another participant did not share this view. Sarah (19-year old Black female; Sociology Major; Freshman) expresses, "Protesting against it, which we are pretty much doing already and keeping supporting the Black lives matter movement. It will hit us harder (in terms of its impact) because we have Black males walking around our campus. *Do you think the protests are effective?* Yes and no. I say yes because we are being heard and now because with the Black Lives Matter movement, people keep trying to take away from it. For instance, you have other people saying 'White lives matter,' but they are not the ones who are being shot down by police."

Question #12: Is there anything else that you would like to share?

Grounded theory analysis of Question 12 (Is there anything else that you would like to share?) reveals that while the majority of participants (21 participants, or 70 percent) did not provide additional information, nine participants (30 percent) believe additional education and training are essential for members of law enforcement. In particular, participants mentioned the need for changes in the criminal justice system. The *Change in the Criminal Justice System* theme relates to words and/or phrases that relate to participants' belief that the criminal justice system should do a better job of ensuring the safety of African Americans. This theme also includes increasing the number of Black police officers, and the need for members of law enforcement to follow the same protocols that they expect others to observe, which includes, but is not limited to mandatory reporting of individuals they murder.

Three individuals (33 percent of those that provided a response) used the phrase "criminal justice system" when describing what is needed to minimize police brutality. Cassie (21-year old Black female; Public Administration; Graduate Student) believes, "I feel as though we (African Americans) argue and fight for change but the change can only start from within the criminal justice system." Leah (21-year old Black female; Health Science; Pre-occupational Therapy; Senior) says, "No. I just think the police should do better. The criminal justice as a whole should do a better job of serving all people." Aaliyah (20-year old Black Female; Sociology Major; Sophomore) shares, "No, but I do think that it would help if more of our law enforcement officers were educated with post-secondary degrees to better understand the criminal justice system. It is more than just protecting and serving and they have an obligation to understand the social implications of their job and what it means to people of color and what law enforcement represents as a social institution."

Three individuals (33 percent of those that provided a response) believe that mandatory procedures, in regards to required training in regards to CPR and firearms, will minimize police brutality against African Americans. Jewel (21-year old African American and Native American female; Criminal Justice Major) explains: "It needs to be mandatory for law enforcement agencies to report information on whomever they kill." Makala (23-year old Black female; Criminal Justice; Graduate Student) says, "Protocols, for the police, are there for a reason. Law enforcement officers should have to follow their protocols because I have never heard of any officer shooting a Black man and then give him CPR when they are supposed to." Eduardo (29-year old; African American/Hispanic; Male; Pre-Physical Therapy Major; Junior) remarks, "One of the biggest things that I have always said is, 'In the military, I get firearms training all of the time.' And to expect a police officer who may be fired once in the academy and twice a year, is not going to know how to react to a sudden movement of a suspect."

Zoe (21-year old African American/Black; Female; Physical Therapy Major; Junior) shares, "I do not think that it is fair that a select group of people (Blacks) have to go through this being the fact the vast majority of people feel this way about police brutality, so what is holding back the change. There are more of us instead of more of the people in power." D'Andre (21-year old Black male; Interdisciplinary Studies; Junior) believes, "I personally feel like every student should take Race, Class, and Justice-related courses. *Why do you feel this way?* Um, it teaches you about the history of police and why they act the way they do towards minorities."

One individual (11 percent of those that provided a response) believes increasing the number of African American police officers will minimize police brutality against Blacks. James (24-year old Black male; Criminal Justice Major; Senior) asserts, "One way to cut down on police brutality against unarmed Blacks is if more African Americans become police officers. We will be policing our own communities instead of White police officers who do not know our culture and it will build more trust within the African American community because the police officer will look like them."

NOTE

1. D'Andre, Interviewee #28 (21-year old Black male; Interdisciplinary Studies; Junior) did not provide a response to this question.

Chapter Five

Discussion

In this chapter, we offer critical, scholarly dialogue of participants' views regarding law enforcement. Specifically, this chapter explores five w's (who, what, when, where, why) that relate to perceptions of police. Therefore, the *"who"* are two entities: (a) minorities and how they perceive police; (b) how members of law enforcement relate to minorities. The *"what"* are the circumstances in which interactions with police occur; the *"when"* are the times when minorities interact with police; the *"where"* is the place minorities and law enforcement meet; the *"why"* is the rationale for why police say they target Blacks and other racial minorities. In the paragraphs that follow, we present each interview question and critically flesh out responses to these eight qualitative questions[1] and four quantitative questions. Since there were fewer of them, we will first discuss the quantitative responses.

QUANTITATIVE RESPONSES

Although most participants have never personally experienced excessive force (23 percent) [Question 8—Has a police officer ever used an excessive amount of force on *you*?], they are aware of police using excessive force on someone they know (77 percent) [Question 9—Has a police officer ever used an excessive amount of force on *someone that you know*?]. While the term "excessive force" may mean different things to different people, the law provides concrete definitions of this term. Acknowledging these definitions is important because it situates participants' views of and responses to police's use of excessive force within an individual, familial, and communal milieu.

Extant scholarship has given much attention to excessive force.[2] What is excessive force? Cornell Law School defines "excessive force" as "force in excess of what a police officer reasonably believes is necessary."[3] US Legal.com defines "excessive force" like this:

> Excessive force by a law enforcement officer(s) is a violation of a person's constitutional rights. The term "excessive force" is not precisely defined; however, the use of force greater than that which a reasonable and prudent law enforcement officer would use under the circumstances is generally considered to be excessive. In most cases, the minimum amount force required to achieve a safe and effective outcome during law enforcement procedures is recommended.[4]

Study.com defines "excessive force" in this way:

> *Excessive force* can be defined as force that is used which exceeds what is necessary to gain compliance or control a situation. The force used is usually physical, but it could also be verbal or just mere intimidation.
>
> Police throughout the United States are legally allowed to use the force necessary to control whatever situation they are faced with. The idea is that the police should use the lowest level of force possible to gain compliance and maintain control of a situation. All police officers are taught to follow a basic use of force continuum. This starts with verbal commands, then moves to physical restraint, increases to less-than-lethal force, and ends with the use of deadly force. The training dictates that a police officer should start at the level of force that is just above the situation he is trying to control [5]

Overall, these definitions propose "excessive force" relates to an officer's use of reason (Cornell, Law School), violates an individual's constitutional rights (US Legal), and can be physical, verbal, or intimidation (Study.com). Added to this, certain aspects of excessive force deserve attention. For example, the one Cornell Law School provides stresses reason ("force in excess of what a police officer reasonably believes is necessary"). Therefore, effective exercising of police duties requires a high level of reason, or being level headed. This means that even in highly stressful situations, the officer must remain in control of his actions. Furthermore, the definition of US Legal.com defines "excessive force" in regards to upholding the constitutional rights of citizens. Essentially, police officers that do not demonstrate reason or a level head when assuming their duties are violating the constitutional rights of citizens. In addition to this, US Legal.com, like Cornell Law School stresses qualified officers use the lowest form of physical force to detain an individual. Thus, while "the minimum amount force required to achieve a safe and effective outcome during law enforcement procedures is recommended," this does not necessarily mean that officers will go beyond what is reasonable to detain an individual.

Lastly, Study.com advocates that police first start with lower forms of interaction and then graduate to more advanced ones. In particular, this definition recognizes that although physical force is usually the method for control, police may use intimidation, and verbal commands as well. Police throughout the United States can legally use force to control whatever situation they face. The idea is that the police should use the *lowest level of force possible* to gain compliance and maintain control of a situation. All police officers learn to follow a basic use of force continuum. This starts with verbal commands, then moves to physical restraint, increases to less-than-lethal force, and ends with the use of deadly force. The training dictates that a police officer should start at the level of force that is just above the situation he is trying to control.

Personal Experience with Excessive Force

When responding to Question 8 (Has a police officer ever used an excessive amount of force on *you*?), five individuals (17 percent of participants) recount an incident in which he/she personally experienced excessive force by a member of law enforcement. For three of these individuals, the physical assaults they experience at the hands of law enforcement occur during times when individuals typically relax and recreate. Malcolm (23-year old Black male; Criminal Justice Major) was enjoying himself at a party with his girlfriend, when, due to being "in the wrong place at the wrong time," is slammed to the ground by a police officer who wrongly believes he is fighting. It is unfortunate that even during a time when a Black person would not ordinarily think of being a victim of excessive force such is the case.

In the case of Cassie (21-year old Black female; Public Administration Graduate Student), she was waiting for a ride home from the movie theatre, when "a violent fight" occurs. While waiting for her friends on the sidelines, a White female officer asks her to leave. When she explains she is waiting on her friends, the police officer uses physical force (grabbed arm, squeezed arm, lifts arm, and causes contents to spill from her pocket) on Cassie and then releases her. Lorenz (22-year old Black male; Psychology Major; Senior), while on his way to play basketball with three friends, is pulled over at a traffic light, and forced to sit on the sidewalk while their car was searched. When Lorenz and his friends inquire about the reason for the search, which was their legal right, police simply tell them it was because they reside in a "drug-infested neighborhood." So, although this Black male and his friends were legal residents of the neighborhood where they were stopped, they were indirectly told they do not belong there and were told to "move" to another neighborhood. Unlike Malcolm, Cassie, and Lorenz, Samuel was speeding in his vehicle. When four police cars approached him, he received instructions to step out of the car. When he inquires about the reason for this request, one of the police officers "grabbed him by the arm, pushed his face to the ground" and told him the cause of his delay is because they "smelled an odor in his car." After the police raise him from the ground and hold him in the back seat of the police car, they search his car and release him. Even when the police find nothing to validate the alleged "odor," they do not apologize to Samuel for detaining him.

Personal Experience with Aggressive Behavior

While the aforementioned five participants were certain they were victims of excessive force, another three individuals (10 percent of participants) were not victims of excessive force, per se, but recount the verbally aggressive nature by which members of law enforcement treated them. What makes these instances especially problematic is the mental, emotional, and spiritual degradation of the Black targets. For example, Angela (21-year old Black female; Pre-Physical Therapy Major) and Chadwick (21-year old Black male; Psychology Major; Junior) report instances of this level of degradation. While Angela says the police "were really demanding and aggressive" with her, Chadwick shared times when police demand that he "Pull his fucking hands up!" and "Get against the wall," to only have the police shine their lights on him and then drive away. The emotional trauma experienced by Jewel (21-year old African American and Native American female; Criminal Justice Major) occurs because a bystander got the wrong impression and called the police. When Jewel and her boyfriend are "play fighting" on their way to CVS (a drug store) for snacks, they immediately find themselves surrounded by "six or seven [white] cops" who, due to not believing their account of what happened, question them separately. In this emotionally charged situation, Jewel mentions that the police did not share with them the reason for their line of questioning "until the end." Although the bystander may have believed Jewel was in distress, one must question why the police would ask Jewel about her safety while her alleged attacker (boyfriend) was present.

Personal Knowledge of Excessive Force

When responding to Question 9 (Has a police officer used an excessive amount of force on *someone that you know*?) the majority of participants (28 or 93 percent of participants) recount an incident in which he/she knows someone who was a victim of excessive force by a member of law enforce-ment. In some cases, it is because the individual fails to comply with the officer's direction. Michelle (21-year old; Black female; Public Administra-tion; Graduate Student) shares a situation when the police beat a person up because he did not comply with the police's direction ("Yes, it was actually influenced because the individual ran. The police just beat him up."). Even arguing with a police officer could have been potentially more dangerous and/or fatal for one of Malcolm's (23-year old Black male; Criminal Justice Major) friends who was "slammed" to the ground. Others share police officer's slamming the body of an individual. Chadwick's (21-year old Black male; Psychology Major; Junior) cousin, while coming from the train station one night, was "stopped, searched, and slammed to the ground." Police, at times, may react to protect their own safety. Brendon's (24-year old Black male; Criminal Justice; Senior) account speaks to the reaction of the officer due to his friend keeping his hands in his pocket. Although Brendon's friend may have kept his hands in his pocket because of nervousness, the police grab him, throw him on the hood of his car, and handcuff him.

Even when a Black male engages in a physical altercation (fight) with another person, interactions with police can quickly escalate. Cassie (21-year old Black female; Public Administration Graduate Student) relates her "older cousin got into a fight at a friend's house, yet when the police came to settle the situation, instead of talking to him or trying to negotiate, he shot him." D'Andre's (21-year old Black male; Interdisciplinary Studies; Junior) "cousin was shot by the police 16 times for a disturbance call." The friend of Idris (19-year old Black male; Criminal Justice; Sophomore) was also a victim of excessive force. This participant states: "Yes. My friend was fighting. The fight was over for an hour and we were still at the park chilling. Then, the police grabbed him and slammed him and they were twisting his arms behind his back and he was yelling in pain." Samuel (23-year old Black male; Criminal Justice Major) shares, "Yes, but I do not know all of the details. My friend just told me that he got slammed by an officer."

Even when a Black male is engaged in illegal activity, he may be subject to assault, post-arrest. This was the scenario Lorenz (22-year old Black male; Psychology Major; Senior) paints when describing how the police "slams one of his friends to the ground" because "he had some drugs on him" yet punch him "after he had been handcuffed." The account that Lorenz offers in some respects mirrors that of the one that Paul provides regarding his cousin and his father. Even though his father "was selling narcotics," he is not in possession of narcotics when the police question him. Instead of accepting his word, they forcibly grab him from the home. After going back into the home to search for narcotics, the police allow him to go back into the home.

In an exceptionally disturbing instance, the victim is first subject to robbery and then assault by police. Rachel (28-year old Black female; Sociology Major; Junior) tells of an incident where her friend, who was a convicted felon, *robbed and shot*, calls the police for protection and is thrown to the floor of his home. Incidents such as this send the clear message that convicted felons will not receive police protection, which may motivate these individuals (many of whom have had multiple run-ins with the law) to take the law into their own hands. Thus, due to being motivated to engage in "street justice," these convicted felons may re-enter the legal system. This reality may be especially real for convicted felons who reside in blighted neighborhoods where crime and violence levels are exceptionally high. African Americans who are unaware there are warrants for their arrest may find themselves in compromising positions with police. This reality supports commentary offered by Sarah and Anita. Sarah's male cousin had a history of being "in and out of jail," and had "warrants out." When the police find him, they are "really rough with him," choking him and slamming him to the ground. Of note, Sarah did not regard this situation as unusual, but rather "stuff that they usually do to people, like on the show Cops." In another incident involving a Black male that had a troubled relationship with the law (including a warrant), Anita's (18-year old Black female; Criminal Justice; Junior) cousin relates that when the police come to take him to jail, a simple request to "hug his daughter," turned into a verbal war between this man's family and police. In this case, the lone, Black officer disagreed with how the other officers (who were White) handled this situation. No doubt, the highly charged emotions between this man, his family, and his young daughter will forever etch in their minds. When a child sees their parent (and family members) visibly upset, yet the parent attempts to calm them through physical contact (via hugging), yet do not have the opportunity to do so, this creates feelings of distrust for police.

Several participants offer examples where they believe police exercise "force in excess of what a police officer reasonably believes is necessary." According to Karen (23-year old Black female; Health Science; Pre-Physical Therapy; Senior), her cousin "was not running or resisting," yet the police still use excessive force with him. Given the increase in individuals who suffer from untreated mental illness,[6] it is imperative that law enforcement de-escalate conflict with persons with a mental illness. According to Denise (20-year old Black female; English Major; Junior), police found it difficult to restrain her male cousin, who has autism, ADHD, and schizophrenia. While it may seem individuals are being deliberately defiant, one or more of these mental conditions may cause social communication impairments (autism), inattention or hyperactivity and impulsivity (ADHD),[7] hallucinations, delusions, thought (unusual or dysfunctional ways of thinking) and movement disorders (agitated body movements).[8] Clearly, while law enforcement agents are not medical professionals, this does not mean that a basic knowledge of symptomatology would not benefit police as they carry out their jobs. Having a rudimentary knowledge of the thoughts, speech, and actions of individuals with a mental illness may help police protect the community and keep the individual who is mentally ill safe.

The appearance of certain Black men may make them targets of police. Recall that Faye (21-year old Black female; Criminal Justice; Junior) recounts an incident when her brother is "racially profiled" by a Caucasian officer because of his hairstyle (dreadlocks), his clothing, and his speech.

While Faye does not go into detail about the clothing that her brother was wearing when this officer stops him, this story recognizes the potential for Whites to associate certain physical qualities with a negative impression of Black men. Apparently, the overall appearance of this Black male motivates this White officer to associate him with illegal drug activity and gangs. Thus, being Black and wearing a particular hairstyle that is not mainstream, not worn by most African Americans, or Whites, equals criminality. The experience of Curtis (21-year old Black male; Criminal Justice; Junior) also speaks to the likelihood for some members of law enforcement to perceive Black males as criminal. For a friend of Curtis, an officer's request to pull over and provide names is justification to search for illegal drugs (marijuana). Since police treated this Black male so roughly ("he pushed my friend on the wall pretty hard"), it makes one wonder why this Black male was not treated with more respect. Curtis used the term "racial profiling" to describe what happened to his friend. The experience of Makala's (23-year old Black female; Criminal Justice; Graduate Student) father illustrates how White police can dehumanize Black males. Even after her father complies with the officer's request that he vacate his vehicle and "put his hands up," he receives a racial slur ("Boy") and receives the reminder they would "find what was in his car." When the victim starts laughing, the police officer, suffering a knee to his back and a busted face, physically abuses him. Conversely, some found they were in the wrong place at the wrong time. Angela (21-year old Black female; Pre-Physical Therapy Major), her roommate, and one of her close friends (a Black male) are on their way to get something to eat when they are stopped by police. Since the car smelled of marijuana, police instruct everyone to exit the vehicle, and then call for the assistance of two other officers (Black cop and White cop). According to Angela, these officers "automatically assume there were more drugs and weapons in the car" simply because they were Black. This participant's use of the word "aggressive" to describe the actions of the officer indicates the use of excessive force with the target of their search.

Still others relate situations when they believe the police did not handle the situation in an appropriate manner and escalate the situation. According to Elijah (19-year old Black male; Political Science Major; Senior), one of his friends was pulled over by police for "driving too close to a car." Even though his friend complied with the officers' request, he and his friends had to get out of the car, placed in handcuffs, and put "on the side of the road." Like Elijah, police antagonize Whitney's (20-year old African American female; Pre-Physical Therapy Major) friend. Guilty of "super-speeding" (15 miles over the speed limit, which is an additional $300), police accuse Whitney's friend and his companions of smoking (marijuana), make them exit the vehicle, and search his car. Whitney believes the physical appearance of her friend may have motivated the police to assume that he was guilty of more than "super-speeding" and her belief has scholarly merit. Historically and contemporaneously, individuals tend to associate Black males with a dark-complexion, and a massive height and weight with criminality, even if they are not breaking the law.[9]

It is especially tragic when the excessive force police use has a fatal outcome for the victim. According to James (24-year old Black male; Criminal Justice Major; Senior), his cousin and his girlfriend was pulled over by a police officer because he was "swerving a bit because he was sleepy." When the police make the request for his cousin to exit the car, he complies and later sits on the curb. When the police starts to yell at this man's girlfriend, he becomes angry, and stands up (while handcuffed). The police shoot him twice and due to the extreme delay of the ambulance, he bleeds to death.

QUALITATIVE RESPONSES

Qualitative analysis of Question 1 (When you hear the word "police," what words immediately come to mind?) reveals participants associate police with the following five themes: law enforcement, negativity, conflict, racism, and police brutality.

Law Enforcement[10]

Since the purpose of law enforcement is to "protect and serve," it is not surprising that some immediately associate police with enforcers of the law. Whether participants refer to them as "gatekeepers of the criminal justice system," associate them with what they carry (a "12-gauge shotgun"), or authority figures ("they are looked as someone with a higher power in society"), people recognize police for their visibility and ability to affect crime. Faye acknowledges the influence that police have when she associates them with "Law enforcement, crime" and later explains, "Police officers enforce the law and they also either hinder or help when it comes to crime." Fundamentally, this means police largely determine the outcome when they interact with individuals who they know or suspect commit crimes.

Conflicting[11]

Several respondents make a distinction between the oath that officers take and *the way that they actually perform their jobs.* While Leah (21-year old Black female; Health Science; Pre-occupational Therapy; Senior) acknowledges police "take an oath to serve and protect, it does not mean that they actually do." What real or perceived barriers may make it difficult for police to do their job in the most effective manner? Leah thinks "preconceived notions" and "prejudice" may be strong motivators. Another narrative reveals minorities who once had positive impressions of police may lose these over time. Although Elijah's (19-year old Black male; Political Science Major; Senior) father was a retired police officer and he grew up seeing law enforcement as protectors, the negative ways in which his friends are treated has stained his once glowing perception. Elijah's story is interesting because he sees a clear difference in how he and his friends are treated. While he believes his physical appearance is not threatening (5'3 height), Elijah realizes that police may automatically assume Black men as dangerous even when they are not. A large physical size should not necessarily suggest danger and Elijah speaks to personal experience when he says, "Some of the biggest people I know are some of the nicest people that I know."

While Keri sees police as "authority" figures who confine lawbreakers (putting them in jail), she first uses the term "White Supremacy" to label police before describing them in other ways. She draws from "statistics and experience" to determine her assessment of police. Mentioning "White Supremacy" before authority recognizes the individuals primarily responsible for enforcing laws are White. With this power, they determine whether minorities should stop, if a situation will escalate or deescalate, or whether the minority will lose his or her life. When one factors the possibility of racism with police officers' legal power to carry a weapon, this makes African Americans particularly susceptible to police violence. Like Keri, Michelle's (21-year old; Black female; Public Administration; Graduate Student) perspective unapologetically blames White Supremacy, without specifically using these words. For Michelle, police are an amalgam of race (White people), discrimination, and safety and believes White officers "treat African Americans differently because they feel that we are lower than them." According to this Black female, White officers "basically belittle" Blacks and "feel that they deserve more input in terms of what goes on in the [Black] community." Michelle's outlook speaks to the core regarding why Blacks and other minorities receive negative treatment from police: Police believe Blacks are cognitively, intellectually, economically, and socially inferior to them. Therefore, *police actions can only change when police perceptions of African Americans and other minorities change.*

Goff et al.[12] reveals officers are more likely to view Black children as older and less innocent than they do White children. Malcolm's (23-year old Black male; Criminal Justice Major) experience makes this clear. He was about 13 or 14 years old at the time and Malcolm and his friends "were playing games at Game Stop" [a video games and electronics store] and begin their journey home, walking to the subway through a predominantly White neighborhood. When one trooper sees him and his friends, three other police officers appear in the subway, "kick tables, throw them on the floor, and search them." When providing a reason why they behaved the way that they did, the White officers state they "thought they were older." Perhaps severe differences in regards to how police treat Blacks may lead them to believe, as Whitney says, some police officers are merely "cowards with guns." Idris (19-year old Black male; Criminal Justice; Sophomore) describes most of the campus police that he comes in contact with as Caucasian and Makala (23-year old Black female; Criminal Justice; Graduate Student) notes negative incidents between police and minorities are now being broadcast on social media, revealing the officers' "true colors." Essentially, these incidents speak to the "Trouble and corruption" that exists within many law enforcement entities. When inquired why she uses these words, she says, "Because I feel that now social media captures the majority of the incidents that have taken place and it reveals the officers' true colors."

Has social media been this influential in police brutality? Most definitely. Social media has been especially prominent in uncovering law enforcement malfeasance. The most popular example of social media's illumination of police brutality occurs 25 years ago. Shortly before 1:00 a.m. on Sunday, March 3, 1999, the squeal of sirens and the buzz of helicopters wake George Holliday, the 31-year-old owner of a small plumbing company, company, and resident of the Lakeview Terrace Suburb in the San Fernando Valley of Los Angeles. From his terrace, Holliday sees Los Angeles police officers beating a big black man and records the incident with his new camcorder. Although Holliday takes the tape to local television station, KTLA-TV, the beating of Rodney King becomes an international sensation after CNN broadcasts Holliday's footage on Tuesday. [13]

Another example of the influence of social media is the fatality of a Black male by a police officer in South Carolina. Officer Michael Slager stops Walter Scott, a Black man for a traffic stop. As Scott is running away, in an empty field, a bystander records (via cell phone) the entire incident and posts it to social media. Not surprisingly, this video sets off "protests against the U.S. as demonstrators said it was another egregious example of police officers mistreating African-Americans." In the Old West, there were standards for those who carry firearms. [14] For example, on television westerns such as "Gunsmoke," "Bonanza," or "The Rifleman" or western films such as "Tombstone," "High Plains Drifter," "The Good, The Bad, and The Ugly," a "fair" fight occurs when two individuals have the same weapon and shoot at the same time. Since real men stood face-to-face, it was the height of cowardice to shoot an individual in the back. Therefore, law enforcement agents that shoot unarmed individuals in the back are indeed acting as cowards.

Negative[15]

Several individuals draw attention to the propensity of police to make individuals feel inferior. Rachel's (28-year old Black female; Sociology Major; Junior) comment recognizes that when police make citizens feel inferior, they automatically assert their superior ("God complex") and social standing. Returning to the *Law Enforcers* theme, D'Andre (21-year old Black male; Interdisciplinary Studies; Junior) acknowledges a divide between what police officers swear to do and what they actually do. On the one side, "police are people who are supposed to help" but on the other hand, "they are harmful to my community." Of note, Chadwick and Curtis use the word "gang" to refer to police. Chadwick (21-year old Black male; Psychology Major; Junior) is a native of California, and the Los Angeles Police Department (LAPD), which came to infamy during the Rodney King beating in 1992. He associates law enforcement with "Brutality. Gangs" and explains it is Los Angeles culture to "see the police as the biggest gang in America." Curtis also describes the police is "almost like a gang," yet acknowledges the role of technology (i.e., mobile phones, social media) in bringing police brutality to light.

The reference to police as gangs may seem misplaced but consider three correlates. For one, gang members and law enforcement agents are highly loyal to the interests of their respective groups. This means that highly committed members of the gang refrain from legally testifying against the members of their group. Notice that police and members of gangs rarely testify against one of their own members. Second, gang members and law enforcement agents are willing to protect members of their group. Consider occasions when both groups will engage in physical combat (fighting) or using firearms to protect a member of their group. Finally, donning particular colors or engaging in certain tactics (verbal and non-verbal gestures) signal to other individuals who are part of their group. Overall, the following lend credence to the "police as gangs" perspectives offered by Chadwick and Curtis.

Police Brutality [16]

Eight individuals (27 percent of participants) use words and/or phrases that relate to police using excessive force or being physically brutal with African Americans. Denise (20-year old Black female; English Major; Junior) makes a critical connection between police "brutality and trust," in that police brutality of African Americans minimizes individual and collective trust in police. Interestingly, Brendon (24-year old Black male; Criminal Justice; Senior) and Asia (22-year old African/Native American female; Psychology Major; Junior) associate breaking the law with police brutality. This is unfortunate since police officers receive training to use reasonable judgement when approaching a criminal. Law enforcement is not the same as police brutality; however, for this Black male, the terms are synonymous. Asia, in particular, mentions Kendrick Lamar's most recent album, which "talks a lot about police brutality." [17]

For several participants, the long arm of White Supremacy privileges Whites, ensuring they receive protection and service first and in a timely manner. Anita (18-year old Black female; Criminal Justice; Junior) notes police cruelty ("brutality") as well as their failure to act promptly during a time of need. This female notes special treatment afforded Whites ("Because when they [police] have to come to White communities, they are there in 5 minutes or less"), while their tardiness in responding necessitates that Blacks "handle it themselves." This assessment mirrors that of Jewel (21-year old African American and Native American female; Criminal Justice Major) who links police to "brutality, violence, hypocrites, biased" as well as the power to "pick and choose who they want to protect." Conversely, Angela (21-year old Black female; Pre-Physical Therapy Major) blends police's job to "protect us and to ensure our safety" with the police brutality that spurred the Black Lives Matter (BLM) Movement.

In the second chapter, we discuss the historicity of the marginalization of African and/or people of African descent. These historical experiences include, but are not limited to, plantation overseers, the Tulsa Riot, Rosewood, the St. Louis Race Riot, and the Rodney King, Rekia Boyd, and Alton Sterling incidents. Zoe (21-year old African American/Black; Female; Physical Therapy Major; Junior) places current negative experiences with police within a historical context when she says, "Historically African Americans have not had a great relationship with police officers or law enforcement throughout the lower income communities, which I come from." As a resident of a "lower income community," Zoe has seen the high levels of unemployment, crime, and violence that generally bring police. [18]

Racist [19]

The fact that 23 percent of participants use words and/or phrases such as "racist," "racially profiling," and "bias" to describe police is evidence of their historical and contemporary negative experiences with Blacks, and in particular, Black males. Sarah (19-year old Black female; Sociology Major; Freshman) makes this point clear when she says, "Racist. Because they prejudge Black people in general, but especially Black males. They just assume Black men are 'thugs' or 'gangsters' even if they are dressed nicely. They just assume Black men are bad like they have something against them." Essentially, Sarah and Karen (23-year old Black female; Health Science; Pre-Physical Therapy; Senior) concede even if a Black male is "dressed nicely" or driving "nice cars," they are targets because they are African American. This assessment is not just a general one, but also a personal one. Although Eduardo (29-year old; African American/Hispanic; Male; Pre-Physical Therapy Major; Junior) has "lived in great places," the possibility of being "a threat" is real. Paul (36-year old Black male; Public Administration; Graduate Student) experienced this at age 24 when "driving in an upscale community." A police officer stops him and advises him he is driving with a suspended license. When Paul tells the officer he was not aware his license was suspended, the officer accuses him of lying, issues him a $300 ticket, and advises he abandon his car and "find his way home." Although his stop was allegedly for a suspended license, Paul is convinced he "got stopped because he was in a nice neighborhood."

What kind of psychological damage has this caused African Americans? Like Zoe, Aaliyah (20-year old Black Female; Sociology Major; Sophomore) draws attention to "The history of police in America. Them being a part of the problem in terms of racism in general" brings attention to the African American's past relationship with law enforcement, but more important, the emotions that police brutality evokes. Aaliyah "grew up having a fear of police" and Lorenz (22-year old Black male; Psychology Major; Senior) uses the word "fear" to describe the connection between the police brutality that he sees on social media and how he is made to feel. While "video footage" increases negative feelings of police among African Americans, Celeste (22-year old Black female; Sociology; Junior) believes personal experiences relating to "arrest, stop and frisk" occur because the police officer fails to "identify with the victim." What is interesting about this comment is that Celeste believes that negative assumptions lead to negative consequences. In other words, if a police officer assumes "a Black man is carrying a weapon or poses a threat to his life," this person will be more likely to shoot and/or murder the Black person. Stated more succinctly, these officers will be less inclined to use "the minimum amount force required to achieve a safe and effective outcome during law enforcement procedures."[20]

Question 2: In general, how do you view police?

Qualitative analysis of Question 2 ("In general, how do you view police?) reveals participants generally have negative feelings about crime squads (negative), see police as possessing positive and negative qualities (conflicting), regard them as law enforcers, and their propensity to perceive Black people in negative ways and discriminate against them (racist).[21] Several participants perceive police as law enforcers. Angela, a 21-year old Black female; Pre-Physical Therapy major says she has "never had any bad encounters with them" (police), and Michelle (21-year old; Black female; Public Administration; Graduate Student) perceives them as "certain individuals who take on the role of patrolling our communities and making sure that we are safe." Another individual's perspective has more nuance because it acknowledges the role of police as well as discrepancies in the enforcement of law. Recall that Aaliyah (20-year old Black Female; Sociology Major; Sophomore) shares: "I view them as a necessary evil. We need police to enforce laws, protect, and serve. On the other hand, those laws are not all inclusive in regards to their enforcement and content. Some of them are targeted toward people of color." Examples of laws and policies created that target people of color are divergent sentencing in regards to crack and cocaine possession, and more recent, Stop and Frisk.

Stop and Frisk

The Supreme Court case *Terry v. Ohio* (1968) was responsible for introducing the practice that we now know as "stop and frisk." This practice requires police officers to stop and frisk anyone they suspect of criminal activity who is armed and dangerous.[22] It is also important to explicate that the court, in laying down its ruling, disagreed with John Terry's notion that even a limited pat down be analogous to a search. Therefore, in the eyes of the court, stop and frisk at the time of the ruling in *Terry v. Ohio* (1968) does not constitute an unreasonable search.[23] Nevertheless, it was not until the 1900s that the introduction of "stop and frisk" occurs in major cities in America.[24] The policy implements with such veracity in minority neighborhoods amid reports of escalating crime rates that it becomes the predominant form of police-citizen contact in many urban areas. Case in point: In Chicago, during a three-month period in 2014, May-August, police stop more than 250,000 persons. In Philadelphia, since 2009, police stop between 215,000 and 253,000, and in New York City, more than 5 million persons were subject to "stop and frisk" between 2004 and 2013.[25] Further, the policy of "stop and frisk" is not effective policing, especially when one examines empirical data. In a 2012, Quinnipiac study, 70 percent of African Americans opposed stop and frisk. A 2013 Marist study finds 75 percent of African Americans desire an overhaul of the policy. In 2015, the American Civil Liberties Union of Illinois finds that despite comprising less than one-third of the population of Chicago, African Americans make up 75 percent of stop and frisk halts. A 2013 New York University study provides no evidence that misdemeanor stop and frisk arrests reduce violent crime. A January 2014 Yale Law School study posits "stop and frisk" reduces the legitimacy of the police in the eyes of African American men.[26]

Several individuals (10 percent of the total number of participants) describe police as racists that have negative opinions of African American people, and many of these experiences are deeply personal. This was the case for Whitney (20-year old African American female; Pre-Physical Therapy Major), who categorizes the "male Caucasians" with whom she has interacted as racist. What makes Whitney believe they are racist? Essentially, "their mannerisms, their tone, their demeanor all changes once they see the color of my skin." What makes Whitney's perspective especially noteworthy is that even though she is consistently respectful, she has never received this treatment in kind. Even when she asks questions, which is her legal right, [27] she never receives responses, is the victim of disrespect, and receives "high tickets when she is pulled over for something small." Interestingly, one individual speaks of "Black cops who will treat their fellow brothers the same as a white cop would or sometimes even worse." The assertion of the possibility that Black cops can "treat their fellow brothers the same as a white cop would or sometimes even worse" speaks to the current number of African Americans that are on the force, compared to Whites. According to Charles Ramsey, "there are approximately 18,000 police departments in the United States." [28] Although they are in a position of power, male officers of color are themselves a minority within law enforcement ranks. Consider that female officers of color are a double-minority within law enforcement ranks. Since African Americans do not head most police departments it is possible that Blacks and other minority officers will be painfully aware of *their limited power*.

In addition, Sarah (19-year old Black female; Sociology Major; Freshman) draws attention to White privilege in society (related to healthcare, home buying) and even technology images on search engines like Google. Idris (19-year old Black male; Criminal Justice; Sophomore) uses the word "unfair" to describe the way that police generally treat African Americans. He draws a parallel between a White and Black male walking down the street with a gun and differences in how law enforcement agents treat both.

Almost half of the men and women in this study (43 percent of the total number of participants) describe police in negative ways, largely because police abuse their power by making others feel inferior. It is important to note that many of these negative views are based on personal experiences. Such was the reality of Paul, Lorenz, and Malcolm. Consider that Paul (36-year old Black male; Public Administration; Graduate Student) finds, "Nine times out of ten, negative. Because of my own experiences" and Lorenz (22-year old Black male; Psychology Major; Senior) "negative view of police" is "due to his personal interactions with police." Even while Malcolm (23-year old Black male; Criminal Justice Major) acknowledges the "some good ones" his overall view of police is negative because "every experience that he had with police growing up has been bad." The dichotomy between what police are supposed to do and how African Americans perceive them is telling. D'Andre (21-year old Black male; Interdisciplinary Studies; Junior) acknowledges that even though police are "supposed to help" he sees them as "basically harmful to his community." Essentially, this harm, whether real or perceived, minimizes the trust Blacks have in police. Brendon's (24-year old Black male; Criminal Justice; Senior) lack of trust links to the lack of transparency when a police officer detains him. If a member of law enforcement does not clearly explain the reason for their detainment of the person of color, this will cause the minority to view them as targets of harassment, especially when placed in handcuffs "during a routine traffic stop and detained."

Members of law enforcement have a tremendous amount of power, and many cases in the media are evidence that many officers exploit this power. Participants like Celeste (22-year old Black female; Sociology; Junior) believe the ability to abuse their power is what attracts some police to law enforcement ("It often seems like an abuse of power on their end. It seems like some police officers go into the field just so they can carry a gun and badge and police others."). Like Celeste, Karen (23-year old Black female; Health Science; Pre-Physical Therapy; Senior) believes the "majority of police officers abuse their power" and because they fail to "think before they retaliate," they "end up hurting innocent individuals, or stereotyping individuals." Similar to Celeste and Karen, Cassie (21-year old Black female; Public Administration; Graduate Student) feels the "abuse of power" of some police tarnishes how people generally view members of law enforcement. Like Celeste, Karen, and Cassie, Zoe (21-year old African American/Black; Female; Physical Therapy Major; Junior) also sees police as individuals who "abuse their power." In contrast to the other participants, Zoe believes the physical training that police go through gives them an "advantage" over members of the general population ("they have the advantage over us regular people").

Several participants report negative perceptions of police because of the negative treatment they receive by police. Such was the case for Denise (20-year old Black female; English Major; Junior) who does not generally trust police because they target people of color ("Umm, I do not really trust them because who they target. They target Black and Brown bodies and they really do not do right by the people."). Some experiences were directly personal. Chadwick (21-year old Black male; Psychology Major) does "not like the police" because "from a young age," he has been the target of their harassment. Chadwick says that as a pre-teen ("around 11 or 12"), he would be on his way to play sports and police "would just pull him over and ask him where he was doing." This young Black male may specifically mention the destination (on his way to play basketball) to demonstrate that even when participating in an enjoyable activity that enhances his physical performance, he is the unjust mark of police. By "assuming that he was doing something" wrong, at an early age, Chadwick learned that even when an African American is not engaging in criminal or suspicious activity (holding a basketball or football in his hand), he still elicits negative treatment from police. Consider this mistreatment by law enforcement started "around 11 or 12" and Chadwick is now 21, which essentially means this young Black male has experienced this mistreatment for half of his life. Therefore, it is not surprising that Chadwick, and other Black males who experience the same treatment, have a less than positive view of police.

Another participant, Leah (21-year old Black female; Health Science; Pre-occupational Therapy; Senior) uses the metaphor of "bad apples" to refer to police persons "that abuse their authority." Sadly, the actions of some "bad apples" make it difficult for Leah to see law enforcement as an entity whose oath is to "protect and serve." The mass incarceration hurts the males who are part of the penal system and their families. Keri (22-year old African American/Black female; Psychology Major; Junior) points to this reality when she asserts many of her incarcerated family "should be out." Furthermore, this 22-year old Black female advantages Caucasians yet disadvantages Black people because "drug war targets inner-cities."

Conflicting[29]

Recall 11 participants (37 percent of the total number of participants) that describe the police as possessing positive and negative qualities seem to, in some respects, be at odds with law enforcement. Interestingly, Anita, Elijah, and James use the word "good" or "doing a good job," yet Elijah provides a unique view: law enforcement as "a good organization that has flawed tactics" that "is often tainted by people's bias and ignorance." Essentially, Elijah's view suggests public bias and ignorance may in many respects link to law enforcement's abuse of power via excessive force or murder. The "abuse of power" phrase appears when Samuel (23-year old Black male; Criminal Justice Major) speaks of police. Like Elijah, he "sees them as good and bad," yet draws attention to inequities in the justice system. Psychological conflict may explain why it is so difficult for many to trust the police. Jewel supports this statement and sees police as "a double-edged sword." While she "wants to trust them," when she realizes the "hundreds, perhaps thousands of reports" of members of law enforcement "beating and killing people," this reality makes it difficult for her to trust them. No doubt, for participants like Faye (21-year old Black female; Criminal Justice; Junior), although police "assist and help with justice" she calls them "a threat." Although George Zimmerman was not a member of law enforcement, he was a non-Black, acting as a law enforcement agent/neighborhood protector, who was responsible for the death of Trayvon Martin. Interestingly, Faye uses the phrase, "I cannot allow myself to forget cases like Trayvon Martin and many others where innocent African Americans, mostly males, were either beaten, shot down, or racially profiled for reasons that still cannot be explained today." According to Faye, there are two reasons why it is difficult for her to forget the atrocities committed on Black bodies. For one, in many cases these Black victims were innocent, and in many cases, unarmed.[30] Second, the threat of police violence, particularly for Black males, is an ever-present danger. For James, "all these cop killings in the media" contribute to distrust of police among members in the Black community. Therefore, instead of regarding police as generally "good apples," the few, very prominent "bad apples" can "spoil the entire bunch," tainting the good reputations of law enforcement agents who honorably serve and protect.

Perceptions of police are not static and can change, specifically, from positive to negative, especially if Blacks feel they are unfairly targeted because of their race. Notice that Anita believes she is "pulled over for really stupid things" or the propensity for police to "pull you over for anything." Curtis (21-year old Black male; Criminal Justice; Junior) shares that his once-positive view of police ("I saw the police as a great unit that protects and serves and actually do their jobs") is currently more negative, particularly since the 10th grade. This less than constructive view of police may relate to personal experiences in which he, his family, and friends are targets of police and his greater awareness via the media regarding the inequitable treatment of Blacks.

James, Asia, and Eduardo use the phrase "bad apples" to describe police they do not trust. Consider Asia (22-year old African/Native American female; Psychology Major; Junior) who admits to not recoiling in the presence of police, yet admits to keep her distance via turning if one is driving behind her. Eduardo (29-year old; African American/Hispanic; Male; Pre-Physical Therapy Major; Junior) juxtaposes police officers that do their job with honor against those that are perpetrators of excessive force. For this 29-year old African American/Hispanic male, "Police have an honorable job, but the people behind the job give policing a bad stigma" and provides support for this view by mentioning the "five or six officers that beat up Rodney King." In contrast to these officers, Eduardo specifically names Tommy Norman, an officer known for "going out in the community and helping his community."

What makes Norman so different from his contemporaries? According to recent reports, "Norman is known for positive community policing. Individuals know Norman for positive community policing. His unorthodox approach to policing includes thousands of video posts, pictures and daily interactive engagement at the Boys & Girls Clubs and the Police Athletic League with those that he protects and serves. He receives credit for presenting 50 NLRSD students with backpacks and $50 gift cards from Shoe Carnival in August to purchase shoes, starting the 'Shop with a Cop' program to help financially struggling students or just dancing with the children."[31] Atlanta activist and rapper Killer Mike says Norman is "doing something right" which gives clear evidence that police can balance being seen as enforcers, servants, and protectors who enjoy their work and the communities they serve.

Unlike Eduardo, Rachel (28-year old Black female; Sociology major; Junior) does not provide the name of any particular law enforcement agent, however, she acknowledges how police have personally helped her. In particular, conscientious officers have assisted her with changing the tire on her vehicle, giving her a warning instead of a ticket, or following her home when she suspected a man was following her after leaving a club. Essentially, this example shows that several "bad apples" do not necessarily "spoil the bunch."

While the aforementioned men and women generally describe officers as agents of good, one participant has conflicted feelings regarding law enforcement because of the length of their training. After describing police as "untrained and uneducated men who have more authority over your life than you actually do," Makala (23-year old Black female; Criminal Justice; Graduate Student) asserts a 5–6 month training time is not sufficient. For her, post-training, officers may not necessarily be accurate when they believe "a human being is being defiant," which is particularly valid if a perpetrator/alleged perpetrator has a mental illness. In situations such as this, police may "use excessive force," largely because they have not been adequately trained in regards to what to do.

Question 4: When you hear of incidents of police brutality, does it influence how you feel about the police? If not, why not? If so, how so?

Recall qualitative analysis of this question reveals two themes, namely: (a) Affirmative;[32] (b) Negative.[33] Only two females, 10 percent of the total number of participants, did not perceive the police in a negative way. However, Anita finds it difficult to separate the job police perform from the uniform that police wear. Recall she says, "I know what the police are here to do; it is just the people in the uniform that I do not trust." Anita's perspective might make more sense when we compare it with Asia's (22-year old African/Native American female; Psychology Major; Junior). Both of these Black females recognize the unfairness of judging "all police on the actions of one," yet Asia, in particular, expresses disappointment in officers who "do not do anything." She notes strong motivations for why police should "stand up" for what they believe is right.

Since individuals are not born with particular thoughts regarding individuals in society, the *Affirmative* theme recognizes negative personal, familial, or communal actions of police causing participants to have a less than favorable perception of law enforcement. The overwhelming majority of the men and women in this study (28 participants, or 90 percent of the total number of participants) had one or more negative experiences with law enforcement, which in turn, has influenced their general attitudes toward police. Students like Keri (22-year old African American/Black female; Psychology Major; Junior) who values "justice and equality" reports having a diminished view of police and Michelle "cannot trust them to protect us and our Black community." Sadly, negative experiences with police supports pre-existing thoughts. Denise says that she "kinds of expects" to not be honored by police. Furthermore, this 20-year old Black female English Major mentions police's "history with brutalizing people" which has "affected her to the point that she cannot trust them the way that she would like." Even Malcolm makes this clear when he uses the phrase "I just think here it goes again." However, the more one learns about police brutality, the more normal it becomes, which in turn contributes to distrust of police. This connection, with the associating normality of police violence, Jewel (21-year old African American and Native American female; Criminal Justice Major) expresses when she states, "The more I hear about these types of incidents (brutality/ shootings), I feel like it is becoming the norm and people are getting complacent. I would say, "I am just tired of hearing about this type of violence. I am just 'over' the police." That is where the distrust comes in. Therefore, increased incidents of police brutality directly minimize trust in law enforcement.

Distrust in police is a process that some participants understand all too well. The 29-year old African American/Hispanic, Pre-Physical Therapy Major, Eduardo has a military background and has training in police officer tactics, such as "detaining suspects." However, this male recognizes that "when police officers cross the line they burn that trust," which in turn, causes "the community you are serving can no longer trust you." The cyclical nature of police distrust occurs when "a police officer roughs up someone, the community basically turns its back on the police force itself," which causes "even more problems" for police. This view recognizes that although police swear, "to protect and serve" their communities, communities can in turn, protect their safety.

The phrases "here it goes again" and "I feel like it is becoming the norm" suggests incidents of police violence and murder against minorities have become so common that members of this group must accept inequality as their reality, and accept that more often than not, justice will not prevail. Paul (36-year old Black male; Public Administration; Graduate Student) makes this clear when he says, "Yes, because it reinforces what I already think about police. Stuff that I see and stuff that I do not see." Whitney (20-year old African American female; Pre-Physical Therapy Major) proclaims, "Of course. It is psychologically detrimental to the Black community just to know that our lives still are not valued." Karen (23-year old Black female; Health Science; Pre-Physical Therapy; Senior) states: "Yes, it does. Because it is just hard to hear stories about them killing individuals because they are Black. You do not trust them, just shoot kill first."

Faye admits that police brutality "confuses" her, and articulates ambivalent feelings toward law enforcement. On the one hand, she regards police as agents to whom she can go to "for help," yet does not trust them because they are perpetrators of discrimination, physical abuse, and murder of Blacks due to "the color of their skin." Even Elijah (19-year old Black male; Political

Science Major; Senior) finds that his respect for law enforcement diminishes when stories of excessive force by police come to light ("It takes me a minute to have respect for them. I do not really have too much to say. My respect for them leaves a lot.") Rachel (28-year old female Sociology Major) says, "Most definitely. Because when you think of the police, you think of people who are supposed to protect and serve. I feel that there has been more profiling than protecting that has been taking place lately." Because of their actions, some individuals may find it difficult to see the police as "good guys." Curtis (21-year old Black male; Criminal Justice; Junior) drove this perspective home when he makes a comparison between how people should perceive police, and how the actions of police, warp that perspective. While this young Black male recognizes society should see police as "people who are out there to get the bad guys that deserve to be in jail," "in reality, the police are the bad guys who deserve to be in prison or jail." However, some participants recognize there is little accountability for police brutality. After sharing police brutality "fuels the fire," Zoe (21-year old African American/ Black; Female; Physical Therapy Major; Junior) expresses the frequency of police brutality ("Because police brutality has always been evident and there are not laws in place enforcing that"). However, she also recognizes the lack of accountability of police in these murders ("So, they do what they please and get off on administrative leave with no consequences").

Participants find video evidence of police brutality and murder particularly disturbing. Leah (21-year old Black female; Health Science; Pre-occupational Therapy; Senior) remarks, "The videos you see are traumatic" and these incidents are especially painful when police "are murdering people for simple infractions." To illustrate the profound effects of murders of Blacks portrayed in the media, Leah mentions Philandro Castille (July 16, 1983–July 6, 2016), "the guy who got shot in the car with his daughter," who "did not even do anything" and whose daughter was "crying in the background" as her father is murdered. Like Leah, Sarah (19-year old Black female; Sociology Major; Freshman) expresses frustration with "waking up every day" to "any innocent Black man being shot for being black who is unarmed." Mirroring the perspective of Sarah, James (24-year old Black male; Criminal Justice Major; Senior) recognizes racism is a "hot-button issue" exacerbated by daily news reports that "literally every night" bring some form of racism to light. For this Black woman, "the case of Philandro Castille whose girlfriend filmed the entire thing" resonates strongly with her. Video evidence causes other participants to distrust police. Celeste (22-year old Black female; Sociology; Junior) mentions that when she sees "a video of police brutality it reinforces" her "negative view of police officers." Sadly, being taught, "that police officers are not to be trusted" gives credence to videos of police brutality and murder. Chadwick's (21-year old Black male; Psychology Major; Junior) confidence diminishes "especially when there is video proof that there was no type of harm done." This young Black male mentions times when "the victim could have his hands in the air, presenting no harm, and still get killed." Occurrences such as this one were the impetus for the "Hands Up, Don't Shoot" motto adopted in many Black, marginalized communities.

The frequency of incidents of excessive force and murder is a constant reminder of the instability of Black life. Idris (19-year old Black male; Criminal Justice; Sophomore) admits: "Yes. It's because it happens too often. It was not a rare thing to hear. Now, when it happens, I am just like 'again.' Aaliyah (20-year old Black Female; Sociology Major; Sophomore) remarks: "Yes. It reinforces my strong feelings that the system victimizes people of color. Modern police brutality give off the essence of Jim Crow type punishments." Cassie (21-year old Black female; Public Administration; Graduate Student) mentions the actions of police cause her to have "a negative outlook about them" and "If those incidents never happened, she would not have a negative influence about them."

Several participants do not feel they or their family members are safe. As "a young Black male," Brendon (24-year old Black male; Criminal Justice; Senior) identifies "with many of the victims of police brutality. Makala (23-year old Black female; Criminal Justice; Graduate Student) simply states, "Yes, because I look at the situation and I think, 'That could have been me.' Lorenz (22-year old Black male; Psychology Major; Senior) 'pictures the individuals being brutalized as myself,'" and D'Andre (21-year old Black male; Interdisciplinary Studies; Junior) recognizes his position as a Black male, in regards to the police is tenuous. He recognizes, "I feel as if police can do it to another black man in the same situation, they can do it to me as well." Acts of police brutality and murder deeply affect the Black males and females in this work. In particular, the Koryn Gaines incident forces Angela (21-year old Black female; Pre-Physical Therapy Major) to think about the possibility of her mother or brother being in a similar situation.

As a Criminal Justice Major, Samuel (23-year old Black male; Criminal Justice Major) is keenly aware of the relationship between law enforcement and the justice system. While he recognizes "the justice system is supposed to be fairly equal . . . blacks and minorities get treated fairly different." He recounts how the race of the police officer influences his feelings toward police. This young Black male notices, "The talk is very different" between the White police officer and the Black police officer, which directly relates to his level of personal discomfort ("I got pulled over by the university police, the officer was Black, and he did not make me fearful of being pulled over").

Question 6: When you become aware of an incident where a police officer used excessive force and he/she said, "I feared for my life!" what do you think?

Grounded theory analysis of Question 6 (When you become aware of an incident where a police officer used excessive force and he/she said, "I feared for my life!" *what do you think*?) reveals three emergent themes: (a) Racism;[34] (b) Disbelief; and (c) Fabrication.

Racism

Six individuals (20 percent of the total number of participants) use words and/or phrases that relate to the belief that race, being a racial minority, or African American as the reason why the police fear for their life. Unanimously, the males and females in this study believe Blacks and other minorities are targets of police and the inclination to shoot first receives priority over other detention methods. Sarah (19-year old Black female; Sociology Major; Freshman) believes police associate being Black with criminality ("I think they felt like the person was bad because they were Black person. They just assume and then they shoot first."). Like Sarah, Leah (21-year old Black female; Health Science; Pre-occupational Therapy; Senior) draws attention to the inclination of police to shoot as the seeming only viable option ("I think, come on, really. You chose this job. You know what this job entails. Why did you not use another tactic? When you subdue the individual, the first idea is to shoot if you are a person of color. It is like there is no other option. There is no scale to judge their level of fear, I mean they (the cops) can be fabricating. That is where it gets sticky.")

Although many law enforcement agents publicly state they shot the perpetrator and/or suspect because they feared for their life, many question the validity of these claims. For example, Celeste, a 22-year old Black female, Sociology major believes "it makes no sense" when trained officers make these claims. Recall that she says, "I do not understand how you fearing for your life leads to an unarmed civilian getting killed. It makes no sense; you are a trained officer. That is how a lot of America sees Black people as super predators, so they believe that excuse. Why not reach for your Taser or pepper spray? Why shoot to kill?"

Even though police assert shooting a minority was the only and/or best way to subdue a suspect, this Black female recognizes that their assertion may not necessarily be based on facts ("I mean, they [the cops] could be fabricating."). The propensity for police to lie is supported by Elijah (19-year old Black male; Political Science Major; Senior), who connects skin tone with threatening behavior ("I think that it is false. Simply put, I feel police officers are liars and the only threatening thing is a Black person's skin tone. When you look at the things that go on in the live videos [of police shootings], their stories never add up."). Even worse, Samuel (23-year old Black male; Criminal Justice Major) finds it problematic that police justify the

murder of Blacks ("It is possible, but when White officers shoot Black people it is always justifiable and it should not be like that."). Overall, police
shootings of unarmed individuals negative affect the mental health of Blacks.
Whitney (20-year old African American female; Pre-Physical Therapy Major) expresses that she feels a combination of emotions that cause her to
worry about family members and loved ones who fit the "racist profile of
criminality." She shares that she feels "frustrated," "depressed and imprisoned" because her boyfriend and siblings are dark-skinned.

Disbelief

Seven individuals (23 percent of the total number of participants) use words
and/or phrases that relate to the participant having doubt that the member of
law enforcement is being truthful regarding fearing for their life.[35] For example, Makala states, "I think if you feared for your life, how did the situation
start and what events led up to you deciding to take your gun?" Her comments speak to every event that results in the murder as well as the decision
of law enforcement to take their guns. Furthermore, Rachel (28-year old
Black female; Sociology Major; Junior) finds a contradiction in fearing the
very individuals police swear to protect ("Why are you a police officer, if
you fear for your life? I mean how can you protect someone who you are
afraid of?") Curtis (21-year old Black male; Criminal Justice; Junior) believes fear and doing the work of policing are incompatible. He shares, "I
understand they are trained to fight those type of situations. Basically, you
put your life on the line every day for those type of situations. You should
not fear anything because that is your job." Others believe fear has no place
in the work of law enforcers who "sign up" for the job. Case in point:
Eduardo (29-year old; African American/Hispanic; Male; Pre-Physical Therapy Major; Junior) feels, "It is what you signed up for. So basically, the job
description is to protect and serve the people. If you did not want the fear of
your life being in danger then you do not sign up for it." While police make
the claim that they fear for their lives, James (24-year old Black male; Criminal Justice Major; Senior), draws attention the clear advantage that police
have over civilians. He asserts, "I do not believe it is true, mainly because the
person is unarmed but you have a gun, a Taser, some pepper spray, a baton,
and all this equipment on. You have all these things to protect yourself
against this person and one could argue with all of the police shootings going
on, that the suspect should be fearing for their life." The phrase "*the suspect
should be fearing for their life*" makes clear the many weapons police have at
their disposal as well as their heightened level of skill in using these weapons. Like James, Brendon (24-year old Black male; Criminal Justice; Senior)
knows that police have other weapons "other than a gun" to protect himself:
"First thing I start to think of is did the person who he used deadly force on

have a weapon. And, if not, then I do not think he should have feared for his life because he has weapons other than a gun himself." Regardless of whether police fear for their life or not, one thing is clear: those are who dead cannot relate *their story* of what happened. Lorenz (22-year old Black male; Psychology Major; Senior) says, "I think, so did the person they killed (feared for their life). The individuals who feared for their life did not get to live to tell their story."

Fabrication

Seventeen individuals (57 percent of the total number of participants) use words and/or phrases that relate to the participant believing that fear is an excuse, justification, and/or cover-up for wrongdoing.[36] While Asia (22-year old African/Native American female; Psychology Major; Junior) believes police may fear Black people because they "are naturally bigger, strong, and faster than White people," police should not use fear to justify murdering them. Others, like Michelle, Malcolm, and Keri had much stronger opinions regarding police's claim that they feared for their life. In particular, Michelle (21-year old; Black female; Public Administration; Graduate Student) does not "really feel that they fear for their life because they are trained to handle these situations." Malcolm (23-year old Black male; Criminal Justice Major) believes the need to defend themselves from legal responsibility motivates fear ("I feel they are making up a justifiable reason for them to shoot someone."). Moreover, like Malcolm, Keri (22-year old African American/Black female; Psychology Major; Junior) uses the word "justification" yet links it to the oath that members of law enforcement take when they enter the force ("Justification. They are just using a justification for whatever they did. When they take the oath, it is something like 'I will risk my own life to save someone else's or something like that.' It something they say to get out of the situation that they are in.").

As previously mentioned, several participants use the word "lie" or "lying" to describe members of law enforcement that blame fear for why they murdered a Black person. Jewel (21-year old African American and Native American female; Criminal Justice Major) uses the words "copout" and "excuse" to describe the actions of untruthful police ("I think they are lying. They are liars! It is a copout. An excuse."). In addition, Karen (23-year old Black female; Health Science; Pre-Physical Therapy; Senior) and Chadwick (21-year old Black male; Psychology Major; Junior) use the phrase "cover up" to describe the claim of police who shoot because their lives are in danger.

Negative "preconceived notions" of Blacks as criminal may cause police to shoot first and give a "generic" response regarding why they behave the way they do. Anita's (18-year old Black female; Criminal Justice; Junior) perspective makes a link between colorism and the perceived criminality of African Americans. She states, "I think that they are lying. *Why do you feel this way?* I just think the media portrays us as negative people. So, whenever you look at a dark-skinned person, you think something bad is going to happen." A Black male supports the idea that police associate Blacks with law breaking. Paul (36-year old Black male; Public Administration; Graduate Student) says, "They are lying. I think they (police) already have precon- ceived notions about other cultures and races. I think the "I feared for my life," is just a generic answer. I mean, how can you fear for your life when you are a police officer. You are the law and 9 times out of 10 the courts will believe the law enforcement officer." Paul's perspective draws particular attention to the propensity for the law to believe the police officer over the civilian. Sadly, even when many witnesses are present, and videotaped evi- dence exists, it is rare for police officers to receive a trial and conviction. [37]

Other participants use the term "bull" and "bullshit" to describe the ac- tions of police. However, like James and Brendon above, they give attention to the advantage that police have over civilians. Recall that Idris (19-year old Black male; Criminal Justice; Sophomore) exclaims, "I think it is bull be- cause you are the one with a gun in the situation. You are the one with the vest on in the situation. You are the one with training on how to defuse the situation. So you are the one fearing for your life when this is the primary thing that you do." In essence, this Black male specifically outlines a gun, vest, and "training on how to defuse the situation" as tools for law enforce- ment. Of note, the onus should be on police to use their skill to "defuse the situation" instead of react by shooting to kill. In support of Idris, another Black female mentions the training law enforcement should actually utilize "for situations that get out of hand." Zoe (21-year old African American/ Black; Female; Physical Therapy Major; Junior) states, "I think it is bullshit because you are trained and equipped for situations that get out of hand and you vow to protect serve, not to take innocent lives away. So, that is just an abuse of power to me. And, if they fear for their lives in situations like that, then they do not need to be police officers because they are not serving or protecting anyone." Zoe brings up an interesting point: Officers that "fear for their lives in situations like that" "do not need to be police officers because they are not serving or protecting anyone." This statement does not assert police officers should never experience fear, but rather, that they not allow their own fears to cause them to abuse their power. In short, the potential exists for fearful police to be more likely than police who lack such fear to behave in ways that escalate conflict, rather than reduce it.

Merriam-Webster defines a "scapegoat" as "one that bears the blame for others" or "one that is the object of irrational hostility"[38] while the English Oxford Dictionary defines a "scapegoat" as "a person who is blamed for the wrongdoings, mistakes, or faults of others, especially for reasons of expediency."[39] Two participants use the term to describe the actions of police. Faye's (21-year old Black female; Criminal Justice; Junior) comment supports the one Paul provides in that accountability is a rarity among police ("They are using the phrase as a scapegoat. It is just an excuse to forcefully attack the victim and because of their position they always escape, so they continue to use it.") Another individual makes a comment regarding why lack of accountability among police is common. Aaliyah (20-year old Black Female; Sociology Major; Sophomore) provides this view, "I think that if they did fear for their life, I think it is a scapegoat. I think by saying that, if the person is of color, they are acknowledging stereotypes about Black people and that would also suggest within their line of work they are trained to fear a person of color. Which means the criminal justice system is racist." Based on the aforementioned definitions of scapegoating, police officers blame others and primarily do so for reasons of expediency or convenience.

Faye and Aaliyah's perspectives suggest police may escape legal responsibility in two ways. First, law enforcement agents may mention the (real or perceived) reason or reasons they detain the Black person. Second, claiming they fear for their life simultaneously allows police to blame the victim and avoid any legal accountability. There are several noteworthy examples of police officers that claim they fear for their life, and thus avoid all legal responsibility. Consider some noteworthy examples. Officer Darren Wilson uses this claim when he murders Michael Brown on August 9, 2014; Officer Ray Tensing does the same when he murders Sam DuBose on July 19, 2015; and Officer Yeronimo Yanez uses this defense when he executes Philandro Castile on July 6, 2016. Thus, in a country that touts "life, liberty, and the pursuit of happiness," lack of legal accountability further deepens the mistrust that many African Americans have for law enforcement.

It is important to note that an "excuse" may be valid or invalid, and several individuals use this word to describe the actions of law enforcement who claim they fear for their life when fatalities occur. Cassie (21-year old Black female; Public Administration; Graduate Student) feels, "I think that the police use that excuse to protect themselves from their wrong doing." D'Andre (21-year old Black male; Interdisciplinary Studies; Junior) feels, "I view it as an excuse to try and cover-up the wrong that they have done." Denise (20-year old Black female; English Major; Junior) says, "I take that as an excuse to brutalize people. For instance, Tamir Rice. They shot twelve-year-old boy in 2 seconds. They say it to excuse their actions. The stand your ground law protects them from consequences when they shoot them." Angela (21-year old Black female; Pre-Physical Therapy Major) states, "I believe that it is an excuse. I think that they are more scared of us (African Americans) than we are scared of them. They feel like when they approach us that we may appear intimidating which leads to them feeling as though they have to protect themselves."

Question #7: When you become aware of an incident where a police officer used excessive force and he/she said, "I feared for my life!" what do you feel?

Grounded theory analysis of Question 7 (When you become aware of an incident where a police officer used excessive force and he/she said, "I feared for my life!" *what do you feel?*) reveals two emergent themes: (a) Fabrication; (b) Frustration and Anger.

Fabrication[40]

Members of law enforcement must be aware that although they say they use excessive force because they are concerned for their lives, many African Americans do not believe these officers. However, in addition to not believing these officers they believe these law enforcement agents are lying. Although only one participant, namely Samuel (23-year old Black male; Criminal Justice Major) shares, he is unaware of what caused the officer fear ("I really do not have any feeling because I do not know what the officer was fearful of"), he stood alone.[41] In particular, sixteen individuals, or over half of participants (53 percent of participants; one person did not provide a response to this question) used words and/or phrases that relate to the participant believing that fear is an excuse, justification, and/or cover-up for wrongdoing of law enforcement. Some believe public perception influences the police narrative on excessive force. In particular, this narrative centers on the minority as the perpetrator and the law enforcement agent as the victim. Notice what Michelle (21-year old; Black female; Public Administration; Graduate Student) says, "I feel disappointed because they are trying to switch the situation around to make it seem like they are a victim."

Of note, five participants use the word "excuse" to describe the actions of police. It is especially important to note four Black females and one Black male share this assessment. Karen (23-year old Black female; Health Science; Pre-Physical Therapy; Senior) shares: "I feel like he is lying. He is trying to cover up. I feel as though they are just making excuses." Cassie, (21-year old Black female; Public Administration; Graduate Student) remarks: "I feel as though it is an excuse they [police] use to protect themselves. I also feel as though they are not really threatened by the suspect." Denise (20-year old Black female; English Major; Junior) says, "Tired. Because how many more officers are going to use that excuse. It is exhausting. They say that one thing and they are let off the hook. Just tired and angry." Brendon (24-year old Black male; Criminal Justice; Senior) says: "I feel upset. Because I feel as though the officer is just using that as an excuse for the amount of force he used because it may have not been necessary." Rachel

(28-year old Black female; Sociology Major; Junior) makes this point clear when she says, "I feel like sometimes that is an excuse for the excessive force. I feel like them saying that their life is in danger will make it justifiable to the public to kill someone."

Other participants draw attention to the total lack of accountability for police. Anita (18-year old Black female; Criminal Justice; Junior) has such little confidence in the justice system that she knows they will not be accountable for their actions ("I feel numb because when they [police] say that you know that they are going to get away."). Another participant, Faye (21-year old Black female; Criminal Justice; Junior) refers to excessive force as "obnoxious behavior" and Curtis (21-year old Black male; Criminal Justice; Junior) believes the training of police should exempt them from fear ("I understand they are trained to fight those type of situations. Basically, you put your life on the line every day for those type of situations. You should not fear anything because that is your job.").

One participant mentions how the legal system has no accountability for law enforcement's justification of murder, yet if the perpetrator were a minority, the minority would be accountable. Consider Eduardo (29-year old African American Hispanic; Male; Pre-Physical Therapy Major; Junior) who mentions the usual outcomes of investigations of police who murder. ("It's upsetting to me, because it is no longer, hey, I am in fear for my life. It is a copout. Because after the shooting and after the investigation, they go to court and say, 'I was in fear for my life,' then the police officer gets away with murder. But, if as an African American I do the same thing, I get put away for murder."). Another participant, Jewel (21-year old African American and Native American female; Criminal Justice Major) mentions the propensity for police to evade accountability for their actions. Although she claims she "rolls her eyes or laughs," at her core, she feels disgust because police believe "acts of brutality are acceptable" and "because they continue to get away with it." I roll my eyes or laugh. I feel disgusted that they think that is acceptable. Now that I think about it. They think it (acts of brutality) are acceptable because they continue to get away with it. Essentially, the comments provided by Eduardo and Jewel shine light on three realities. First, the infrequent convictions for police that murder a minority (Black) civilian.[42] Second, Blacks are painfully aware the legal system holds them to a harsher standard than police. Finally, the legal system is more likely to penalize a Black that murders than police officers that murder.

Over the past four decades, African American children are more likely than any other racial or ethnic group to be born in single-parent (mother-headed) homes. Related to this, is the mass incarceration of Black males. One female in particular, drew a connection between the excessive force of police on minorities and the structure of families. Zoe (21-year old African American/Black; Female; Physical Therapy Major; Junior) admits to feeling "hurt, because of the fact that these are innocent lives being taken away from families." She is pained that "children are growing up without their parents because of the situation that got out of hand." As a result, her trust in officers "continues to diminish." Excessive force by police is personal, causing some individuals to be deeply concerned for their safety. Notice that Angela (21-year old Black female; Pre-Physical Therapy Major) says that she feels "scared" and wonders about the outcome if she was in the same predicament. However, it appears that Angela is deeply concerned that law enforcement agents may misinterpret her actions ("I feel, maybe scared. I think, 'What if I was placed in this predicament?' They may mistake any of my sudden movements as me trying to target them instead, and that may not be the situation.").

Frustration and Anger[43]

Thirteen individuals (43 percent of participants) use words and/or phrases that relate to participants' resentment of police who use excessive force yet claim they fear for their life. Pauline Boss (2002) describes ambivalence as experiencing two emotions simultaneously, and this was most certainly the feelings of many of the men and women in this study. For example, Lorenz, (22-year old Black male; Psychology Major; Senior) says: "I feel sad. Sometimes anger." Paul (36-year old Black male; Public Administration; Graduate Student) says: "I feel anger, frustration, and a sense of disbelief." James (24-year old Black male; Criminal Justice Major; Senior) experiences "frustration and anger" because police claims of fearing for their lives are common and these claims allow them to escape legal accountability ("It frustrates and angers me. Because I feel like, I am hearing more and more police officers use the phrase and seems like it is all that they have to say to get away with killing an unarmed Black person.") Malcolm (23-year old Black male; Criminal Justice Major) admits: "I feel a little angry because of the simple fact that I know he is going to get off for it." Elijah (19-year old Black male; Political Science Major; Senior) admits: "Angry. Initially, I become angry. Because I feel is they are so easily scared then maybe it is not the job for them." Chadwick (21-year old Black male; Psychology Major; Junior) states: "It makes me very angry and causes me to think of the steps I could take to prevent this from happening in the future." Makala (23-year old Black female; Criminal Justice; Graduate Student) shares: "I feel anger, especially when the (victim) is unarmed and you (officer) are armed because you have a deadly weapon so how can you (officer) fear your life when they are unarmed."

Not only does Idris (19-year old Black male; Criminal Justice Sophomore) feel "disgust and anger," he believes claiming their lives were in danger affords law enforcement agents "the get out of jail free card." In addition to anger, it is difficult for some individuals to sympathize with police. Aaliyah (20-year old Black Female; Sociology Major; Sophomore) expresses lack of sympathy, anger, and lack of surprise when she learns of police brutality, hurt, and frustration. She feels that it (police brutality) "did not need to happen" and inequities in the legal system allow these incidents to continue to happen ("Towards the police officers, I feel unsympathetic. I feel angry, but not surprised. Towards those people that have been brutalized, I feel a hurt for them and their families. I know that regardless of what happens, this was going to happen to them or to someone else. It did not need to happen, but because of the way the system is set up, it continues to happen.")

The murder of African Americans has received much scholarly attention, but one particular work examines the murder of unarmed Blacks as well as the outcome for police in these situations. Not only are Blacks more likely to be victims of police brutality, with few exceptions (Officer Michael Slager in the murder of Walter Scott) the overwhelming majority of police escape legal accountability. Keri (22-year old African American/Black female; Psychology Major; Junior) states, "I feel pissed, especially when they (the victim) is unarmed. If that person being harmed is not trying to harm someone else, I feel even more pissed." While members of the racial majority may find it difficult to understand the frustration of Blacks murdered by police, one participant puts this in perspective by reversing the social position of the races. In addition to feeling "insulted," Sarah (19-year old Black female; Sociology Major; Freshman) draws attention to the lunacy of assuming a Black person is bad, or assuming that all Whites are bad. What is especially interesting about this Black female's perspective is that she acknowledges the likelihood for White males to be perpetrators of "all of the mass shootings in society."

Clearly, the anger and disappointment these men and women feel relates to concerns for the safety of their family. Celeste's (22-year old Black female; Sociology; Junior) commentary has four noteworthy points. First, Black people connect police brutality to their immediate family members, namely brothers, or uncles ("Anger. Because as a Black person, I understand that could have been my brother or uncle"). Second, due to being members of the same race, Black people feel the pain of other Black victims of police brutality ("I can see the pain that the families go through."). Third, even when videotaped evidence exists, Black people rarely see police tried and convicted for police brutality ("And for these killings to not result in at least a conviction, even when they are caught on film, is insulting."). Finally, many Black people believe Whites have more concern for the plight of animals than African Americans ("White people care more about animal abuse than Black people.")

Although she does not specifically mention it, Celeste may be referring to the Michael Vick incident as an example of White people's greater concern for animals. Michael Dwayne Vick (born June 26, 1980) is a former American football quarterback who played 13 seasons in the National Football League, primarily with the Atlanta Falcons and the Philadelphia Eagles. Although he holds the record for the most career rushing yards by a quarterback (6,109) and the most rushing yards by a quarterback in a season (1,039), Vick's NFL career came to a halt in 2007 after he pleaded guilty for his involvement in a dog-fighting ring and spent 21 months in federal prison. His arrest and subsequent conviction garnered Vick notoriety with the public, which lasted throughout the rest of his career.[44] Sadly, even after completing his prison sentence and filming a Public Service Announcement (PSA) for People for the Ethical Treatment of Animals (PETA),[45] many Whites still regard his actions as unforgivable and do not believe he deserves another chance. Incidents such as this one are evidence that many of the same individuals that deem Vick's actions morally irresponsible do not have the same view when police murder Blacks.

One participant acknowledges circumstances where a Black person's actions may have led to their death. While Asia (22-year old African/Native American female; Psychology Major; Junior) feels anger and disappointment, she states she feels "anger because it should not happen. It is wrong. Disappointment because the person did not choose or try to choose another option."). From this comment, this young participant makes a distinction between Black murders. In particular, differentiating between "circumstantial" murders and those that are self-contributory via "irate and ignorant" behavior.

Question #10: What steps, if any, do you believe law enforcement agencies should take to deal with issues related to police brutality?

Grounded theory analysis of Question 10 (What steps, if any, do you believe law enforcement agencies should take to deal with issues related to police brutality?) reveals four emergent themes: (a) Stricter Hiring and Training Practices; (b) Reevaluate Current Laws and Policies; (c) Required Body Cameras; (d) Nothing Will Change.

Stricter Hiring and Training Practices

Nineteen participants (63 percent of the total number of participants) use words and/or phrases that relate to participants' assertion that stricter hiring and training practices will help prevent police brutality.[46] However, one must recognize the eligibility requirements that law enforcement already has in place. What are the requirements to be a police officer?

According to Law EnforcementEDU.net, there are general police academy requirements as well as ones that specifically relate to physical fitness requirements, cognitive requirements, and character requirements. Regarding the general requirements, examples include, but are not limited to being at least 21 years at the time of police academy graduation, being a United States citizen, no felony convictions, nor domestic violence convictions.[47] Physical fitness requirements involve the physical capability to perform the many duties expected of any law enforcement professional. In particular, physical fitness relates to stamina, strength, and dexterity and coordination. Related to the latter, LawEnforcementEDU.net states, "Dexterity and coordination are critical to police service. The ability to properly discharge and reload a firearm is contingent upon the dexterity of the officer. In many cases, the lives of officers and bystanders are dependent upon the ability to properly aim and fire a weapon at a dangerous individual." Cognitive requirements involve "The ability to analyze a situation and formulate a response strategy is critical to job performance. It is possible to possess such life-saving skills naturally, but most police officers develop their cognitive skills through education and training. Education at the collegiate level emphasizes critical skills like problem solving, analytical thinking, and logic, which is why so many police agencies are willing to incentivize college graduates to apply for positions." Finally, the following relates to character requirements, "Within the dynamic environment of law enforcement there are numerous opportunities to betray the public trust. These actions, however, can significantly undermine the organization's ability to perform its duties. Law enforcement authorities can successfully operate within their communities only because they have earned the respect and trust of its members." As it relates to police officers being a single member of a law enforcement body, note the following: "Character is also important to the organization itself. The lives of fellow officers may be in the hands of a law enforcement professional, so it is of paramount importance that they have confidence in the judgment and actions of each other."

The number of individuals entering the force has seen a strong and steady rise over the past few years. The number of people employed as police officers has been growing at a rate of 1.01 percent, from 737,263 people in 2015 to 744,674 people in 2016,[48] so this suggests the need to actively screen, and equally important, weed out individuals who are not fit to protect the public. Several respondents believe preemptive measures should occur during the hiring and training process. This was the perspective of Malcolm (23-year old Black male; Criminal Justice Major) ("They need to develop better communication skills and properly train officers to use force.") and Denise (20-year old Black female; English Major; Junior) ("I feel like they should go through in-depth background screenings. Also, the way they are trained."). This young Black male and Black female see the need for police to get the best training possible, yet they were not the only ones. This was the view of Samuel (23-year old Black male; Criminal Justice Major) ("Yes, practice more tactics so they can be more trained.") as well as Leah (21-year old Black female; Health Science; Pre-occupational Therapy; Senior) who says, "I think more thorough training should be given. Some type of audit. Look at their records or files and any citations for brutality or doing something awful. Then they should be fired. The hiring process should be standardized. They should have more thorough background checks. I also think they should have rigorous sensitivity training." Karen (23-year old Black female; Health Science; Pre-Physical Therapy; Senior) says, "I feel like they should do some type of training on how to handle certain situations. The police officer is taking his power and running with it. They should do some sort of mental training to see if something is wrong with them."

Although they are part of the legal system, it is not the job of law enforcement agents to make determinations regarding innocence or guilt. This means the ability to enforce the law, via detaining a suspect, should be expedient and fair. Eduardo (29-year old; African American/Hispanic; Male; Pre-Physical Therapy Major; Junior) makes this point clear when he says, "Police officers need to realize that they are not the judge, jury, and executioner. If you cannot put someone down with two shots from your pistol, then you do not need to be on the force." In a related vein, another respondent describes a systematic approach that police officers must consciously take when they detain someone. Sarah (19-year old Black female; Sociology Major; Freshman) says, "They should question someone before they put their hands on them. They should make sure the person knows what they are getting in trouble for before they get violent. They should be certain that they have probable cause before they take their gun and shoot it. They should have to call back up before they shoot someone who is unarmed, so they will have someone there to validate why they shot an unarmed man or woman."

Eduardo and Sarah's commentary speak to the lunacy of police officers that shoot an individual multiple times, or do not make it clear to the suspect the consequences for certain actions. Sarah's comment especially speaks to this point. If law enforcement agents would follow specific protocols as it relates to questioning, understanding, probable cause, and telephoning back-up before shooting, this can validate the officer's claims and make civilians feel safe. Since there is a high level of distrust among members of the African American community and police, an especially important point is the need for police to inform the suspect why they detain them as well as what could happen should the suspect become violent. This level of transparency may mentally redirect the minority suspect or minority criminal to recognize the negative consequences of speech or behavior that make police feel provoked.

Some individuals recommend that members of law enforcement have a better understanding of the African American culture. Paul (36-year old Black male; Public Administration; Graduate Student) feels, "I think they should take more classes on cultural awareness. It will make them more aware of the cultures of other groups. The course should not last a day or two; it should last about a week." Faye (21-year old Black female; Criminal Justice; Junior) says, "The steps I feel that law enforcement should take, starts with getting feedback about the way they make African Americans feel. Do not look at it like it is a form of bashing or making their name look bad, but really consider how their approach affects others." Idris (19-year old Black male; Criminal Justice; Sophomore) feels, "First, they have to address the fact that there is a difference in how the treat white people compared to Black people. Secondly, if you can see the difference, treat them equally." Lorenz (22-year old Black male; Psychology Major; Senior) simply says, "I feel like that they should psychologically test officers for racial biases." Curtis, (21-year old Black male; Criminal Justice; Junior) feels, "First, they must provide counseling for officers regarding anger management and racial profiling. They should have something before they go out and patrol."

One participant wants law enforcement to create a new training course. Chadwick (21-year old Black male; Psychology Major; Junior) says, "I feel like they should create a new training course. And, I feel the placement of cops should be taken into consideration. For example, cops that grew up in the 'hood,' or the 'inner city,' should service those areas because they would know how to deal with those areas." Anita (18-year old Black female; Criminal Justice; Junior) says, "They (police) should take psychology courses to teach them how to deal with people. They need to follow the lead of Starbucks and provide police with extensive diversity training."

Rachel (28-year old Black female; Sociology Major; Junior) says, "I feel like a police officer should not police a neighborhood that he or she is unfamiliar with. I feel like police should do more community service to get to know people and build trust. They should actually go out to different neighborhoods and introduce themselves to build a better rapport with the citizens in the community. I believe those community service hours should be done before they are sworn." Greater police involvement with minority neighborhoods could build trust. Keri (22-year old African American/Black female; Psychology Major; Junior) expresses police should "take the integrity training seriously. They should interact with the neighborhood so that they can have a better relationship, better trust. I think they should learn and understand Black culture more." When questioned regarding why this is important, Keri says, "So they can better understand what causes certain negative deviant behavior. If they can better understand it, they will be less violent or brutal when addressing it."

Although law enforcement do not require applicants to graduate from college, one Black female has very strong opinions regarding how law enforcement agencies can deal with police violence. Jewel, (21-year old African American and Native American female; Criminal Justice Major)[49] feels strongly that college should be "a requirement" and the screening process delve deeply into the "types of experiences these guys have had, mental health issues." Since racial diversity in America has seen a steady increase over the past several decades,[50] it is imperative that officers understand "how to deal with all types of people from all different walks of life." She also feels "there needs to be a much greater focus on de-escalated situations as opposed to resorting to using force," and that police must be held accountable for their actions. In particular, this young woman believes "it needs to be a crime for officers to shoot and kill someone. It should not be justified by their badge. There are hundreds of dangerous jobs in the world and they are held accountable."

Reevaluate Current Laws and Policies

Five individuals (17 percent of the total number of participants) use words and/or phrases that relate to the belief that laws and policies should make police accountable when they use excessive force and/or murder a Black person.[51] For D'Andre (21-year old Black male; Interdisciplinary Studies; Junior) one such policy relates to firearm prevention ("Umm, pass laws to where policemen's gun not show up with loaded guns."). Two Black females use the word "consequences" to stress police officers must pay a price when they do not follow decorum. Notice that Whitney (20-year old African American female; Pre-Physical Therapy Major) says, "Umm, have their officers suffer consequences when they do not follow proper protocol, not make excuses." In addition, Cassie (21-year old Black female; Public Administration; Graduate Student) relates, "I honestly think they should take the same route that they would with any other citizen. If you are in a position of authority or not, there should always be consequences for your actions." Essentially, both of these comments stress two realities. First, law enforcement agents should experience the same consequences as the general populace. Second, being in a position of authority to enforce the law does not exert police from experiencing the consequences of their actions.

An additional policy involves self-defense that is not necessarily contingent on having a weapon. Celeste (22-year old Black female; Sociology; Junior) feels, "They should re-evaluate stop and frisk because it disproportionately impacts Black communities. They should know how to defend themselves besides using their gun." While all of these men and women provide insightful thoughts, one Black male provides a comprehensive approach to eradicating excessive force. James (24-year old Black male; Criminal Justice Major; Senior) says, "There should be some classes taken regularly by officers with video footage illustrating what to do and what not to do and potentially volatile situations. Police officers who use excessive force should receive stiffer and harsher punishments. If they feel there are harsh punishments, they will not do that again." Three things make James' comment especially noteworthy. First, he recognizes that training should be a frequent process ("There should be some classes taken regularly by officers"). Second, he recommends visual examples that help reiterate what should (and should not) be done during "potentially volatile situations. Finally, he recognizes that "harsh punishments" are a powerful impetus to reduce police violence against citizens ("If they feel there are harsh punishments, they will not do that again.").

Required Body Cameras

Four individuals (13 percent of the total number of participants) use words and/or phrases that relate to the participant believing that if members of law enforcement were required to wear body cameras and/or dash cameras, this would minimize police brutality.[52] For the most part, the males and females who advocate for these forms of surveillance see this as part of responsibility and accountability. Angela (21-year old Black female; Pre-Physical Therapy Major) definitely believes they can be effective. She specifically mentions "body camera" as a step that has already been "taken to calm to resolve the issue."). One Black male feels video cameras would allow attorneys and prosecutors to conduct "checks and balances." Elijah (19-year old Black male; Political Science Major; Senior) says, "I think every police officer should have a body camera in use at all times. I also feel that the attorneys and prosecutors should have more checks and balances." When asked to elaborate on what he means, he says, "I feel like each party should be held accountable by all of the evidence. I feel that when the attorneys see the evidence they should seek to serve the citizens and find them justice instead of working with their friends [the police]."

Another respondent recommends another way to increase accountability in law enforcement, besides body cameras. Brendon (24-year old Black male; Criminal Justice; Senior) feels, "They should either have body cams or having a journalist or a ride along person with a camera to document things. Because they do that in the army when soldiers are deployed." Previously, we mention the cognitive requirements for individuals interested in becoming a member of law enforcement. One of these was the cognitive requirement and one participant goes into depth regarding her stance on body cameras as well as determining racial bias within applicants that should disqualify them from the job. Makala (23-year old Black female; Criminal Justice; Graduate Student) feels, "They should go through training. Specifically, a psychological examination. A White cop should not view a Black person any differently than they view a White person. Taxpayers spend money on this equipment (dash cams, body cams) and it should be used without any exceptions. Your vehicle should not go out into the field if the dash cam is not working."

Nothing Will Change

Three individuals (10 percent of the total number of participants) use words and/or phrases that relate to participants' belief that racism in society and members of law enforcement is so deep that will nothing will eradicate police brutality.[53] For example, Zoe (21-year old African American/Black; Female; Physical Therapy Major; Junior) says, "Honestly, law enforcement agencies they won't take any steps." On the other hand, Michelle (21-year old; Black female; Public Administration; Graduate Student) recognizes the ability of individuals to be self-determining, ("I do not feel like they can really do anything. I feel that each individual has their own thoughts and that individual is going to do what they think is right."). Since racism has existed since slavery, and Aaliyah (20-year old Black Female; Sociology Major; Sophomore) believes that the problem of racism is so profoundly intertwined with Blacks' reality that she does not believe real change will occur in her lifetime ("Well, the issue related to police brutality is racism. I feel like it is so deeply interwoven into the system that there is really no true rectification that will happen in my lifetime.").

There are three reasons why these participants have such a bleak outlook in regards to change. For one, the forced enslavement of Africans set in motion a racial power dynamic that disadvantaged Blacks and advantaged Whites. Second, numerous cases where police do not receive a trial and/or conviction for using excessive force or murdering an African American may cause these Black women to have little faith in the legal system. Finally, since individuals are self-determining, and have the right to make decisions, this grants Whites legal protection, especially when they claim they did "what they thought was right."

Question #11: What steps, if any, do you believe universities and colleges should take to deal with issues related to police brutality?

Grounded theory analysis of Question 11 (What steps, if any, do you believe *universities and colleges* should take to deal with issues related to police brutality?) reveals four emergent themes: (a) University-Led Education on Interacting with Law Enforcement; (b) University-Led Law Enforcement Community Efforts; (c) University-Advocating Attitudinal and Policy

Changes in Law Enforcement; (d) University Accountability of Law Enforcement.

University-Led Education on Interacting With Law Enforcement[54]

Fourteen individuals (47 percent of the total number of participants) use words and/or phrases that relate to participants' belief that universities and colleges should initiate seminars, workshops, and courses that advise students of their legal rights as well as how to interact with members of law enforcement. Even though police receive training in de-escalation tactics, Curtis (21-year old Black male; Criminal Justice; Junior) and Lorenz (22-year old Black male; Psychology Major; Senior) use the same verbiage ("Colleges should teach students how to de-escalate a situation.") to express the need for colleges to assist students in this way. While these males speak to the responsibility of colleges and universities to educate their students, others describe this activity as a form of community outreach. Samuel (23-year old Black male; Criminal Justice Major) makes this clear when he says, "Just provide seminars and trainings to prevent police brutality within the community." This statement may reveal Black students' propensity to view colleges and universities as a microcosm of the Black community, more broadly. Such community efforts may invariably bridge some of the distrust that exists, especially among Primarily White Institutions (PWIs) and marginalized communities.

While the above students offer recommendations on how to de-escalate conflict, Malcolm (23-year old Black male; Criminal Justice Major) advocates that seminars teach students "how to avoid conflict altogether." Knowledge in this area may help African Americans learn how to circumvent situations that may lead to excessive force or murder. Added to this, Michelle (21-year old; Black female; Public Administration; Graduate Student) advocates for the dual education of "students and faculty." The purpose of this collective effort is to change their current attitude toward police (from negative to positive) as well as result in less hostile interactions ("I feel that they should educate the students and faculty more. Because it would change the way they view officers and also when it comes to being in contact with them.") Cassie (21-year old Black female; Public Administration; Graduate Student) states, "I feel like they should take the same steps that they would for any other citizens. It does not matter if you are on campus or outside in the regular world, there should always be consequences for your actions. I also believe more awareness for police brutality should be given on campuses because students and police officers interact with one another on a daily basis."

Several participants believe individuals should know their rights. Keri exclaims, "Umm, I guess classes like Sociology of law in which students can learn more about their rights and which laws are what." Anita (18-year old Black female; Criminal Justice; Junior) says, "Students need to be coopera-tive and taught their rights. A lot of Black people do not know their rights." Elijah (19-year old Black male; Political Science Major; Senior) says, "They should make students aware of their rights and let them know what they have and have not to do when they are pulled over by police." Karen (23-year old Black female; Health Science; Pre-Physical Therapy; Senior) expresses, "All you can do is inform the students of the situations and teaching what not to do. So that they will not end up dead. Honestly, there is not anything that you can do."

Other contributors see a connection between education and actions in the field. Idris (19-year old Black male; Criminal Justice; Sophomore) expresses, "I guess educate more people on their rights and in law related majors try to put out more educated people in the law enforcement field. I feel the more educated you are the more level headed and work oriented you will be. You will be able to focus on the job on hand and make you less biased." Aaliyah (20-year old Black Female; Sociology Major; Sophomore) states, "I feel like the college should educate the people interested in changing the system in a way that is inclusive and recognizes the faults in the system of law enforce-ment. Attempt to not perpetuate the same tropes about people of color that exist in law enforcement."

Another participant believes civilian education on interacting with police would be beneficial. Chadwick (21-year old Black male; Psychology Major; Junior) remarks, "Possibly more seminars that explain police brutality and the steps you should take to prevent things like altercations when you get pulled over or like being searched." James (24-year old Black male; Criminal Justice Major; Senior) offers this perspective: "They should educate some students with how to engage with police officers on one traffic stops. They should teach students to do whatever they have to do to get out of that one on one encounter, so they can deal with that on the other side (the legal end)." Still another participant stressed the importance of education. D'Andre (21-year old Black male; Interdisciplinary Studies; Junior) shares, "They should educate students on how to act when they encounter policemen. Have police-men come to the classrooms to educate student how to act in certain situa-tions."

University-Led Law Enforcement Community Efforts[55]

Since service is one of the core missions of land-grant institutions,[56] it is fitting that five individuals (17 percent of the total number of participants) use words and/or phrases that relate to participants' belief that universities should bridge the acrimonious relationship between minority communities and members of law enforcement. Several males and females put service or providing valuable information to the community at large forth. Faye (21-year old Black female; Criminal Justice; Junior) regards "having more positive interactions" with police. In addition, Brendon (24-year old Black male; Criminal Justice; Senior) says, "I think that the universities should reach out to the local police departments in their cities, so that officers could come and talk to the students and hold seminars so they and the students can build a positive relationship." Leah (21-year old Black female; Health Science; Pre-occupational Therapy; Senior) also places the onus squarely on the shoulders of higher learning institutions to initiate "seminars and panel discussions." She specifically states, "The university officers should take a step to reach out to students and explain what they do from their perspective." Paul's (36-year old Black male; Public Administration; Graduate Student) words "They should have police officers come to the university and give courses so that students will know about them and their purpose in the community," resonate deeply with Leah's. Furthermore, transparent discussions, such as the ones Jewel (21-year old African American and Native American female; Criminal Justice Major) offers (regarding what they do and why they do it) can clarify the role and presence of law enforcement.[57]

Law enforcement taking the initiative could have three potential benefits. For one, by doing so police demonstrate they acknowledge socio-historical distrust and are interested in healing that distrust. Second, police coming to the university campus signals to students that they honor their space and have made a concerted effort to come to them. Finally, explaining "what they do from their perspective" can help students (and faculty) understand the rationale for some of the decisions they make. Students who believe that all law enforcement agents use violence when not appropriate, after such transparent discussion, may learn why the police officer uses some methods and not others.

University Advocating Attitudinal and Policy Changes in Law Enforcement[58]

Five individuals (17 percent of the total number of participants) use words and/or phrases that relate to participants' belief that universities should ensure that members of law enforcement change how they perceive African Americans and abide by laws and policies that protect all citizens.

Since attitudes directly affect behaviors, police must change what they think of Blacks. Two participants, namely Denise and Makala, stress why this is important, albeit for different reasons. Denise (20-year old Black female; English Major; Junior) believes the problems spring from the early distrust of police, which occurs when teachers call police for student issues ("I feel like the problem is that this dislike/trust of police officers starts at an early age. Not having so many schools on high school campuses. I feel that when teachers are having a hard time with a student they call police."). On the other hand, another Black female asserts refraining from consciously placing Blacks in a criminal pigeonhole is a mark of respect. Makala (23-year old Black female; Criminal Justice; Graduate Student) says, "I feel the first step any law enforcement officer should take is to not view any African American male as the same. In other words, they should not stereotype them. They should treat them with respect." Herein lies the connection between what police think of African Americans and how they actually treat African Americans. Essentially, while disrespectful thoughts lead to disrespectful actions, respectful thoughts lead to respectful actions.

Some males and females believe institutions of higher learning have a responsibility to clearly define "excessive force" and make law enforcement agents aware of the consequences for such. Therefore, in addition to attitudinal changes, three participants believe university policy should take a firm stance and not condone police violence. Eduardo[59] (29-year old; African American/Hispanic; Male; Pre-Physical Therapy Major; Junior) makes it clear that once universities ensure "their police force knows what excessive force is," that the officer must "be on their own" if they exercise excessive force. The establishment of policies that force police to take full responsibility for their actions, without the aid of the PWI or HBCU may minimize cases of police brutality, particularly on college campuses. Rather than protesting, Celeste (22-year old Black female; Sociology; Junior) recommends "research that can lead to policy changes." Furthermore, this young woman points to instances where protesting, in the wake of the Trayvon Martin murder were not effective. Since the Civil Rights movement during the 1950s and 1960s was responsible for many policy changes, she demands organizational efforts that galvanize communities. While Celeste discusses change via a macro lens, Zoe (21-year old African American/Black; Female; Physical Therapy Major; Junior) speaks of personal responsibility. This young Black female sees "the younger generation" as "our future" and impels individuals to change something that they do not like. Instead of waiting for others to bring about positive change, she encourages individuals to "focus more on bettering" themselves in order to bring about the change they seek.

University Accountability of Law Enforcement[60]

Four participants (13 percent of the total number of participants) use words and/or phrases that relate to participants' belief that universities and colleges should be at the forefront of making law enforcement accountable for police brutality. Included within this theme is the view that universities should take the lead in organizing protests against law enforcement in the wake of police brutality. While one Black female did not experience police brutality on her college campus,[61] some individuals believe institutions of higher learning, specifically Primarily White Institutions (PWIs), and Historically Black Colleges and Universities (HBCUs) have a responsibility to eradicate police brutality. Historically deep images of Blacks as criminals have caused many Whites to fear Blacks, and institutions of higher learning can help address and eradicate this fear. Which institution should primarily bear the responsibility of educating Blacks, PWIs or HBCUs? The narratives of two Black females reveal that it depends on whom you ask.

Whitney (20-year old African American female; Pre-Physical Therapy Major) puts this responsibility on Primarily White Institutions ("Mainly PWIs. Predominantly White Institutions) need to break psychologically chains of having white people "scared."). On the other hand, Rachel (28-year old Black female; Sociology Major; Junior) believes, "HBCU's especially should be at the forefront of leading the movement to have police officers be held accountable. They can do it by. Well, I have not really thought about it. I mean protesting does not help. I do not feel any real changing of laws come out of protesting. Sometimes a lot of community damage comes from protesting and that is not conducive to the movement to bring about change." While Rachel (28-year old Black female; Sociology Major; Junior) believes "protesting does not help," another Black female, who was coincidentally a Sociology major, had a somewhat different perspective. Sarah (19-year old Black female; Sociology Major; Freshman) recommends continued support of the Black Lives Matter movement yet realizes these efforts may lessen because of counter-race movements like "White Lives Matter." However, Sarah puts these counter-race movements in perspective by mentioning "but they [whites] are not the ones who are being shot down by police."

Quantitative Findings

As mentioned in the previous section, four questions were subject to numerical analysis.[62] As evidenced by the response to Question 3 (On a scale of 1-10, with 1 being lowest and 10 being highest, how much do you trust the police?), the men and women in this study generally have little confidence in police. When responding to a question that ranks their level of trust ("1 being lowest and 10 being highest"), the average score was 1.26, which is evidence of negligible faith in law enforcement. In regards to Question 5 (Do you believe the police treat Black people better than, equal to, or worse than White people?), participants unanimously believe police treat Black people worse than they treat White people and this belief no doubt, relates to law enforcement's use of excessive force on people of color. With that said, while the majority of participants have never personally experienced excessive force (23 percent) [Question 8—Has a police officer ever used an excessive amount of force on *you*?], they are aware of police using excessive force on someone they know (77 percent) [Question 9—Has a police officer ever used an excessive amount of force on *someone that you know*?]. These findings align with extant scholarship that reveals minorities, and in particular, African Americans are substantially more likely to have negative encounters with police.[63]

SUMMARY

Earlier, we outline in this chapter explores five w's (who, what, when, where, why) that relate to perceptions of police. Recall the *"who"* are two entities: (a) minorities and how they perceive police; (b) how members of law enforcement relate to minorities. The *"what"* are the circumstances in which Blacks' interactions with police occur; the *"when"* are the times when minorities interact with police; the *"where"* is the place minorities and law enforcement meet; the *"why"* is the rationale for why police say they target Blacks and other racial minorities.

Who. Who is the focus of this examination? The focus of this investigation is African Americans' opinion of police. The results of this section reveal Blacks generally have very little faith and confidence in police. While some individuals base their views on second-hand accounts, most base their views on personal experience. Being called a "Boy," being slammed to the ground, not responding to their questions, and being treated in a harsh manner are examples of law enforcement's systematic disrespect of African Americans.

What. What are the circumstances where police interact with African Americans? It is the responsibility of police to enforce the law and police will detain an African American that is in possession of illegal drugs.

When. During what times do police interact with African Americans? Not surprising, many Blacks interact with police while driving. However, members of this group come in contact with police during family gatherings, while recreating (attending the movies or playing basketball with friends), or while joking with friends in a public place.

Where. What is the location where police interact with African Americans? Law enforcement agents encounter members of this group on the streets, in stores, and even in their home.

Why. What is the rationale for police target of African Americans? Law enforcement target African Americans, through excessive force or murder, because they believe the Black person in question has a weapon. Another reason is the growing narrative of police that they fear for their own lives and safety.

NOTES

1. *Qualitative Findings*. Qualitative analysis was conducted on the following eight questions: (1) When you hear the word "police" what words immediately come to mind? (2) In general, how do you view the police? (4) When you hear of incidents of police brutality, does it influence how you feel about the police? If not, why not? If so, how so? (6) When you become aware of an incident where a police officer used excessive force and he/she said, "I feared for my life!" *what do you think*? (7) When you become aware of an incident where a police officer used excessive force and he/she said, "I feared for my life!" *what do you feel*? (10) What steps, if any, do you believe law enforcement agencies should take to deal with issues related to police brutality? (11) What steps, if any, do you believe *universities and colleges* should take to deal with issues related to police brutality? (12) Is there anything else that you would like to share?

2. Alpert, G.P. and Smith, W.C., 1994. How reasonable is the reasonable man: Police and excessive force. *J. Crim. L. & Criminology*, *85*, p.481. Gerber, Monica M., and Jonathan Jackson. "Justifying violence: legitimacy, ideology and public support for police use of force." *Psychology, Crime & Law* 23, no. 1 (2017): 79–95. Skolnick, Jerome H., and James J. Fyfe. *Above the law: Police and the excessive use of force*. New York: Free Press, 1993. Ajilore, Olugbenga, and Shane Shirey. "Do# AllLivesMatter? An evaluation of race and excessive use of force by police." *Atlantic Economic Journal* 45, no. 2 (2017): 201–212. Jacobsma, Michael J. "Non-Contact Excessive Force by Police: Is That Really a Thing." *U. Rich. L. Rev.* 52 (2017): 1.

3. Cornell Law School. Excessive Force. Retrieved from: https://www.law.cornell.edu/wex/excessive_force

4. US Legal. Excessive Force Law and Legal Definition. Retrieved from: https://definitions.uslegal.com/e/excessive-force/

5. https://study.com/academy/lesson/excessive-force-definition-cases-statistics.html

6. Schomerus, Georg, Susanne Stolzenburg, Simone Freitag, Sven Speerforck, Deborah Janowitz, Sara Evans-Lacko, Holger Muehlan, and Silke Schmidt. "Stigma as a barrier to recognizing personal mental illness and seeking help: a prospective study among untreated persons with mental illness." *European Archives of Psychiatry and Clinical Neuroscience* (2018): 1–11. Merikangas, Kathleen R., Evelyn J. Bromet, and Benjamin G. Druss. "Future surveillance of mental disorders in the United States: count people, not disorders." *JAMA Psychiatry* 74, no. 5 (2017): 431–432.

7. Healthline (2018). The Relationship between ADHD and Autism. Retrieved from: https://www.healthline.com/health/adhd/autism-and-adhd

8. National Institute of Mental Health (2018). Schizophrenia. Retrieved from: https://www.nimh.nih.gov/health/topics/schizophrenia/index.shtml

9. Delgado, Richard, and Jean Stefancic. *Critical race theory: An introduction*. NYU Press, 2017. Johnson, Jason Kyle. "Who's Afraid of the Big Black Man?." *Educational Studies* 54, no. 2 (2018): 229–236. Rutbeck-Goldman, Ariela, and L. Song Richardson. "Race and Objective Reasonableness in Use of Force Cases: An Introduction to Some Relevant Social Science." *Ala. CR & CLL Rev.* 8 (2017): 145. Spence, Lester K. "Images of black people in general, and black men in particular, have long." *Contours of African American Politics: Volume 2, Black Politics and the Dynamics of Social Change* (2017): 281.

10. The *Law Enforcers* theme relates to the participant using words and/or phrases that describe the police as those who ensure that members of society follow the law.

11. The *Conflicting* theme relates to the participant using words and/or phrases that describe the police as possessing positive and negative qualities. In particular, this theme relates to the participant using words or phrases that describe the police as protectors and aggressors.

12. Goff, Phillip Atiba, Matthew Christian Jackson, Brooke Allison Lewis Di Leone, Carmen Marie Culotta, and Natalie Ann DiTomasso. "The essence of innocence: Consequences of dehumanizing Black children." *Journal of Personality and Social Psychology* 106, no. 4 (2014): 526–545.

13. Troy, Gil. Filming Rodney King's Beating Ruined His Life, March 3, 2016, Accessed on July 31, 2018, https://www.thedailybeast.com/filming-rodney-kings-beating-ruined-his-life

14. Hess, Judith. "Genre films and the status quo." *Film Genre: Theory and Criticism*, edited by B. Grant. Metuchen, NJ: Scarecrow (1977): 65–95.

15. *The Negative* theme relates to the participant using words and/or phrases that describe the police in negative ways. In particular, this theme relates to police using their authority to make citizens feel inferior.

16. The *Police Brutality* theme relates to the participant using words and/or phrases related to the police using excessive force or being physically brutal with African Americans.

17. https://mashable.com/2015/07/01/kendrick-lamar-alright-video-police-brutality/#_J7PdoxQHgqo

18. Han, Bing, Deborah A. Cohen, Kathryn P. Derose, Jiang Li, and Stephanie Williamson. "Violent crime and park use in low-income urban neighborhoods." *American Journal of Preventive Medicine* 54, no. 3 (2018): 352–358. Brantingham, Paul J., and Patricia L. Brantingham. "Notes on the geometry of crime." In *Principles of Geographical Offender Profiling*, pp. 97–124. Routledge, 2017.

19. The *Racist* theme relates to the participant using words and/or phrases that describe the police as racists that immediately have negative perceptions of African American people.

20. Cornell Law School. Excessive Force. Retrieved from: https://www.law.cornell.edu/wex/excessive_force

21. *The Negative* theme relates to the participant using words and/or phrases that describe the police in negative ways. In particular, this theme relates to police using their authority to make citizens feel inferior. The *Conflicting* theme relates to the participant using words and/or phrases that describe the police as possessing positive and negative qualities. In particular, this theme relates to the participant using words or phrases that describe the police as protectors and aggressors. The *Law Enforcers* theme relates to the participant using words and/or phrases that describe the police as those who ensure that members of society follow the law. The *Racist* theme relates to the participant using words and/or phrases that describe the police as racist, or immediately having negative perceptions of African American people.

22. Meares, Tracey L. "The Law and Social Science of Stop and Frisk." *Annual Review of Law and Science* 10, no. 1 (2014): 335–52.

23. Ibid.

24. Huq, Aziz. "The Consequences of Disparate Policing: Evaluating Stop and Frisk as a Modality of Urban Policing." *Minnesota Law Review* 100, no. 6 (2017): 2397–2480.

25. Ibid.

26. Graham, David A. "Stop and Frisk: Trump's Bad Idea for Fighting Crime," *The Atlantic*, September 21, 2016, https://www.theatlantic.com/politics/archive/2016/09/trump-stop-and-frisk-ineffective-unconstitutional/501041/

27. Miller, Reuben Jonathan, Lester Jackson Kern, and Ayanna Williams. "The Front End of the Carceral State: Police Stops, Court Fines, and the Racialization of Due Process." *Social Service Review* 92, no. 2 (2018): 290–303.

28. Charles Ramsey on Sunday, July 10th, 2016 in an interview on "Meet the Press."

29. The *Conflicting* theme relates to the participant using words and/or phrases that describe the police as possessing positive and negative qualities. In particular, this theme relates to the participant using words or phrases that describe the police as protectors and aggressors.

30. Chaney, Cassandra, and Ray V. Robertson. "Armed and Dangerous? An Examination of Fatal Shootings of Unarmed Black People by Police." *The Journal of Pan African Studies* 8, no. 4 (2015): 45–78. Chaney, Cassandra, and Ray V. Robertson. "Can We All Get Along? Blacks' Historical and Contemporary (In) Justice with Law Enforcement." *Western Journal of Black Studies*, 38, no. 2 (2014): 108–122. Chaney, Cassandra, and Ray V. Robertson. "Racism and Police Brutality in America." *Journal of African American Studies*, 17, no. 4 (2013): 480–505.

31. Tommy Norman, Wikipedia, Accessed on July 20, 2018, https://en.wikipedia.org/wiki/Tommy_Norman

32. The *Affirmative* theme refers to words and/or phrases that relate to negative personal, familial, or communal actions of police causing participants to have a less than favorable perception of law enforcement as a whole.

33. The *Negative* theme refers to words and/or phrases that relate to participants not allowing the actions of some police to cause them to have a less than favorable perception of law enforcement as a whole.

34. The *Racism* theme refers to words and/or phrases that relate to participants' belief that race, being a racial minority, or African American as the reason why the police fear for their life.

35. The *Disbelief* theme refers to words and/or phrases that relate to the participant having doubt that the member of law enforcement is being truthful regarding fearing for their life.

36. The *Fabrication* theme refers to words and/or phrases that relate to the participant believing that fear is an excuse, justification, and/or cover-up for wrongdoing.

37. Park, Madison (March 22, 2018). Police Shootings: Trials, Convictions are Rare for Officers. Accessed on Wednesday July 26, 2108, https://www.cnn.com/2017/05/18/us/police-involved-shooting-cases/index.html

38. Merriam-Webster, Scapegoat Definition, Accessed July 29, 2018, https://www.merriam-webster.com/dictionary/scapegoat

39. English Oxford Dictionary, Scapegoat Definition, Accessed July 29, 2018, https://en.oxforddictionaries.com/definition/scapegoat

40. The *Fabrication* theme refers to words and/or phrases that relate to the participant believing that fear is an excuse, justification, and/or cover-up for wrongdoing of law enforcement.

41. D'Andre, Interviewee #28 (21-year old Black male; Interdisciplinary Studies; Junior) did not provide a response to this question.

42. For examples of indictments and non-indictments of police, see Cassandra Chaney and Ray V. Robertson. "Armed and Dangerous? An Examination of Fatal Shootings of Unarmed Black People by Police." *The Journal of Pan African Studies* 8, no. 4 (2015): 45–78.

43. The *Frustration and Anger* theme refers to words and/or phrases that relate to participants' resentment of police who use excessive force yet claim they fear for their life. This theme also refers to words and/or phrases that relate to the participant believing police use "fear for their life" as a way to obstruct justice.

44. Michael Vick, Accessed on July 26, 2018, https://en.wikipedia.org/wiki/Michael_Vick

45. Mike Vick Dogfighting TV Commercial (March 30, 2012), Accessed July 28, 2018, https://www.youtube.com/watch?v=rk3TbAUDBd8

46. The *Stricter Hiring and Training Practices* theme refers to words and/or phrases that relate to participants' assertion that stricter hiring and training practices will help prevent police brutality.

47. General Police Academy Requirements: Being at least 21 years at the time of police academy graduation; being a United States citizen; No misdemeanor convictions within the three years prior to applying; valid driver's license; No felony convictions; No DWI Convictions in the five years prior to applying; No domestic violence convictions; Sixty credit hours from an accredited college or university (College credit requirements may be waived for those with at least three years of military service and an honorable discharge)

48. Data USA, Police Officers, 2018. Accessed on July 15, 2018, https://datausa.io/profile/soc/333050/

49. Jewel's Narrative: I think that college needs to be a requirement, not a bonus (in terms of pay). The screening process needs to be more in depth in terms of finding out what types of experiences these guys have had, mental health issues. The training needs to be much more extensive and consistent. For example, officers need to be trained on how to deal with all types of people from all different walks of life. And, there needs to be a much greater focus on de-escalated situations as opposed to resorting to using force. Finally, it needs to be a crime for officers to shoot and kill someone. It should not be justified by their badge. There are hundreds of dangerous jobs in the world and individuals that hold these jobs assume accountability.

50. Frey, William H. *Diversity explosion: How new racial demographics are remaking America*. Brookings Institution Press, 2014.

51. The *Reevaluate Current Laws and Policies* theme refers to words and/or phrases that relate to participants' belief that laws and policies should make police accountable when they use excessive force and/or murder a Black person.

52. The *Required Body Cameras* theme refers to words and/or phrases that relate to the participant believing that if members of law enforcement were required to wear body cameras and/or dash cameras, this would minimize police brutality.

53. The *Nothing Will Change* theme refers to words and/or phrases that relate to participants' belief that racism in society and members of law enforcement is so deep that will nothing will eradicate police brutality.

54. The *University-Led Education on Interacting with Law Enforcement* refers to words and/or phrases that relate to participants' belief that universities and colleges should initiate seminars, workshops, and courses that advise students of their legal rights as well as how to interact with members of law enforcement.

55. The *University-Led Law Enforcement Community Efforts* theme refers to words and/or phrases that relate to participants' belief that universities should bridge the acrimonious relationship between minority communities and members of law enforcement.

56. Scott, John C. "The mission of the university: Medieval to postmodern transformations." *The Journal of Higher Education* 77, no. 1 (2006): 1–39.

57. Jewel (21-year old African American and Native American female; Criminal Justice Major) states, "I think they (police) should be more transparent. Like community policing. I mean, on campus I see 15 cop cars, but I have no idea what they are doing. So, in that sense, it seems like they are harassing students as opposed to fighting crime and protecting us."

58. The *University-Advocating Attitudinal and Policy Changes in Law Enforcement* theme refers to words and/or phrases that relate to participants' belief that universities should ensure that members of law enforcement change how they perceive African Americans and abide by laws and policies that protect all citizens.

59. "Make sure that their police force knows what excessive force is and to make sure that they (the university) will not stand by you (the brutal officer), you are going to be on your own."

60. The *University Accountability of Law Enforcement* theme refers to words and/or phrases that relate to participants' belief that universities and colleges should be at the forefront of making law enforcement accountable for police brutality. Included within this theme is the view that universities should take the lead in organizing protests against law enforcement in the wake of police brutality.

61. Angela, a 21-year old Black female; Pre-Physical Therapy Major, states, "There is not a lot of incidents of police brutality that I know of on University campuses."

62. (3) On a scale of 1–10, with 1 being lowest and 10 being highest, how much do you trust the police? (5) Do you believe the police treat Black people *better than, equal to,* or *worse than* White people? (8) Has a police officer ever used an excessive amount of force on *you*? (9) Has a police officer ever used an excessive amount of force on *someone that you know*?

63. Chaney, Cassandra, and Ray V. Robertson. "Armed and Dangerous? An Examination of Fatal Shootings of Unarmed Black People by Police." *The Journal of Pan African Studies* 8, no. 4 (2015): 45–78. Chaney, Cassandra, and Ray V. Robertson. "Can We All Get Along? Blacks' Historical and Contemporary (In) Justice with Law Enforcement." *Western Journal of Black Studies*, 38, no. 2 (2014): 108–122. Chaney, Cassandra, and Ray V. Robertson. "Racism and Police Brutality in America." *Journal of African American Studies*, 17, no. 4 (2013): 480–505.

Conclusion

At this point, we highlight the auxiliary comments provided by participants in response to the final question (Question 12), "Is there anything else that you would like to share?" While most did not provide parting comments (21 participants, or 70 percent) and did not provide additional information, nine participants (30 percent) did. In particular, these men and women seek modifications in the criminal justice system and law enforcement systems that do a better job of ensuring the safety of African Americans. For these participants, these changes involve increasing the number of Black police officers, and the need for members of law enforcement to follow the same protocols that they expect others to observe, which include, but are not limited to mandatory reporting of individuals they murder.

Three individuals (33 percent of those that provide a response) use the phrase "criminal justice system" when describing what is needed to minimize police brutality. Some advocate police service from a general perspective (Leah, 21-year old Black female; Health Science; Pre-occupational Therapy; Senior, says, "No. I just think the police should do better. The criminal justice as a whole should do a better job of serving all people."). Essentially, Leah's comment recognizes three things. For one, it does not assert police are not doing a good job. Second, it recognizes the criminal justice's ability to "do a better job of serving all people." Finally, we stress "*all people*" as current inequalities in the criminal justice system operate through the lens of White Supremacy, favoring Whites and disadvantaging Blacks. On the other hand, Cassie (21-year old Black female; Public Administration Graduate Student) believes the change must come from within the system. She states, "I feel as though we (African Americans) argue and fight for change but the change can only start from within the criminal justice system." Still for others, internal change involves placing police in communities, based on their race, which might minimize police brutality against Blacks. Recall that James (24-year old Black male; Criminal Justice Major; Senior) says, "One way to cut down on police brutality against unarmed Blacks is if more African Americans become police officers. We will be policing our own communities instead of White police officers who do not know our culture and it will build more trust within the African American community because the police officer will look like them." Here, James mentions racial trust would be more likely to occur if officers of the same race were serving communities.

Advanced education may foster positive internal change. This was the view of 20-year old, Sociology Major, Aaliyah who believes obtaining post-secondary degrees will help police "better understand the criminal justice system." For this female, this information is key because "protecting and serving" links to comprehending "the social implications" of serving communities of color. Like Aaliyah, D'Andre, (21-year old Black male; Interdisciplinary Studies; Junior) believes "every student should take Race, Class, and Justice-related courses" because it teaches them "about the history of police and why they act the way they do towards minorities." Teaching new and seasoned police officers about the socio-historical relationship between law enforcement and communities of color has three benefits. For one, it helps these officers recognize that current attitudes are rooted in past actions. Second, it helps these officers to recognize current actions increase or decrease feelings of trust in police. Finally, it helps these officers to understand that the actions of one or a few officers may lead to widespread negative feelings toward police.

Since the Federal Bureau of Investigation (FBI) does not require law enforcement agencies to submit shooting data,[1] establishing such a policy may bring immediate systemic change because it establishes a verifiable pattern of behavior. In other words, police officers or police units that have an exceptionally high number of incidents of excessive force or murder may signal a culture in that unit that devalues Black lives. This was most certainly the case when the Department of Justice (DOJ) investigated the Ferguson Police Department. What caused this particular unit for an investigation? On August 9, 2014, Darren Wilson, an officer with the Ferguson Police Department (FPD) shoots 18-year old Michael Brown who is African American.[2] In the wake national protests and a public outcry, on September 3, 2014, the Justice Department announced that it would open a broad civil rights investigation that would examine whether the Ferguson police had a history of discrimination or misuse of force beyond the Michael Brown case. On March 4, 2015, Attorney General Eric H. Holder Jr. publicly criticized the Ferguson Police Department for "implicit and explicit racial bias" and "routinely violating the constitutional rights of its black residents."

Several key events occur between September 3, 2014 and March 4, 2015. For one, the FPD targets Black residents for excessive force ("Nearly 90 percent of documented force used by FPD officers was used against African Americans"). In addition, only African Americans experience canine bites ("In every canine bite incident for which racial information is available, the person bitten was African American"). Even the dissemination of justice was a needlessly long process via municipal court practices that harmed Blacks ("African Americans are 68 percent less likely than others to have their cases dismissed by the court, and are more likely to have their cases last longer and result in more required court encounters. African Americans are at least 50 percent more likely to have their cases lead to an arrest warrant, and accounted for 92 percent of cases in which an arrest warrant was issued by the Ferguson Municipal Court in 2013."). Furthermore, African Americans were targets for racial bias among police and court staff ("Emails circulated by police supervisors and court staff that stereotype racial minorities as criminals, including one email that joked about an abortion by an African-American woman being a means of crime control").[3]

Recall that three individuals (33 percent of those that provide a response) believe mandatory procedures, in regards to required training for CPR and firearms, will minimize police brutality against African Americans. This most certainly was what Jewel (21-year old African American and Native American female; Criminal Justice Major) believes ("It needs to be mandatory for law enforcement agencies to report information on whomever they kill."). In addition to reporting incidents of death, another participant asserts police should make a conscious effort to keep the victim alive and receive training in this respect. Makala (23-year old Black female; Criminal Justice; Graduate Student) says, "Protocols, for the police, are there for a reason. Law enforcement officers should have to follow their protocols because I have never heard of any officer shooting a Black man and then give him CPR when they are supposed to." The mention of Cardiopulmonary Resuscitation (CPR)[4] is appropriate and aligns with the mission of police to protect and serve. If law agents find that an individual is in need of CPR, keeping the individual alive via this way *protects the individual from future harm* (physical, mental, emotional), and by tending to their crisis, *gives the law enforcement agent an opportunity to serve the person in need.*

Still others advocate officer training should be a frequent practice, not just during a specific training period. Eduardo (29-year old; African American/ Hispanic; Male; Pre-Physical Therapy Major; Junior) says, "One of the biggest things that I have always said is, 'In the military, I get firearms training all of the time.' And to expect a police officer who may be fired once in the academy and twice a year, is not going to know how to react to a sudden movement of a suspect." Eduardo's view suggests two realities. First, that solitary training may be insufficient. Second, that training makes officers aware how to deal with the unexpected, which may increase their confidence in the field.

Since the skin tone and phenotypical characteristics of African Americans make it impossible for them to avoid racism,[5] this reality means that the skin that Black people live in, makes their lives more difficult than those who do not share their race. This point was beautifully articulated by Zoe (21-year old African American/Black; Female; Physical Therapy Major; Junior) who shares she does not think it "fair that a select group of people (Blacks) have to go through this being the fact the vast majority of people feel this way about police brutality." This woman recognizes the growing distrust in police and appropriately wonders, "What is holding back the change?"

Antwon Rose II was a seventeen-year old, African American male shot and killed on June 19, 2018 by East Pittsburgh police officer Michael Rosfeld as he fled a car after a traffic stop. According to the criminal complaint filed against Rosfeld by Allegheny County District Attorney Steve Zappala, Rose II receives one shot to the face, one in his right arm, and one in the middle of his back as he ran away from Rosfeld.[6] The criminal complaint charges Rosfeld with criminal homicide, which according to Pennsylvania law includes murder, voluntary manslaughter, and involuntary manslaughter. Further, Zappala assert Rosfeld made inconsistent statements (which eyewitnesses later contradict) regarding whether the unarmed Rose II had a gun. Finally, and perhaps most controversial, the judge grants Rosfeld a $250,000 bail which was unsecured (meaning Rosfeld does not pay one cent to get out of jail), despite Zappala's argument against an unsecured bail for such a serious offense.[7] The aforementioned compounds Rosfeld's troubling past with other police departments and he had not completed one full day of patrolling the streets of East Pittsburgh.[8]

Excessive force threatens the physical, mental, and emotional health of African Americans and their families. Consider the case of Davinna Simmons. In June 2018, the Chicago City Council approved a $2.5 million settlement to the family of then three year-old Davinna Simmons for holding a gun to the young African American girl's chest on August 29, 2013.[9] The police raids the family home allegedly to search for Davinna's mother, Aretha Simmons and her boyfriend, Alonzo McSpadden. Although McSpadden did not live at the family's home, he was not present at the time of the raid. Nevertheless, police, according to court documents, knock down the front and back doors to the home in order to gain entry, hold a loaded gun to the chest of young Davinna and handcuff both her mother (Aretha Simmons) and grandmother (Emily Simmons). As the emotional grandmother begs the officer to remove the gun from the child's chest, one of the officers commands that she "shut up!"[10] Although finding no drugs in the home, because of sustaining rough actions from an officer, this child's mother receives an injured eye socket, and this results in the dismissal of all charges. Lastly, a psychiatrist who evaluates Davinna after the incident suggests she had one of the worst cases of Post-Traumatic Stress Disorder (PTSD) syndrome that he had ever seen.[11]

The PTSD suffered by young Davinna Simmons is indeed tragic and no one should have to endure this level of trauma, especially in his or her own home. Unfortunately, African Americans collectively suffer mental health issues from exposure via reading, watching a video, or personally witnessing excessive force by police.[12] In their study of the impact of police killings on the mental health of African Americans, Bar et al. (2018) surmise the killings of unarmed black Americans by police have a deleterious effect on the mental health of African Americans. Additionally, the authors assert that the implementation of programs, which decrease the regularity of such events, could mitigate the mental health problems experienced by African Americans when these events occur. Moreover, police killings of unarmed African Americans can compromise the mental health of African Americans in the following ways: 1) heightened perceptions of systemic racism and a lack of fairness; 2) loss of social status; 3) increased fear of victimization and mortality expectations; 4) increased vigilance; 5) activation of prior traumas; and 6) diminished trust in social institutions.[13]

For the reasons we mention above, this chapter will emphasize how to remedy the problem of police use of excessive force. Thus, this chapter will critically explore viable solutions in hopes of creating a just and humane society in which African Americans can flourish. Specifically, chapter 5 will explore the following: 1) the efficacy of better training; 2) community policing and its prospects for positive change; 3) body cameras and dashboard cameras; 4) strategies to reduce police excessive force that have showed promise; 5) policy recommendations and areas for future research.

THE EFFICACY OF BETTER TRAINING

When individual police officers or police departments use excessive force, that public appeals for better training.[14] However, one might ask, "Will better training make a difference?" There are many reasons why African Americans would consider the effectiveness of better training with cynicism. Why? Because police have brutalized African Americans since the establishment of police in America.[15] A recent case of police malfeasance that cause many African Americans to wonder if training can make a difference comes from the suburban Miami, Florida town of Biscayne Park. In June of 2018, former Biscayne Park Police Chief Raimundo Atesiano, along with former officers Raul Fernandez and Charlie Dayoub, receive federal civil rights indictments for falsely accusing a sixteen-year-old, black Haitian American youth, referred to the indictment as "T.D.," of four unsolved burglaries with no evidence.[16] Furthermore, during 2013 and 2014, the Biscayne Park Police Department implicate Black males in nearly all 30 burglaries during this period. Atesiano possibly faces eleven years in prison for instructing his officers to arrest "anyone Black" to achieve a perfect crime clearance rate. Further, Officers Fernandez and Dayoub were following the orders of Atesiano in gathering information for the four unsolved burglary cases, creating a false narrative that T.D. burglarized four unoccupied residences.[17] The indictments were the result of a 2014 internal probe during which Atesiano resigns.[18] It is important to note that in the wake of the reform efforts of the Biscayne Park Police Department, Atesiano has the choice to resign. Since police departments generally allow officers to retain their retirement benefits when they resign, this prevents officers from facing the maximum punishment for their transgressions.[19] Furthermore, following the chief's resignation, the Biscayne Park Police Department does not clear any of the 19 burglary cases that occur in 2015.[20]

Even though the previous example of unethical police behavior did not involve acts of brutality, one can logically deduce this illegal and unethical behavior by police can transcend to other areas. In other words, if, for the purpose of producing perfect crime clearance statistics, this group blames burglaries on innocent citizens, it is highly likely they would also conceal acts of brutality/excessive force. Next, that the highest-ranking official in the department would sanction such acts against Blacks, speaks to the lengths lower-ranked officers would go to protect their fellow officers against accusations of brutality, which could only lead to questions regarding the prospects of the effectiveness of better training.

Some police training methods show a great deal of promise, however. In terms of research regarding the effectiveness of police training, Owens et al. (2018) draw from the fields of psychology and economics to present an experimental evaluation of a procedural justice-training program designated to slow down police officers' thought processes during encounters with citizens in the community. The authors find officers arbitrarily assigned to participate in training were as engaged in the community as similarly situated officers, but were less likely to resolve incidents with an arrest or be involved where force was present. In addition, police officers who connect to their communities can reduce crime through general deterrence or merely by their presence. The above-mentioned finding provides a glimmer of hope for training and its prospects for excessive force reduction. Likewise, this finding comes with a caveat because of two ancillary findings. First, those excessive discretionary arrests can increase the likelihood of potentially violent encounters between police and citizens, which can reduce the public's trust of the police. Secondly, there is little scholarly evidence regarding how police departments can decrease the gulf that exists between law enforcement and trust in police.[21]

Stoughton (2015) presents a dilemma that engenders a unique concern for law enforcement. Essentially, the quandary emerges when police officers face performing the dual roles of "warrior" and "guardian" of the public's safety. The aforementioned involves striking a balance between procuring high arrest rates and maintaining the warrior persona.[22] Unfortunately, the "warrior" persona is not consistent with principles of "protecting and serving" the public. It makes sense that when police officers patrol a community, particularly a predominantly Black community, as an occupying army, there are essentially no benefits. Further, practicality mandates that when officers interact with citizens, who pay their salary, and to whom they have a duty to protect and serve, it will only further fracture the historically acrimonious relationship between the police and community and make it more difficult for police to solve serious and non-serious crimes.[23] Recall that White Supremacy asserts the values, beliefs, attitudes, and behaviors of White people are superior to those of non-White people.[24] Finally, it invokes curiosity regarding whether police see affluent White communities as "warriors" fighting an enemy, and who is the enemy?

Research by Tyler offers hope regarding effective police training and its possible impact on excessive force against African Americans.[25] Particularly, the prospects for better training reside in the area of procedural justice. Essentially, procedural justice is concerned with how police officers and other law enforcement personnel interact with the public and how the complexities of those interactions shape the public's view of the police, their willingness to obey the law, and affect actual crime rates.[26] Thus, Tyler sees the role of procedural justice as important in fomenting police legitimacy in the eyes of the public in general. We surmise three ways where procedural justice may produce positive relations between police and African Americans. First, implementing and encouraging procedural justice in training and holding police accountable to follow its mandates can reduce the potential for officer malfeasance. This can serve to raise expectations of the public when it comes to police behaving fairly and improve the public's view of police. Furthermore, it can encourage voluntary respect for police authority. Respect for police authority is important because one of the primary precipitators of police use of excessive force is officers feeling that are not receiving the proper amount of respect, especially from African Americans.[27] Second, emphasizing procedural justice in training (along with holding officers accountable for their actions) can alter officer behavior. So, when officers are more respectful with African Americans, the respect will be reciprocated and ameliorate the possibility of the types of encounters that can culminate in accusations of excessive force and make crime solving easier because of more community assistance in solving crimes.[28] Third, requiring procedural justice to be a fundamental component of police training can promote the redesigning of the internal organization of police departments which ultimately lessen not only the strength of the "blue wall of silence" but also motivate department personnel to treat members of the communities they serve more fairly.[29] Moreover, Tyler suggests adhering to the principles of procedural justice can aid in maintaining social order, which contributes to making policing more effective.[30]

In the article titled "How to Reduce Police Violence," Maron (2016) offers a critique on the potential effectiveness of better police training and its prospects for reducing police brutality.[31] The author questions whether training can ever have any positive impact in reducing excessive force because of the deeply ingrained stereotypical views that police hold of those they patrol. To buttress her point, she points to the lack of usefulness of implicit bias training.[32] Implicit bias is concerned with mental associations that individuals generally have about racial and ethnic groups and the traits/characteristics that accompany those associations. Many assume the previously mentioned mental cognitions, which fuel implicit biases, can exist in opposition to what the person consciously claims to believe.[33] Accordingly, she asserts that better training can raise an officer's awareness of their implicit bias. However, she cautions that being aware of a bias does not prevent an officer from acting on those biases in the field.[34] Moreover, the prevailing literature on police training reveals officers do not view departmental training as transferring to what happens when they are "walking the beat."[35] In addition, in a study of young Black men and urban policing, Brunson and Miller (2006) point out the impact of negative police perceptions of citizens and their influence on police brutality. Specifically, the authors contend negative police perceptions of African American men encourage law enforcement officers to be less responsive to crime in Black communities. These views act as a stimulus in acts of police brutality and the use of deadly force.[36] To add, police view African American men as "symbolic assailants" which essentially means that even if an African American man does not commit a crime, police still regard him as fully capable and likely to commit a crime.[37] Lastly, in an examination of the connection between perceived minority threat and policing, criminologists find two things happen when more African Americans move into integrated communities. First, Whites view the threat of crime as more succinct. Second, police presence becomes more visible and their subsequent treatment of African Americans in those communities becomes more punitive.[38] Ultimately, we must deliberately ponder the following questions: Will police training ever be effective in preventing acts of police brutality and excessive force against African Americans? Most importantly, has police training ever been able to prevent police from brutalizing African Americans?

COMMUNITY POLICING AND ITS
PROSPECTS FOR POSITIVE CHANGE

Until approximately the first half of the twentieth century, policing in America followed the "professional model."[39] The professional model consists of an organization, a strict adherence to standardized protocols, and a hierarchical structure.[40] Social upheavals of the 1950s and 1960s, particularly, the Civil Rights movement, the Black power and consciousness movement, and the urban riots (which were primarily the result of massive economic inequality and rampant, unchecked, police brutality) were dynamic calls for a new form of policing which requires law enforcement agents to interact positively with the Black community.[41] Community-oriented or simply, community policing, stresses more straightforward participation with constituents that law enforcement officers serve, fewer unyielding procedures, and an earnest attempt to address the indigenous origins of crime and disruption in communities of color.[42] It is important to note that although the social milieu lays the foundation for a divergence from the professional model, the actual implementation of community-oriented policing did not take place until the 1970s. Nevertheless, the popularity of inserting some variant of community-oriented policing into the standard operating procedures in police departments across the country has not wavered. For instance, by 1997, an estimated 58 percent of departments integrated some form of community policing and by 2003, 81 percent of law enforcement agencies professed to contain some element of community-oriented policing.[43]

Considering the widespread popularity of community-oriented policing begs the question "If community-oriented policing has been implemented to such a degree, why the need to write this book?" In other words, if community-oriented policing is so prevalent, why is police use of excessive force, i.e., police brutality, still such a massive problem in American communities of color today?" One possible explanation, despite an attempt that the authors make earlier at a succinct definition of community-oriented policing, is that there is no standard, universal definition as to what constitutes community-oriented policing.[44] Case in point: The Department of Justice asserts that community-oriented policing is a strategy for building trust between police and the communities that they serve.[45] The definition also involves law enforcement agencies fostering positive relationships with local business owners, community groups, non-profits, schools, churches, and other similar entities. Further, community-oriented policing consists of such methods as data sharing, body-worn cameras, police athletic leagues for youths, etc. Put succinctly, no standard systematic procedures characterize community-oriented policing.[46] Conversely, since the 1960s, the remedy for poor community-police relations should involve three steps: 1) a move to guardian policing. Essentially, guardian policing entails eschewing the military boot-camp, get ready for war type training that the typical police recruit receives to a more de-escalating of potentially conflict producing situations approach;[47] 2) overcoming bias; and 3) replacing hopelessness, which is often a feature of blighted communities, with hope and justice.[48]

An example of community-oriented policing is the East Los Angeles' Police Department's Community Safety Partnership Unit, which operates in one of this city's worst housing projects.[49] It involves officers adhering to several mandates. First, patrolling the different housing projects on foot and getting to know the residents by name. Second, officers foster confidence by community members via engaging in such activities as purchasing eye glasses for elder members of the community who cannot afford them, creating sports leagues for children, aiding in the creation of a farmer's market with healthy fruits and vegetables and local residents, and, perhaps most importantly, providing incentives for positive engagement with community members. Likewise, officers receive promotions for actions that minimize community distrust and heighten community trust. In particular, these officers receive promotions when they help divert a child from jail instead of making more arrests. Moreover, it begins with buy-in from community leaders and ends in an apology from the police to the community for past wrongs. Similarly, grieving parents must join officers who have jailed or killed their child during their efforts to combat drugs and gangs. While we do not know whether programs are panaceas, they are a step in the right direction.[50]

One issue that is a major impediment to the success of community-oriented policing initiatives across the country is officer support. Patrol officers, and officers in general, are likely to view community-oriented policing as synonymous to social work.[51] Now on the surface, the average citizen might consider this a good thing. Why? Because to an extent, it can be perceived as analogous to the popular police moniker of "protect and serve." However, once one embarks upon deconstructing the notion of community-oriented policing, as being similar to social work, individuals must understand there is a strong possibility that the individual who goes to college to major in social work or to be a community organizer, is not the same individual who attends college to become a law enforcement officer.[52] Officers generally receive training in the police academy in a military style manner, and the subculture of policing has an ethos where the officer views himself/herself as a soldier who is going to war. Unfortunately, the enemy combatants are those individuals whom the officer has sworn to protect and serve.[53] To add, when the typical police recruit can be characterized as young, conservative, white-male from a working-class background, with some or no college credits, one can easily discern why this individual may easily reject doing something he considers social work in communities of color, especially predominantly black communities.[54]

Lastly, taking into account that community-oriented policing, in one form or another, was integrated into police departments since the 1970s, why is police brutality such a pressing problem against African Americans? Besides, from the issue of officer accountability, which we discuss later in-depth, one can construe few laypersons and public officials truly understand what they are subjecting communities to. Put another way, community-oriented policing often entails placing more "warriors" into the "war." Community-oriented policing often places officers, at least when we are speaking of African Americans, into communities in which they have little cultural competence, who are not held accountable, who have a lot of discretion, and are full of implicit biases regarding African Americans, and are expected to respect them as they do themselves. [55] Thus, you have pain inflicted upon black communities, subsidized by these communities via tax dollars.

Body-Worn Cameras and Dashboard Cameras

Laypersons, scholars, and politicians, and others frequently tout body-worn cameras and dashboard cameras as a positive step towards limiting acts of police excessive force. These methods are gaining support as a necessary component of effective policing and police accountability. For instance, stationary cameras provide police with greater surveillance power. Additionally, cameras mounted inside police automobiles along with body-worn cameras have value in the areas of encouraging better behavior by police and citizens during their encounters. [56]

There are five reasons why police departments should implement car/dashboard cameras. First, video surveillance enhances an officer's safety by producing undeniable evidence to verify what actually happened in a questionable situation. Consider the murder of Cedric Chatman. On the same day that presidential hopeful (January 14, 2016), Donald J. Trump makes the statement, "The police are the most mistreated people in this country" a horrific video puts law enforcement in a particularly negative light. On the same day that Trump makes this declaration, the Chicago Police Department releases a video showing Officer Kevin Frye killing Cedric Chatman in 2013. The teen was sprinting away at the time of the shooting, unarmed except for a stolen cellphone box (which Fry claims he thinks is a weapon). The officer has faced no consequences for his death. [57] Second, video surveillance can reduce police liability by giving police departments the ability to film an entire situation, which can eliminate the possibility of potential lawsuits against the police. Third, video surveillance is conducive to police transparency for the community, which has potential to foster a modicum of trust between police and the community. Fourth, police cameras can possibly improve police/law enforcement conviction rates by producing, via video evidence, ancillary evidence that escalates the likelihood of conviction. Finally, police cameras improve police training by demonstrating good and bad aspects regarding how police officers handle specific situations. [58]

Police body-worn cameras have been the subject of three major empirical studies. The studies took place at the Rialto (California) Police Department, the Mesa, Arizona Police Department, and the Phoenix Arizona Police Department. [59] The Rialto study took place from February 2012 through July 2013. It involved 54 officers who wore the TASER AXON body-camera system. There was a 59 percent reduction in use of force incidents, along with 87.5 percent reduction in citizen complaints when compared to the period before implementation of the body-worn camera system. [60] The Mesa, Arizona study took place from October 2012 through September 2013. [61] The 50 participating officers wearing TASER AXON FLEX body-worn cameras, were concerned with the camera's effect on reducing civil liability, and complaints against the department and increasing the prosecution of criminals, compared to officers not wearing cameras. [62] The study produces a 40 percent reduction in complaints against the department and a 75 percent reduction in use of force complaints. [63] Finally, the Phoenix, Arizona Police Department assigned 50 officers to wear the VIEVU camera system. [64] The objective of the study was to determine if cameras could deter unprofessional officer behavior, reduce citizen complaints and resistance, and exonerate officers from allegations made against them. [65] Subsequently, according to official records, the study publishes a 60 percent decrease in self-reported complaints against officers and 44 percent decrease in complaints against officers. [66]

In a study inspired by the significant increase in murders of African Americans by police, Ray et al. (2017) examine how laypersons perceive police body-worn cameras. Situated in Prince George's County, Maryland, the authors conduct 81 interviews with the county's residents. Perhaps not surprisingly, the authors find non-White men, particularly African American men, are substantially more likely to report negative interactions with the police than White men were. Further, the authors find respondents fell into one of two groups regarding their attitudes on the efficacy of police body-worn cameras, supporters and skeptics. The supporters belong to one of two groups, those who support police and those that support citizens. Supporters of police perceive body-worn cameras as delineating the difficulty of being a police officer. Conversely, citizen supporters characterize individuals who see body-worn cameras as protecting citizens because they foment police transparency and buttress community trust of police. Whites were more likely to be police supporters whereas Blacks and other people of color tended to be citizen supporters. Likewise, the skeptics belong to two groups, privacy skeptics and structural skeptics. The former, consist of those that believe police body-worn cameras violate the trust of both the police and citizens. [67] White (2014) corroborates this finding. [68] The latter believe body-worn cameras would not alter the systemic discrimination that Blacks and other minorities face nor alter power inequities between citizens and police.[69] Ultimately, the researcher asserts body-worn cameras might improve dealings between citizens and police but not do anything substantial to alter power inequities that exist between citizens and police.

In a study titled "The Deterrence Spectrum: Explaining Why Police Body-Worn Cameras 'Work' or 'Backfire' in Aggressive Police-Public Encounters," Ariel et al. (2017) examine if the deterrent effect of police body-worn cameras is a function of discretion in terms of their capability to de-escalate or aggravate aggressive encounters. The authors demonstrate that the deterrent effect of body-worn cameras ranges from minimal deterrence to maximum deterrence mitigated by the officer's amount of discretion.[70] Minimal deterrence inversely relates to maximum discretion. In other words, minimal deterrence means that officers have broad discretion and the deterrent effect of body-worn cameras is not great. Conversely, maximum deterrence correlates with little discretion and the effect of body worn cameras is greatest. The authors assert more consideration be given to officers' discretion, training on appropriate use of body-worn cameras, in addition to the willingness of the agency to adopt an evidence-based framework for body-worn cameras to have a positive impact.[71]

A potential drawback associated with body-worn cameras is they can inhibit officers' ability to eliminate police malfeasance, particularly during instances where officers turn off body cameras. Two notable instances of police doing this occur in Baltimore, Maryland and Sacramento, California. In Baltimore, police arrest two citizens in what appears to be a routine drug bust. These officers apparently forgot their body-worn cameras were on when one of the officers squats in front of an empty driver's seat in a car they search for thirty minutes. Moments later, another officer finds, but actually plants, a bag of drugs in the same seat.[72] A separate case in Baltimore involves three officers caught on video engaging in unethical behavior. The body-worn camera footage reveals a Baltimore PD officer planting a bag of pills in an empty lot while two of his colleagues looked on. The damning video results in county prosecutors dropping 34 cases involving both drugs and weapons connected to the officers visible on the camera.[73] The more recent of the two incidents occur in Sacramento, California. Twenty-two-year-old Stephon Clark, an African American male, was unarmed in his grandmother's backyard in March of 2018 after Sacramento PD officers fire twenty shots at him when they alleged they mistook his cell phone for a gun.[74] The officers were pursuing Clark after dispatched to South Sacramento to investigate a report that someone was breaking car windows. An autopsy commissioned by the family reveals Clark was shot eight times, three times in his lower back, which ultimately raises questions as to whether Clark was a threat to officers at the time they murder him.[75] One of the most controversial aspects of the incident was when the officers receive instructions to mute their body-worn cameras approximately seven minutes after the shooting. [76] In addition to the officers muting their body cameras, the officers continue to ask Clark if he was okay after the shooting for roughly three minutes after gunfire instead of immediately rendering first aid. The autopsy asserts Clark lived for approximately three to ten minutes after the shooting. Medical assistance does not arrive until approximately six minutes after the shooting. [77] Ultimately, the officers involved in the Clark shooting do not receive charges.

STRATEGIES TO REDUCE POLICE BRUTALITY

To create a society where African Americans can reach their full potential and thrive, the pertinent question becomes, "How American society can eliminate police brutality against African Americans?" In a study titled "War on Drugs Policing and Police Brutality," scholar Hannah Cooper examined the interconnections between explicit "war on drugs" policing strategies and police use of excessive force against African Americans. [78] More specifically, she explores the historical relationship between race and policing in the United States, the ways in which policies implemented during the war on drugs erode the protections designed to limit police powers, and how attrition of the aforementioned protections results in more instances of police using excessive force against Black Americans.

Thus, based on Cooper's work, we offer several recommendations to reduce the likelihood of police brutality against African Americans. First, bring a nationwide end to stop and frisk. Second, discontinue the use of the Special Weapons and Tactics (SWAT) teams to deal with low-level, non-violent street and drug offenses. Third, restore rights originally protected by the 4th amendment (unreasonable searches and seizures). Fourth, strengthen the Posse Comitatus Act. The Posse Comitatus Act, originally passed in 1878, made it illegal for the Armed Forces to perform duties of police. The process to dismantle it began in 1981, giving law enforcement access to military bases, training, and equipment. The ban on the military's access to train police officers is lifted twelve years later, in 1993. [79] Thus, you have greater and greater military-styled police departments. [80] Military training may be great if you are fighting in an actual war, but is it the best policy being among people whom you are supposed to protect and serve? Will you care about their lives? Will you treat them the same as you would your own family?

POLICY RECOMMENDATIONS
AND AREAS FOR FUTURE RESEARCH

Police brutality against African Americans is a huge problem in contemporary America. Thus, we put forth the following policy initiatives to combat this problem, which has existed as long as there has been law enforcement and police departments:

1. Repeal or end policies associated with the "War on Drugs." The War on Drugs has been a disaster for African Americans. It has resulted in the mass incarceration of thousands of African American men and women, has broken up families, and has decimated Black communities across the United States. Specific "War on Drugs" era policies that merit elimination are Stop and Frisk, reinstatement of the Posse Comitatus Act, and the use of SWAT teams for low-level, non-violent, drug and street offenses.

2. Search for, identify, and remove White Identity Extremists/White nationalists/White supremacist group members from all police departments. In 2006, the Federal Bureau of Investigation (FBI) released a memo positing members of White supremacist groups had infiltrated law enforcement. Since the issuance of the memo, a myriad of police officers in states throughout America, particularly Florida, Louisiana, Alabama, and others, have been terminated due to having membership in White supremacist groups. Additionally, officers have received public condemnation for wearing tattoos affiliated with White supremacist groups such as the Iron Fist and the Celtic cross.[81]

3. Only allow officers to patrol areas where they reside. In other words, when officers come from or live in the areas they patrol, they are more likely to have a stake in the community and the people in it.[82] Although hiring more Black officers is definitely not a panacea, they are less frequently implicated in shooting unarmed African Americans and one can presume they will exhibit a greater willingness to defuse potentially volatile situations involving African Americans;

4. Hold district attorneys and their offices accountable for their questionable decisions. District attorneys have almost unlimited power and their positions require that they work closely with police officers with whom they frequently have an allegiance with and are not likely to indict.[83] Case in point: Former Cook County District Attorney Anita Alvarez overcharges former police officer Dante Servin who shoots and kills Rekia Boyd, an unarmed African American woman. She (Alvarez) presumes to have purposely overcharged Servin with involuntary manslaughter instead of first-degree murder and the presiding judge threw out the case without even hearing from the defense. Con-

sequently, after murdering Boyd, Servin is exonerated and allowed to resign, and retains all of his benefits.[84]

5. Increase police officer accountability. The findings of this study support most African Americans believe police officers should be accountable for instances of police brutality.[85] One novel proposal would be to take the money that victims and their families receive from cities in settlements directly from police retirement funds. Financial settlements such as the ones given to the family of Sean Bell ($3.25 million for a wrongful death lawsuit), Prince Jones ($3.7 million for a wrongful death lawsuit), and Rekia Boyd ($4.5 million for a wrongful death lawsuit), are large and quite costly for a city.[86] Covering settlements to families from police retirement funds may be a strong motivation (financial incentive) for police to act appropriately. Presently, officers are not required to make any financial contribution to the millions of dollars dolled out to victims of police murders and police brutality. Additionally, this policy would save cities millions and save African Americans from being the recipients of police brutality.[87]

6. Make dashboard cameras and body-worn cameras mandatory for all police departments across the United States. While body-worn cameras and dashboard cameras are not without problems, they have shown some success in studies involving the Phoenix, Rialto, and Mesa police departments. Thus, implementing body-worn and dashboard cameras, requiring officers to live in the communities that they serve, and increasing officer accountability, can eliminate incidents of police brutality against African Americans.

LIMITATIONS OF THE CURRENT STUDY

This study had several scholarly parameters. For one, the majority of the participants in this study were Black females (18 females; 12 males). Second, in contrast to the majority of members of this racial group, the participants were highly educated. Third, as it relates to education, half of the males and females in this study were juniors, which means they were toward the end of their undergraduate educations. This means that a group of freshmen or sophomores may have provided different responses than those provided by the men and women in this study.

Fourth, the participants generally had incomes higher than the national average for minorities. Fifth, since almost half (47 percent) of participants were residents of Florida, a state in which the Trayvon Martin murder occurred, residents in other places may have different views of police. Lastly, as a third (33 percent) of participants were Criminal Justice and Sociology

(11 percent) majors, these students may view police through a different lens than non-Criminal Justice and Sociology majors. In contrast to students who are Health Science, Pre-Physical Therapy, English, or Interdisciplinary Studies majors, the core of the Criminal Justice Major is to study primary institutions of the criminal justice system, namely the police, prosecution and defense lawyers, the courts, and prisons. These students invariably have greater insight into when punishment, rehabilitation, and moral support are most appropriate. Like Criminal Justice, Sociology focuses on the systematic understanding of social interaction, social organization, social institutions, and social change. These students customarily have greater insight into how social institutions and how individuals' reactions toward those institutions have changed over time. Overall, these majors provide students a foundation to view social interaction from a law enforcement, defense, rehabilitative perspective, as well as a keen awareness of how race, gender, and class influence police behavior. In spite of these limitations, however, this work highlights how members of the community, who police swear, "to protect and serve" perceive them.

DIRECTIONS FOR FUTURE RESEARCH

We offer several recommendations regarding how scholars can build on the current work. For one, since Black males are substantially more likely than Black females to be targets of excessive force and murder, future studies can specifically explore the views of Black males regarding police. Qualitative work in this area will particularly validate the lived experiences of minority members. In addition, since this study delves into the thoughts of African American college students, scholars can compare the perceptions of police brutality of African American students to those of non-African American students (e.g., Whites, Asians, Latinos, and Native Americans). Scholarly work in this area can reveal how race and racial experiences perceive perceptions of police. Furthermore, as the participants in this study were college-educated, future studies can examine how community members who are not college-educated and approximately the same age, perceive police. Added to this, since this study focuses on the attitudes/perceptions of African American students at a Historically Black College or University (HBCU) in the South, subsequent studies can compare African American students at HBCUs to those African American students at Predominantly White Institutions or colloquially known as PWIs. Such work in this area will highlight differences and similarities regarding how members of each group view law enforcement.

Likewise, scholars can consider studying the phenomenon of police brutality against African Americans by integrating a quantitative component (i.e., survey/questionnaire) to supplement qualitative data. Related to this, qualitative work can lead to the development of new quantitative measures that may be more culturally relevant than current ones. In addition, since several participants report their perceptions of police changed from positive or neutral to negative, future work can examine the opposite effect. In other words, the circumstances that influence individuals to change their views of police from negative to positive merit scholarly consideration. Associated to this, longitudinal studies should provide the needed methodological basis to determine the specific points in time when perceptions of police change. Knowledge in this regard can help police understand the specific actions and behaviors that increase societal respect. Moreover, as many of the men and women in this study recommend colleges and universities advise students regarding the role of police, future work can highlight how institutions of higher learning facilitate trusting relationships with police. Finally, since law enforcement is mostly made up of members who do their jobs with dignity, integrity, and honor, future work should examine police who have earned a positive reputation of service in their communities. Highlighting the good that these men and women consistently do will go a long way in helping bridge the historical distrust that minorities have developed for members of law enforcement.

CLOSING THOUGHTS

Given the amount of time that police departments have behaved with impunity,[88] we are realists. Police brutality against African Americans will not end anytime soon. However, this work addresses, understands, and provides solutions to help minimize or eradicate police brutality against African Americans. It is our hope that Americans of all races and ethnic groups seriously consider this topic through the lens of positive change. However, it requires great effort to change the status quo. This effort involves a growing police force to recognize many African Americans do not feel law enforcement agents desire to "serve and protect" them. In fact, the findings in this study reveal most Black have concerns police will "harass and kill them." Therefore, it is no wonder that African Americans feel their individual, familial, and communal safety is threatened.

Even though the majority of the males and females in this study have negative views of police, this would not be the case if the public associates police with positive community policing. Tommy Norman, an officer known for "going out in the community and helping his community," is a notable exception. When many individuals think of Norman, they do not think of excessive force. They immediately think of a man who consistently works to serve his community, not abuse or murder them. This man is a credit to the force that he represents not because of who he is but rather, how he does his job. This officer has made the conscious decision to serve poor, Black communities with dignity, honor, and respect, and it is because of how he treats others, that he in turn, receives respect. However, we are convinced that Norman is one of many officers whose form of policing makes their job easier and makes a substantial contribution to bridging the distrust between African American communities and law enforcement. Moving forward as a society, we strongly believe community policing can help heal the historically acrimonious relationship between African Americans and law enforcement.

Police must be aware that carrying a firearm makes it easier for them to demand respect; however, when an officer earns respect *without using their firearm*, two things will most likely occur. For one, the officer may find that he or she can successfully use intimidation or verbal commands to de-escalate a situation. Second, and most important, the officer may learn that earned respect makes their job easier because citizens have positive views of law enforcement. Therefore, positive views of law enforcement may invariably help prevent the horrific murders of police, like the ones in Dallas and Baton Rouge, who die honorably while doing their jobs.

As they await greater racial equity, African Americans can take a page from the African American sage, Dr. Claud Anderson who suggests Black folks need to develop economically viable communities, which will allow them to have the money to control city governments and district attorneys to insulate them from the ravages of police brutality.[89] This strategy holds tremendous promise in the quest to eliminate police brutality against African Americans.

NOTES

1. Chaney, Cassandra, and Ray V. Robertson. "Armed and Dangerous? An Examination of Fatal Shootings of Unarmed Black People by Police." *The Journal of Pan African Studies* 8, no. 4 (2015): 45–78.

2. Chaney, Cassandra. "Institutional Racism: Perspectives on the Department of Justice's Investigation of the Ferguson Police Department." *Western Journal of Black Studies* 39, no. 4 (2015): 4.

3. Berman, Mark & Lowery, Wesley. (March 4, 2015). The 12 Key highlights from the DOJ's Scathing Ferguson Report. Retrieved from: http://www.washingtonpost.com/news/post-nation/wp/2015/03/04/the-12-keyhighlights-from-the-dojs-scathing-ferguson-report/

4. Cardiopulmonary resuscitation (CPR) is a lifesaving technique useful in many emergencies, including a heart attack or near drowning, in which someone's breathing or heartbeat has stopped. (Mayo Clinic, 1998–2018).

5. Dixon, Travis L., and Keith B. Maddox. "Skin Tone, Crime News, and Social Reality Judgments: Priming the Stereotype of the Dark and Dangerous Black Criminal 1." *Journal of Applied Social Psychology* 35, no. 8 (2005): 1555–1570.

6. McLaughlin, Elliott C. "East Pittsburgh Officer Charged with Criminal Homicide in Antwon Rose Shooting," CNN.com, June 27, 2018, https://www.cnn.com/2018/06/27/us/michael-rosfeld-charged-criminal-homicide-antwon-rose-east-pittsburgh/index.html

7. Ibid.

8. Haag, Matthew. "Officer Who Shot Antwon Rose Is Charged with Criminal Homicide," *The New York Times*, June 27, 2018. https://www.nytimes.com/2018/06/27/us/antwon-rose-shooting-michael-rosfeld.html

9. Helm, Angela. "Chicago PD Settle for $2.5 Million After Police Point Gun at 3-Year Old," The Root, July 3, 2018, https://www.theroot.com/chicago-pd-settle-for-2-5-million-after-police-point-g-1827325007.

10. Ibid.

11. Ibid.

12. Bar, Jacob, Venkataramani, Atheendar S., Williams, David R., and Alexander C. Tsai. "Police Killings and their Spillover Effects on Mental Health of Black Americans: A Population Based, Quasi-Experimental Study." *The Lancet*, (2018): 31130–31139.

13. Ibid.

14. Dulaney, W. Marvin. *Black Police in America*. Bloomington: Indiana University Press, 1996.

15. Ibid.

16. Colding, Shenequa. "A Florida Police Chief Allegedly told Cops to Arrest 'Anybody Black'," *Vibe*.com, July 15, 2018. https://www.vibe.com/2018/07/florida-police-chief-arrest-anybody-black/

17. Ibid.

18. Hamlin, Clarissa. "Former Florida Police Chief Arrested Telling Cops to Arrest Anybody Black," RickeySmileyMorningShow.com. July 18, 2018. https://rickeysmileymorningshow.com/1927010/former-florida-police-chief-arrested-for-telling-cops-to-arrest-anybody-black/

19. Rector, Kevin. "De Sousa's Resignation Means No Severance, But He Will Receive Accrued Leave According to His New Contract," *The Baltimore Sun*, July 18, 2018, http://www.baltimoresun.com/news/maryland/crime/bs-md-ci-de-sousa-payout-20180515-story.html#

20. Hamlin, Clarissa. "Former Florida Police Chief Arrested Telling Cops to Arrest Anybody Black," RickeySmileyMorningShow.com. July 18, 2018. https://rickeysmileymorningshow.com/1927010/former-florida-police-chief-arrested-for-telling-cops-to-arrest-anybody-black/

21. Owens, Emily, Weisburd, David, Amendola, Karen L., and Geoffrey P. Alpert. "Can You Build a Better Cop?: Experimental Evidence on Supervision, Training, and Policing in the Community." *Criminology and Public Policy* 17, no. 1 (2018): 41–87.

22. Stoughton, Seth. "Law Enforcement's 'Warrior' Problem." *Harvard Law Forum*, 128 (2015): 225–235.

23. Weitzer, Ronald. "Racialized Policing: Residents' Perceptions in Three Neighborhoods." *Law and Society Review* 34, no. 1 (2000): 129–155.

24. Bonilla-Silva, Eduardo. *White supremacy and racism in the post-civil rights era*. Lynne Rienner Publishers, 2001.

25. Tyler, Tom. "Procedural Justice and Policing: A Rush to Judgment?" *Annual Review of Law and Social Science*, 13(2017): 29–53.

26. Tyler, Tom R., Goff, Phillip Atiba, and Robert J. MacCoun. "The Impact of Psychological Science on Policing in the United States: Procedural Justice, Legitimacy, and Effective Law Enforcement." *Psychological Science in the Public Interest* 16, no. 3(2015): 75–109.

27. Balko, Radley. *Rise of the Warrior Cop: The Militarization of America's Police Forces*. New York: Public Affairs, 2013.

28. Weitzer, Ronald. "Racialized Policing: Residents' Perceptions in Three Neighborhoods." *Law and Society Review* 34, no. 1 (2000): 129–155.

29. Balko, Radley. *Rise of the Warrior Cop: The Militarization of America's Police Forces*. New York: Public Affairs, 2013.

30. Tyler, Tom R. "Procedural Justice and Policing: A Rush to Judgment?" *Annual Review of Law and Social Science*, 13(2017): 29–53.

31. Maron, Dina Fine. "How to Reduce Police Violence: Doubts Cast on Implicit Bias Training." Scientific American, July 22, 2016, https://www.scientificamerican.com/article/how-to-reduce-police-violence/

32. Ibid.

33. Spencer, Katherine, Charbonneau, Amanda, and Jack Glaser. "Teaching and Learning Guide for Implicit Bias and Policing." *Social and Personality Psychology Compass*, 9, no. 12 (2015): 705–708.

34. Maron, Dina Fine. "How to Reduce Police Violence: Doubts Cast on Implicit Bias Training." Scientific American, July 22, 2016, https://www.scientificamerican.com/article/how-to-reduce-police-violence/

35. Skolnick, Jerome Herbert and James J. Fyfe. *Above the Law: Police and the Excessive Use of Force*. New York: Free Press.

36. Brunson, Rod K. and Jody Miller. "Young Black Men and Urban Policing in the United States." *The British Journal of Criminology* 46, no. 1 (2006): 613–640.

37. Brunson, Rod K. "Police Don't Like Black People: African American Young Men's Accumulated Police Experiences." *Criminology and Public Policy* 6, no. 1 (2007): 71–101.

38. Smith, Brad W. and Malcolm D. Holmes. "Community Accountability, Minority Threat, and Police Brutality: An Examination of Civil Rights Complaints." *Criminology* 41, no. 4 (2006): 1035–1064.

39. Lawrence, Sarah and Bobby McCarthy. "What Works in Community Policing? A Best Practices Context for Measure Y Effects." *Chief Justice Earl Warren Institute of Law and Public Policy. University of California School of Law*, (2013): 1–17.

40. Ibid.

41. Robertson, Ray V. ed. *Blacks Behind Bars: African Americans, Policing, and the Prison Boom*: San Diego, CA: Cognella Publishing, 2014.

42. Lawrence, Sarah and Bobby McCarthy. "What Works in Community Policing? A Best Practices Context for Measure Y Effects." *Chief Justice Earl Warren Institute of Law and Public Policy. University of California School of Law*, (2013): 1–17.

43. Lawrence, Sarah and Bobby McCarthy. "What Works in Community Policing? A Best Practices Context for Measure Y Effects." *Chief Justice Earl Warren Institute of Law and Public Policy. University of California School of Law*, (2013): 1–17.

44. Starr, Terrell Jermaine. "Community Policing is Not the Solution to Police Brutality. It Makes it Worse," *The Washington Post*, November 3, 2015 https://www.washingtonpost.com/posteverything/wp/2015/11/03/community-policing-is-not-the-solution-to-police-brutality-it-makes-it-worse/?noredirect=on&utm_term=.498975d7899a

45. Ibid.

46. Ibid.

47. Kindy, Kimberly. "Creating Guardians, Calming Warriors. A New Style of Training for Police Recruits Emphasizes Techniques to Better De-Escalate Conflict Situations," *The Washington Post*, December 10, 2015, https://www.washingtonpost.com/sf/investigative/2015/12/10/new-style-of-police-training-aims-to-produce-guardians-not-warriors/?utm_term=.7989ac96eb35

48. Beck, Charlie and Connie Rice. " How Community Policing Can Work," *The New York Times*, August 12, 2016, https://www.nytimes.com/2016/08/12/opinion/how-community-policing-can-work.html

49. Ibid.

50. Ibid.

51. Skolnick, Jerome Herbert and James J. Fyfe. *Above the Law: Police and the Excessive Use of Force* . New York: Free Press.

52. Eldridge, Lance. "The Impending Death of Community Policing," *PoliceOne* .com, July 28, 2010, https://www.policeone.com/community-policing/articles/2147172-The-impending-death-of-community-policing/

53. Ibid.

54. Skolnick, Jerome Herbert and James J. Fyfe. *Above the Law: Police and the Excessive Use of Force* . New York: Free Press.

55. Balko, Radley. *Rise of the Warrior Cop: The Militarization of America's Police Forces*. New York: Public Affairs, 2013.

56. Jennings, Wesley G., Fridell, Lorie A. and Mathew D. Lynch. "Cops and Body Cameras: Officers Perceptions of the Use of Body-Worn Cameras in Law Enforcement." *Journal of Criminal Justice* 42, no. 1 (2014): 549–556.

57. The Blog. U.S. Laws Protect Police But Endanger Civilians, January 29, 2017, Accessed on July 20, 2018, https://www.huffingtonpost.com/the-conversation-us/us-laws-protect-police-wh_b_9018144.html

58. Romig, Hillary. " 5 Reasons Why A Police Department Needs An in Car Video System," *PoliceOne*.com, January 3, 2018, https://www.policeone.com/police-products/body-cameras/articles/468485006-5-reasons-why-a-police-department-needs-an-in-car-video-system/

59. White, Michael D. *Police-Officer Body-Worn Cameras: Assessing the Evidence*. U.S. Department of Justice: Office of Justice Programs Diagnostic Center, Washington, D.C., 2014.

60. Farrar, Tony, and Barak Ariel. *Self-Awareness to Being Watched and Socially Desirable Behavior: A Field Experiment on the Effect of Body Worn Cameras and Police Use of Force* . Washington, D. C.: Police Foundation, 2013.

61. Ibid.

62. White, Michael D. *Police-Officer Body-Worn Cameras: Assessing the Evidence*. U.S. Department of Justice: Office of Justice Programs Diagnostic Center, Washington, D.C., 2014.

63. Jennings, Wesley G., Fridell, Lorie A. and Mathew D. Lynch. "Cops and Body Cameras: Officers Perceptions of the Use of Body-Worn Cameras in Law Enforcement." *Journal of Criminal Justice* 42, no. 1 (2014): 549–556.

64. Ibid.

65. White, Michael D. *Police-Officer Body-Worn Cameras: Assessing the Evidence*. U.S. Department of Justice: Office of Justice Programs Diagnostic Center, Washington, D.C., 2014.

66. Jennings, Wesley G., Fridell, Lorie A. and Mathew D. Lynch. "Cops and Body Cameras: Officers Perceptions of the Use of Body-Worn Cameras in Law Enforcement." *Journal of Criminal Justice* 42, no. 1 (2014): 549–556.

67. Rashawn, Ray, Marsh, Kris, and Connor Powelson. "Can Cameras Stop the Killings? Racial Differences in Perceptions of the Effectiveness of Body Worn Cameras in Police Encounters." *Sociological Forum* 32, no. 51 (2017): 1032–1050.

68. White, Michael D. *Police-Officer Body-Worn Cameras: Assessing the Evidence*. U.S. Department of Justice: Office of Justice Programs Diagnostic Center, Washington, D.C., 2014.

69. Rashawn, Ray, Marsh, Kris, and Connor Powelson. "Can Cameras Stop the Killings? Racial Differences in Perceptions of the Effectiveness of Body Worn Cameras in Police Encounters." *Sociological Forum* 32, no. 51 (2017): 1032–1050.

70. Ariel, Barak, Sutherland, Alex, Henstock, Darren, Young, Josh, and Gabriela Sosinski. "The Deterrence Spectrum: Explaining Why Police Body Worn Cameras 'Work' or 'Backfire' in Aggressive Police-Public Encounters." *Policing: A Journal of Police and Practice* 12, no. 1 (2017): 1–21.

71. Ariel, Barak, Sutherland, Alex, Henstock, Darren, Young, Josh, and Gabriela Sosinski. "The Deterrence Spectrum: Explaining Why Police Body Worn Cameras 'Work' or 'Backfire' in Aggressive Police-Public Encounters." *Policing: A Journal of Police and Practice* 12, no. 1 (2017): 1–21.

72. Weill, Kelly. "Baltimore Cops Caught Turning Off Body Cameras Before 'Finding' Drugs," Daily Beast, August 1, 2017, https://www.thedailybeast.com/baltimore-cops-turned-off-body-cameras-before-finding-drugs.

73. Weill, Kelly. " Baltimore Cops Caught Turning Off Body Cameras Before 'Finding' Drugs," Daily Beast, August 1, 2017, https://www.thedailybeast.com/baltimore-cops-turned-off-body-cameras-before-finding-drugs.

74. Vera, Amir. "Officers Muted Body Cameras in Stephon Clark Shooting. Why?," *CNN*.com, March 26, 2018, https://www.cnn.com/2018/03/25/us/sacramento-shooting-body-camera/index.html

75. Robles, Frances and Jose A. Del Real. "Stephon Clark Was Shot 8 Times Primarily in His Back, Family-Ordered Autopsy Finds," *The New York Times*, March 30, 2018, https://www.nytimes.com/2018/03/30/us/stephon-clark-independent-autopsy.html

76. Vera, Amir. "Officers Muted Body Cameras in Stephon Clark Shooting. Why?," *CNN*.com, March 26, 2018, https://www.cnn.com/2018/03/25/us/sacramento-shooting-body-camera/index.html

77. Robles, Frances and Jose A. Del Real. "Stephon Clark Was Shot 8 Times Primarily in His Back, Family-Ordered Autopsy Finds," *The New York Times*, March 30, 2018, https://www.nytimes.com/2018/03/30/us/stephon-clark-independent-autopsy.html

78. Cooper, Hannah LF. "War on Drugs Policing and Police Brutality." *Substance Use and Misuse* 50, nos. 8–9 (2015): 1188 –1194.

79. Ibid.

80. Balko, Radley. *Rise of the Warrior Cop: The Militarization of America's Police Forces.* New York: Public Affairs, 2013.

81. Downs, Kenya. "FBI Warned of White Supremacists in Law Enforcement 10 Years Ago. Has Anything Changed," October 21, 2016, *PBS*.orghttps://www.pbs.org/newshour/nation/fbi-white-supremacists-in-law-enforcement

82. Eligon, John and Kay Nolan. (2016). "When Police Do Not Live in the City They Serve," *The New York Times*, August 18, 2016, https://www.nytimes.com/2016/08/19/us/when-police-dont-live-in-the-city-they-serve.html

83. Balko, Radley. "The Power of the Prosecutor," *The Huffington Post*.com, January 16, 2013b, https://www.huffingtonpost.com/2013/01/16/the-power-of-the-prosecut_n_2488653.html

84. Sweeney, Annie. "Inside the Failed Prosecution of Dante Servin," *The Chicago Tribune*, July 3, 2015, http://www.chicagotribune.com/news/ct-dante-servin-acquittal-met-20150626-story.html

85. Balko, Radley. *Rise of the Warrior Cop: The Militarization of America's Police Forces.* New York: Public Affairs, 2013.

86. For financial settlements awarded families, see Cassandra Chaney and Ray V. Robertson. "Armed and Dangerous? An Examination of Fatal Shootings of Unarmed Black People by Police." *The Journal of Pan African Studies* 8, no. 4 (2015): 45–78.

87. Wing, Nick. "We Pay A Shocking Amount for Police Misconduct, and Cops Want Us to Accept It. We Shouldn't, *The Huffington Post*.com, May 29, 2015, https://www.huffingtonpost.com/2015/05/29/police-misconduct-settlements_n_7423386.html

88. Associated Press, 14 high-profile police-related deaths of U.S. blacks, December 8, 2017. Accessed on July 31, 2018, https://www.cbc.ca/news/world/list-police-related-deaths-usa-1.4438618

89. Anderson, Claud. *Powernomics: The National Plan to Empower Black America.* Bethesda, Maryland: Powernomics Corporation of America, 2001.

Afterword

Earl Smith, PhD, Emeritus Sociologist,
Wake Forest University

Now that we have read *Police Use of Excessive Force against African Americans: Historical Antecedents and Community Perceptions* what else can be said about POLICE BRUTALITY?

Police brutality has a long history in the United States. It begins in slavery (Aptheker 1946). For this afterword we start in SportsWorld—since the book does not address police brutality in SportsWorld—and start with Jack Johnson who was the first African American to hold the championship in the sport of boxing, and we see police brutality following the July 4, 1910 fight with Jim Jeffries. Johnson won the fight in Reno, Nevada in front of an estimated crowd of 20,000. After the fight, riots took place in more than 25 states and 50 cities, including Houston, New York, St. Louis, Omaha, New Orleans, Little Rock, and Los Angeles. At least twenty people were killed across the US from the riots. Most were African American (Smith 2014).

That was then. This is now. At about 2:00 am on January 26, 2018 Mr. Sterling Brown, a member of the NBA Milwaukee Bucks is harassed, tased, thrown to the ground, and beaten by members of the Milwaukee police department. This incident, which received a lot of attention because Brown is a prominent Black athlete, was filmed on police issue body cameras and now the administration within the police department say they are sorry (https://www.pbs.org/newshour/show/sterling-brown).

No one is sorry for police brutality. It is not implicit bias. It is explicit bias. Police violence has been carried out against Black Americans and with impunity. This book, *Police Use of Excessive Force against African Americans: Historical Antecedents and Community Perceptions* delves into some "meaty" police brutality topics that needed addressing.

Inside are five chapters that address topics from the modern civil rights era and Black Power movements, to the early "race riots" in places until recently little known like Tulsa, Oklahoma in 1921 where 50 Whites and up to 300 Blacks were killed and more than 8,000 were left homeless. The late Professor Jon Hope Franklin, the James B. Duke Professor of History Emeritus at Duke University in Durham, North Carolina, and the author of the immensely important and popular *From Slavery to Freedom* (2018, 10th edition) has researched and written and testified before Congress on the Tulsa and riots had this to say (Franklin 2007):

> By any standard, the Tulsa race riot of 1921 is one of the great tragedies of Oklahoma history.

In the city of East St. Louis, Illinois a race riot ensued in 1917. There, 250 Blacks were beaten and shot by White mobs over issues related to work. The early chapters in *Police Use of Excessive Force against African Americans: Historical Antecedents and Community Perceptions* provide an exhaustive coverage of the riots and other historical events that set up nicely the chapters to come. Without this analysis by professors Robertson and Chaney, it would be hard to ascertain why what we see in police brutality incidents today looks the way it does.

A standard methodology section (chapter 3) provides for the reader the important methodological overview and specific details of the scientific underpinnings of the study. We learn what questions were asked to ascertain answers and of whom. The results are displayed in a clear and systematic manner.

Police brutality comes in many forms such as beatings, killings, stop & frisk, illegal kidnapping, etc. Yet most discussions are about police using excessive force in African American neighborhoods against Black people (Hattery and Smith, 2018). This is correct. We do not see the type of excessive force researched for this book used on a daily basis and for a long period against any other race/ethnic group in America except Blacks. None. This is the essence of sustained police brutality captured in this text.

AFTERWORD BIBLIOGRAPHY

Aptheker, Herbert. 1946. *American Negro Slave Revolts*. New York: International

Franklin, John Hope. 2018. *From Slavery To Freedom*. New York: McGraw-Hill Education

Franklin, John Hope. 2007. "Tulsa Still Hasn't Faced the Truth About the Race Riot of 1921." Delivered before the House Judiciary Committee, Subcommittee on Constitution, Civil Rights and Civil Liberties, April 28, 2007. http://bit.ly/2seTec7

Hattery, Angela and Earl Smith. 2018. *Policing Black Bodies: How Black Lives are Surveilled and How to Work for Change*. Lanham, Maryland: Rowman and Littlefield.

Bibliography

Akers, Elmer and Vernon Fox. "The Detroit Rioters and Looters Committed to Prison." The *Journal of Criminal Law and Criminology* 35, no. 2 (1944–1945): 105–110.

Ajilore, Olugbenga, and Shane Shirey. "Do# AllLivesMatter? An evaluation of race and excessive use of force by police." *Atlantic Economic Journal* 45, no. 2 (2017): 201–212.

Alpert, Geoffrey P., and William C. Smith. "How reasonable is the reasonable man: Police and excessive force." *J. Crim. L. & Criminology* 85 (1994): 481.

Anderson, Claud. *Powernomics: The National Plan to Empower Black America*. Bethesda, Maryland: Powernomics Corporation of America, 2001.

Ariel, Barak, Sutherland, Alex, Henstock, Darren, Young, Josh, and Gabriela Sosinski. "The Deterrence Spectrum: Explaining Why Police Body Worn Cameras 'Work' or 'Backfire' in Aggressive Police-Public Encounters." *Policing: A Journal of Police and Practice* 12, no. 1 (2017): 1–21.

Armour, Jody David. *Negrophobia and Unreasonable Racism: The Hidden Costs of Being Black in America*. New York: University Press, 1997.

Associated Press, 14 high-profile police-related deaths of U.S. blacks, December 8, 2017. Accessed, July 31, 2018, https://www.cbc.ca/news/world/list-police-related-deaths-usa-1.4438618

Aymer, Samuel R. "'I can't breathe': A case study—Helping Black men cope with race-related trauma stemming from police killing and brutality." *Journal of Human Behavior in the Social Environment* 26, no. 3–4 (2016): 367–376.

Balko, Radley. "Once again: There is no 'War on Cops' and those who claim otherwise are Playing a Dangerous Game," *The Washington Post*, September 10, 2015. https://www.washingtonpost.com/news/the-watch/wp/2015/09/10/once-again-there-is-no-war-on-cops-and-those-who-claim-otherwise-are-playing-a-dangerous-game/.

Balko, Radley. "The Power of the Prosecutor," *The Huffington Post*, January 16, 2013, https://www.huffingtonpost.com/2013/01/16/the-power-of-the-prosecut_n_2488653.html

Balko, Radley. *Rise of the Warrior Cop: The Militarization of America's Police Forces*. New York: Public Affairs, 2013.

Bar, Jacob, Venkataramani, Atheendar S., Williams, David R., and Alexander C. Tsai. "Police Killings and their Spillover Effects on Mental Health of Black Americans: A Population Based, Quasi-Experimental Study." *The Lancet*, (2018): 31130–31139.

Bassett, C. Jeanne. "House Bill 591: Florida Compensates Rosewood Victims and Their Families for a Seventy-One-Year-Old Injury." *Florida State University Law Review* 22, no. 10 (1995): 503–523.

Beck, Charlie and Connie Rice. "How Community Policing Can Work," *The New York Times*, August 12, 2016, https://www.nytimes.com/2016/08/12/opinion/how-community-policing-can-work.html

Beck, Elwood M., and Stewart E. Tolnay. "The killing fields of the deep south: the market for cotton and the lynching of blacks, 1882–1930." *American Sociological Review* (1990): 526–539.

Becker, Sarah. "Race and Violent Offender Propensity: Does the Intraracial Nature of Violent Crime Persist On the Local Level?" *Justice Research and Policy* 9, no. 2 (2007): 53–86.

Bell, Derrick. *Faces at the Bottom of the Well: The Permanence of Racism*. New York, NY: Basic Books, 1992.

Bentley, Rosalind. "The Rosewood Massacre: How a Lie Destroyed a Black Town," *The Atlanta Journal Constitution*, February 17, 2017, https://www.myajc.com/news/national/the-rosewood-massacre-how-lie-destroyed-black-town/wTcKjELkGskePsWiwutQuO/

Berman, Mark & Lowery, Wesley. (March 4, 2015). The 12 Key highlights from the DOJ's Scathing Ferguson Report. Retrieved from: http://www.washingtonpost.com/news/post-nation/wp/2015/03/04/the-12-keyhighlights-from-the-dojs-scathing-ferguson-report/

Berger, Ronald J., Free Jr., Marvin D., Deller, Melissa, and Patrick K. O'Brien. *Crime, Justice, and Society: An Introduction to Criminology*. 4th ed. Boulder, CO: Rienner, 2015.

Birth of a Nation. Directed by D. W. Griffith. New York, NY: Epoch Producing Company, 1915.

Bjorhus, Jennifer and Mary Jo Webster. (2017). "Shielded by the Badge, Part 1," *Minneapolis Star Tribune*, October 1, 2017, http://www.startribune.com/minneapolis-police-officers-convicted-of-serious-crimes-still-on-the-job/437687453/

Blow, Charles M. "Crime, Bias, and Statistics," *The New York Times*, September 7, 2014. http://www.nytimes.com/2014/09/08/opinion/charles-blow-crime-bias-and-statistics.html?_r=0.

Blumgart, Jake. "The Brutal Legacy of Frank Rizzo, the Most Notorious Cop in Philadelphia History," *Vice*.com, October 22, 2015, https://www.vice.com/en_us/article/kwxp3m/remembering-frank-rizzo-the-most-notorious-cop-in-philadelphia-history-1022

Bogdan, Robert, and Sari Biklen. "Qualitative research for education: An introduction to theory and practice." Needham Heights, MA: Allyn and Bacon (2007).

Bogus, Carl T. "The Hidden History of the Second Amendment," *U. C. Davis Law Review* 31, no. 80 (1998): 309–411.

Bonilla-Silva, Eduardo. *Racism without Racists: Color-Blind Racism and the Persistence of Racial Inequality in America*. 4th ed. Lanham, MD: Rowman & Littlefield, 2014.

Bonilla-Silva, Eduardo. "The Invisible Weight of Whiteness: The Racial Grammar of Everyday Life in Contemporary America." *Ethnic and Racial Studies* 35, no. 2 (2012): 173–194.

Boyer, Peter J. "Bad Cops: Rafael Perez's Testimony on Police Misconduct Ignited the Biggest Scandal in the History of the L.A.P.D. Is it the Real Story?" *The New Yorker*, May 21, 2001, http://www.asu.edu/courses/fms440mg/total-readings/badcops.pdf

Brantingham, Paul J., and Patricia L. Brantingham. "Notes on the geometry of crime." In *Principles of Geographical Offender Profiling*, pp. 97–124. Routledge, 2017.

Brophy, Alfred L. *Reconstructing the Dreamland. The Tulsa Race Riot of 1921: Race, Reparations, and Reconciliation*. London: Oxford University Press, 2002.

Brunson, Rod K. "Police Don't Like Black People: African American Young Men's Accumulated Police Experiences." *Criminology and Public Policy* 6, no. 1 (2007): 71–101.

Brunson, Rod K. and Jody Miller. "Young Black Men and Urban Policing in the United States." *The British Journal of Criminology* 46, no. 1 (2006): 613–640.

Burrell, Tom. *Brainwashed Challenging the Myth of Black Inferiority*. New York, NY: Smiley-Books, 2010.

Chaney, Cassandra, and Ray V. Robertson. "Armed and Dangerous? An Examination of Fatal Shootings of Unarmed Black People by Police." *The Journal of Pan African Studies* 8, no. 4 (2015): 45–78.

Chaney, Cassandra, and Ray V. Robertson. "Can We All Get Along? Blacks' Historical and Contemporary (In) Justice with Law Enforcement." *Western Journal of Black Studies*, 38, no. 2 (2014): 108–122.

Chaney, Cassandra. "Institutional Racism: Perspectives on the Department of Justice's Investigation of the Ferguson Police Department." *Western Journal of Black Studies* 39, no. 4 (2015).

Chaney, Cassandra, and Ray V. Robertson. "Media Reporting of the Sandy Hook Elementary School Angels." *The Journal of Pan African Studies*, 5, no. 6 (2013b): 74–114.

Chaney, Cassandra, and Ray V. Robertson. "Racism and Police Brutality in America." *Journal of African American Studies*, 17, no. 4 (2013a): 480–505.

Chandler, D. L. "Detroit Race Riots Began on this Day in 1943," *Newsone*, June 20, 2013, https://newsone.com/2605677/detroit-race-riot-1943/

Charles, Christopher, and Yaba Blay. "Skin Bleaching and Global White Supremacy." *Journal of Pan African Studies* 4, no. 4 (2011): 4–46.

Chevigny, Paul, and Paui Chevigny. *Edge of the knife: Police violence in the Americas.* No. 363.2097 C4. New York: New Press, 1995.

Cleaver, Kathleen and George Katsiaficas C. *Liberation, imagination and The Black Panthers and their Legacy.* New York: Routledge, 2014.

"Cointelpro: The FBI's War on Black America," *Originalpeople.org*, November 15, 2012, http://originalpeople.org/cointelpro-the-fbis-war-on-black-america/

Colding, Shenequa. "A Florida Police Chief Allegedly told Cops to Arrest 'Anybody Black'," *Vibe*.com, July 15, 2018. https://www.vibe.com/2018/07/florida-police-chief-arrest-anybody-black/

Cooper, Hannah LF. "War on Drugs Policing and Police Brutality." *Substance Use and Misuse* 50, nos. 8–9 (2015): 1188–1194.

Cooper, S. J. "Holding the police to account: A critical analysis of the structures of police accountability and the introduction and operation of Police and Crime Commissioners." PhD diss., 2018.

Cornell Law School. Excessive Force. Retrieved from: https://www.law.cornell.edu/wex/excessive_force

Cottman, Michael H. "Should the Parents of the Child Who Fell into Gorilla Enclosure Be Charged," BlackAmericaWeb.com, May 31, 2016. http://blackamericaweb.com/2016/05/31/should-the-parents-of-the-child-who-fell-into-gorilla-enclosure-be-charged/.

Crenshaw, Kimberle. "20 Years of Critical Race Theory: Looking Back to Move Forward." *Connecticut Law Review* 43, no. 5 (2011): 1253–1352.

Data USA, Police Officers, 2018. Accessed on July 15, 2018, https://datausa.io/profile/soc/333050/

Davis, Kelly. "CPS Adding Jon Burge Torture Scandal to Curriculum," *WGNTV*.com, August 28, 2017, http://wgntv.com/2017/08/28/cps-adding-jon-burge-police-torture-scandal-to-curriculum/

Delgado, Richard, and Jean Stefancic. *Critical race theory: An introduction.* NYU Press, 2017.

Denzin, Norman K., and Yvonna S. Lincoln. "Major paradigms and perspectives." *Strategies of Qualitative Inquiry*, NYK Denzin and YS Lincoln (eds.) Sage Publications, Thousand Oaks (1998).

Dixon, Travis L. "Network News and Racial Beliefs: Exploring the Connection between National Television News Exposure and Stereotypical Perceptions of African Americans." *Journal of Communication* 58, no. 2 (2008): 321–337.

Dixon, Travis L., and Keith B. Maddox. "Skin Tone, Crime News, and Social Reality Judgments: Priming the Stereotype of the Dark and Dangerous Black Criminal 1." *Journal of Applied Social Psychology* 35, no. 8 (2005): 1555–1570.

Downs, Kenya. "FBI Warned of White Supremacists in Law Enforcement 10 Years Ago. Has Anything Changed,"*PBS*.org, October 21, 2016, https://www.pbs.org/newshour/nation/fbi-white-supremacists-in-law-enforcement

Dottolo, Andrea L., and Abigail J. Stewart. "'Don't ever forget now, you're a Black man in America': Intersections of race, class and gender in encounters with the police." *Sex Roles* 59, no. 5–6 (2008): 350–364.

Dulaney, W. Marvin. *Black Police in America.* Bloomington: Indiana University Press, 1996.

Durr, Marlese. "What is the Difference between Slave Patrols and Modern Day Policing? Institutional Violence in a Community of Color." *Critical Sociology* 41, no. 6 (2015): 873–879.

Dye, Thomas R. "The Rosewood Massacre: History and the Making of Public Policy." *The Public Historian* 19, no. 3 (1997): 25–39.

Eldridge, Lance. "The Impending Death of Community Policing," *PoliceOne*.com, July 28, 2010, https://www.policeone.com/community-policing/articles/2147172-The-impending-death-of-community-policing/

Eligon, John and Kay Nolan. (2016). "When Police Do Not Live in the City They Serve," *The New York Times*, August 18, 2016, https://www.nytimes.com/2016/08/19/us/when-police-dont-live-in-the-city-they-serve.html

Ellawala, Themal. "Pulling the Trigger: Dehumanization of African Americans and Police Violence." *Scholarly Undergraduate Research Journal at Clark University* 2, no. 1 (2016): 2–8.

Embrick, David. (2015). "Two Nations, Revisited: The Lynching of Black and Brown Bodies, Police Brutality, and Racial Control in 'Post-Racial' Amerikka." *Critical Sociology* 41, no. 6 (2015): 835–843.

English Oxford Dictionary, Scapegoat Definition, Accessed July 29, 2018, https://en.oxforddictionaries.com/definition/scapegoat

Farrar, Tony, and Barak Ariel. *Self-Awareness to Being Watched and Socially Desirable Behavior: A Field Experiment on the Effect of Body Worn Cameras and Police Use of Force.* Washington, D. C.: Police Foundation, 2013.

Feagin, Joe. R. *Racist America: Roots, Current Realities, and Future Reparations.* 3rd ed. New York: Routledge, 2014.

Feldmeyer, Ben and Darrell Steffensmeier. "Immigration Effects on Homicide Offending for Total and Race/Ethnicity-Disaggregated Populations (White, Black, and Latino)." *Homicide Studies* 13, no. 3 (2009): 211–226.

Feuer, Alan. "Ex-New York Officer gets 5 years of Probation in Fatal Brooklyn Shooting," *The New York Times*, April 19, 2016. https://www.nytimes.com/2016/04/20/nyregion/peter-liang-ex-new-york-police-officer-sentenced-akai-gurley-shooting-death-brooklyn.html

Frey, William H. *Diversity explosion: How new racial demographics are remaking America.* Brookings Institution Press, 2014.

Friedman, Brandis. "Survivors of Torture under Jon Burge Find a Place," *WTTW*.com, May 25, 2017, https://chicagotonight.wttw.com/2017/05/25/survivors-torture-under-jon-burge-find-place-respite

Fuhrman, Matthew and Wil Cruz. Ving Rhames says officers pulled their guns on him in his own home, July 28, 2018, Accessed on July 28, 2018, https://abcnews.go.com/US/ving-rhames-officers-pulled-guns-home/story?id=56890288

Gabbidon, Shaun L. *Criminological Perspectives on Race and Crime.* 2nd Ed. New York: Routledge, 2010.

Gambacorta, David, Brennan, Chris, and Valerie Russ. "Was Frank Rizzo Racist, or Just a Product of His Time?," *Philly*.com, August 22, 2017, http://www.philly.com/philly/news/philadelphia-statue-legacy-was-frank-rizzo-racist-20170822.html

Garfinkel, Harold. "Studies in ethnomethodology." Prentice Hall, 1967.

Gerber, Monica M., and Jonathan Jackson. "Justifying violence: legitimacy, ideology and public support for police use of force." *Psychology, Crime & Law* 23, no. 1 (2017): 79–95.

Glenza, Jessica. "Rosewood Massacre a Harrowing Tale of Racism and the Road Toward Reparations," *The Guardian*, January 3, 2016, https://www.theguardian.com/us-news/2016/jan/03/rosewood-florida-massacre-racial-violence-reparations

Goff, Phillip Atiba, Matthew Christian Jackson, Brooke Allison Lewis Di Leone, Carmen Marie Culotta, and Natalie Ann DiTomasso. "The essence of innocence: Consequences of dehumanizing Black children." *Journal of Personality and Social Psychology* 106, no. 4 (2014): 526–545.

Gone with the Wind. Directed by Victor Fleming. Beverly Hills, CA: Metro-Goldwyn-Mayer, 1939.

Graham, David A. "Stop and Frisk: Trump's Bad Idea for Fighting Crime," *The Atlantic*, September 21, 2016, https://www.theatlantic.com/politics/archive/2016/09/trump-stop-and-frisk-ineffective-unconstitutional/501041/

Greenwood, Ronni Michelle. "Remembrance, Responsibility, and Reparations: The Use of Emotions in Talk about the Tulsa Race Riots," *Journal of Social Issues* 71, no. 2 (2015): 338–355.

Haag, Matthew. "Officer Who Shot Antwon Rose Is Charged with Criminal Homicide," *The New York Times*, June 27, 2018. https://www.nytimes.com/2018/06/27/us/antwon-rose-shooting-michael-rosfeld.html

Hadden, Sally E. *Slave Patrols: Law and Violence in Virginia and the Carolinas*. Cambridge, Massachusetts: Harvard University Press, 2001.

Hall, Allison V., Perry, Jamie L., and Erika V. Hall. "Black and Blue: Exploring Racial Bias and Law Enforcement in the Killings of Unarmed Black Male Civilians." *American Psychologist* 71, no. 3 (2016): 175–186.

Hamlin, Clarissa. "Former Florida Police Chief Arrested Telling Cops to Arrest Anybody Black, RickeySmileyMorningShow.com. July18, 2018. https://rickeysmileymorning-show.com/1927010/former-florida-police-chief-arrested-for-telling-cops-to-arrest-anybody-black/

Han, Bing, Deborah A. Cohen, Kathryn P. Derose, Jiang Li, and Stephanie Williamson. "Violent crime and park use in low-income urban neighborhoods." *American Journal of Preventive Medicine* 54, no. 3 (2018): 352–358.

Hancock. Directed by Peter Berg. Culver City, CA: Overbrook Entertainment, 2008.

Healthline (2018). The Relationship between ADHD and Autism. Retrieved from: https://www.healthline.com/health/adhd/autism-and-adhd

Helm, Angela. "Chicago PD Settle for $2.5 Million After Police Point Gun at 3-Year Old," The Root, July 3, 2018, https://www.theroot.com/chicago-pd-settle-for-2-5-million-after-police-point-g-1827325007.

Hess, Judith. "Genre films and the status quo." *Film Genre: Theory and Criticism*, edited by B. Grant. Metuchen, NJ: Scarecrow (1977): 65–95.

Higgins, George E., Jennings, Wesley G., Jordan, Kareem, L., and Shaun L. Gabbidon. "Racial Profiling in Decisions to Search: A Preliminary Analysis Using Propensity-Score Matching." *International Journal of Police Science and Management* 13, no. 4 (2011): 336–347.

Hill, Karlos K. *Beyond the Rope: The Impact of Lynching on Black Culture and Memory*. London: Cambridge University Press, 2016.

Hill, Rickey. "The Bogalusa Movement: Self-Defense and Black Power in the Civil Rights Struggle." *The Black Scholar* 41, no. 3 (2011): 43–54.

Hirsch, James S. *Riot and Remembrance: The Tulsa Race War and Its Legacy*. Boston: Houghton Mifflin Company, 2002.

Holmes, Malcolm D. "Minority Threat and Police Brutality: Determinants of Civil Rights Criminal Complaints in US Municipalities." *Criminology* 38, no. 2 (2000): 343–368.

Holsti, Ole R. *Content analysis for the social sciences and humanities*. Addison-Wesley Pub. Co, 1969.

Hunt, Jennifer and Peter K. Manning. "The Social Context of Police Lying," *Symbolic Interaction* 14, no. 1 (1991): 51–70.

Huq, Aziz. "The Consequences of Disparate Policing: Evaluating Stop and Frisk as a Modality of Urban Policing." *Minnesota Law Review* 100, no. 6 (2017): 2397–2480.

Ivkovic, Sanja Kutnak. "To Serve and Collect: Measuring Police Corruption." *Journal of Criminal Law and Criminology* 93, no. 2–3: (2003): 593–650.

Jacobsma, Michael J. "Non-Contact Excessive Force by Police: Is That Really a Thing." *U. Rich. L. Rev.* 52 (2017): 1.

Jennings, Wesley G., Fridell, Lorie A. and Mathew D. Lynch. "Cops and Body Cameras: Officers Perceptions of the Use of Body-Worn Cameras in Law Enforcement." *Journal of Criminal Justice* 42, no. 1 (2014): 549–556.

Johnson, Adam. "5 Times the Media has Smeared Black Victims of Police Killings since Michael Brown," *Alternet.org*, August 6, 2015. http://www.alternet.org/media/5-times-media-has-smeared-black-victims-police-killings-michael-brown

Johnson, Jason Kyle. "Who's Afraid of the Big Black Man?." *Educational Studies* 54, no. 2 (2018): 229–236.

Johnson, Martenzie. "Colin Kaepernick's Parents break Silence: We absolutely Support Him," *The Undefeated*, December 10, 2016. https://theundefeated.com/features/colin-kaepernicks-parents-break-silence-we-absolutely-do-support-him/

Johnson, Richard R. "Community Policing is Not Soft on Crime: The Evidence." (2017).

Jones, Maxine D. "The Rosewood Massacre and the Women Who Survived It." *The Florida Historical Quarterly* 76, no. 2 (1997): 193–208.

Joseph, Peniel. "The Black Power Movement, Democracy, and America in the King Years." *American Historical Review* 114, no. 4 (2009): 1001–1016.

Joseph, Peniel. "Black Liberation Without Apology: Reconceptualizing the Black Power Movement." *The Black Scholar* 31, no. ¾ (2001): 2–19.

Judge, Monique. "No Justice, No Peace, Just Crooked Police," *The Root*, October 6, 2017, http://www.theroot.com/no-justice-no-peace-just-crooked-police-1819237633

Kahn, Carrie. "After Riots, Scandal Sparked Reform in LAPD," *National Public Radio*, April 25, 2012, https://www.npr.org/2012/04/25/151354376/after-riots-scandal-sparked-reform-in-lapd

Karenga, Mualana. *Introduction to Black Studies*. 4th edition. Los Angeles, CA: University of Sankore Press, 2010.

Kayyali, Dia. "The History of Surveillance and the Black Community," *Electronic Frontier Foundation*, February 13, 2014. https://www.eff.org/deeplinks/2014/02/history-surveillance-and-black-community

Kenney, Tanasia. "FBI Director Claims the 'Ferguson Effect' and Black Lives Matter Are To Blame for the Rise in Violent Crimes. . . . Again," *Atlanta Blackstar*, May 13, 2016. http://atlantablackstar.com/2016/05/13/fbi-director-claims-the-ferguson-effect-and-black-lives-matter-are-to-blame-for-the-rise-in-violent-crimes-again/

Kindy, Kimberly. "Creating Guardians, Calming Warriors. A New Style of Training for Police Recruits Emphasizes Techniques to Better De-Escalate Conflict Situations," *The Washington Post*, December 10, 2015, https://www.washingtonpost.com/sf/investigative/2015/12/10/new-style-of-police-training-aims-to-produce-guardians-not-warriors/?utm_term=.7989ac96eb35

King, Shaun. "King: Conservatives Ought to Direct Their Rage toward Angry White Men-Not Beyoncé," *New York Daily News*, February 22, 2016, http://www.nydailynews.com/news/national/king-white-men-killed-7-8-cops-u-s-year-article-1.2539913.

King, Shaun. "King: White Men Killed More American Police than any other Group, But Conservatives will not Address the Facts," *New York Daily News*, May 11, 2016. http://www.nydailynews.com/news/national/king-cops-killed-white-men-conservatives-silent-article-1.2632965.

LawEnforcementNET.edu. Eligibility Requirements for Police Officer Jobs, 2018. Accessed on July 28, 2018 from https://www.lawenforcementedu.net/police-officer/police-officer-requirements/

Lawrence, Sarah and Bobby McCarthy. "What Works in Community Policing? A Best Practices Context for Measure Y Effects." *Chief Justice Earl Warren Institute of Law and Public Policy. University of California School of Law*, (2013): 1–17.

Lee, Trymaine. "A Video Again Casts Doubt on Police Shooting of a Black Man," *NBCNEWS*.com, October 7, 2017, https://www.nbcnews.com/news/nbcblk/video-again-casts-doubt-police-shooting-black-man-n808506

Lee, Trymaine. "Jon Burge, Ex-Chicago Cop Who Ran Torture Ring, Released from Prison," *MSNBC*.com, October 3, 2014, http://www.msnbc.com/msnbc/jon-burge-ex-chicago-cop-who-ran-torture-ring-released-prison

Leonard, Mary Delach. "Legacy of 1917 East St. Louis Race Riot is Etched in Family Trees," *St. Louis Public Radio*, June 30, 2017, http://news.stlpublicradio.org/post/legacy-1917-east-st-louis-race-riot-etched-family-trees#stream/0

Lewis, Michael. *The Blind Side: Evolution of a Game*. New York: W.W. Norton and Company, 2006.

Lieberson, Stanley and Arnold Silverman. "The Precipitants and Underlying Conditions of Race Riots." *American Sociological Review* 30, no. 6 (1965): 887–898.

Linter, Timothy. "Critical Race Theory and the Teaching of American History: Power, Perspective, and Practice." *Social Studies Research and Practice* 2, no. 1 (2007) 103–116.

Loewen, James W. *Lies My Teacher Told Me: Everything Your History Textbooks Got Wrong.* New York: Touchstone, 2007.

Loewen, James W. *Sundown Towns: A Hidden Dimension of American Racism.* New York: The New Press, 2005.

Loveday, Barry, and Sue Roberts. "A time of change: the expanding role of Police and Crime Commissioners in local criminal justice delivery." In *Multi-Agency Working: Policy, Theory and Practice.* Policy Press, 2018.

Lowery, Wesley J. "Study Finds Police Fatally Shoot Unarmed Black Men at Disproportionate Rates," *The Washington Post,* April 7, 2016, https://www.washingtonpost.com/national/study-finds-police-fatally-shoot-unarmed-black-men-at-disproportionate-rates/2016/04/06/e494563e-fa74-11e5-80e4-c381214de1a3_story.html?noredirect=on&utm_term=.df5b4eeaf252

Mac Donald, Heather. "The Ferguson Effect," *The Washington Post,* July 20, 2016, https://www.washingtonpost.com/news/volokh-conspiracy/wp/2016/07/20/the-ferguson-effect/?utm_term=.2b78e042a99f

Madigan, Tim. *The Burning: Massacre, Destruction, and the Tulsa Race Riot of 1921.* New York: Thomas Dunne's Books, 2003.

Maron, Dina Fine. "How to Reduce Police Violence: Doubts Cast on Implicit Bias Training." *Scientific American,* July 22, 2016, https://www.scientificamerican.com/article/how-to-reduce-police-violence/

Marshall, Tony F., and Susan Merry. *Crime and accountability: Victim/offender mediation in practice.* HM Stationery Office, 1990.

McDermott, Maeve. "Rudy Guiliani calls Beyonce's Super Bowl Performance 'Attack' on Cops." *USA Today,* February 9, 2016, http://www.usatoday.com/story/life/people/2016/02/08/rudy-giuliani-criticizes-beyonce-super-bowl-formation-attack-on-cops/80018490/.

McLaughlin, Malcolm. "Ghetto Formation and Armed Resistance in East St. Louis, Illinois." *Journal of American Studies* 41, no. 2 (2007): 435–467.

McLaughlin, Malcolm. "Reconsidering the East St. Louis Race Riot of 1917". *Internationaal Instituut voor Social Gerchiedenis* 47, no. 1 (2002): 187–212.

Meares, Tracey L. "The Law and Social Science of Stop and Frisk." *Annual Review of Law and Science* 10, no. 1 (2014): 335–52.

Meiners, Erica R. *Right to Be Hostile: Schools, Prisons, and the Making of Public Enemies.* New York: Routledge, 2007.

Merikangas, Kathleen R., Evelyn J. Bromet, and Benjamin G. Druss. "Future surveillance of mental disorders in the United States: count people, not disorders." *JAMA Psychiatry* 74, no. 5 (2017): 431–432.

Merriam-Webster, Scapegoat Definition, Accessed July 29, 2018, https://www.merriam-webster.com/dictionary/scapegoat

Miller, Michael E. "Cop Accused of Brutally Torturing Black Suspects Costs Chicago 5.5 Million," *The Washington Post,* April 15, 2015, https://www.washingtonpost.com/news/morning-mix/wp/2015/04/15/closing-the-book-on-jon-burge-chicago-cop-accused-of-brutally-torturing-african-american-suspects/?noredirect=on&utm_term=.1f373fedc58e

Miller, Reuben Jonathan, Lester Jackson Kern, and Ayanna Williams. "The Front End of the Carceral State: Police Stops, Court Fines, and the Racialization of Due Process." *Social Service Review* 92, no. 2 (2018): 290–303.

Morris, John W. "Why is the Rizzo Statue Controversial?" *6abc*.com, August 18, 2017, http://6abc.com/politics/why-is-the-rizzo-statue-controversial/2321718/

Myers, Daniel J. "Racial Rioting in the 1960s: An Event History Analysis of Local Conditions." *American Sociological Review* 62, 1 (1997): 94–112.

National Institute of Mental Health (2018). Schizophrenia. Retrieved from: https://www.nimh.nih.gov/health/topics/schizophrenia/index.shtml

Owens, Emily, Weisburd, David, Amendola, Karen L., and Geoffrey P. Alpert. "Can You Build a Better Cop?: Experimental Evidence on Supervision, Training, and Policing in the Community." *Criminology and Public Policy* 17, no. 1 (2018): 41–87.

Painter, Nell I. *The History of White People.* New York: W. W. Norton, 2010.

Park, Madison, and Holly Yan. "Gorilla Killing: 3 Year-Old Boy's Mother Won't be Charged," *CNN*, June 6, 2016. http://www.cnn.com/2016/06/06/us/harambe-gorilla-death-investigation/

Park, Madison. (March 22, 2018). Police Shootings: Trials, Convictions are Rare for Officers. Accessed on Wednesday July 26, 2108, https://www.cnn.com/2017/05/18/us/police-involved-shooting-cases/index.html

Park, Madison, Grinberg, Emanuella, and Tiffany Ap. "'We'd Make the Same Decision,' Zoo Director Says of Gorilla Shooting," *CNN*, May 31, 2016. http://www.cnn.com/2016/05/30/us/gorilla-shot-harambe/

Pew Research Center (2018). *5 Facts about Blacks in the United States.* Retrieved from http://www.pewresearch.org/fact-tank/2018/02/22/5-facts-about-blacks-in-the-u-s/

Phillips, Charles D. "Exploring Relations among Forms of Social Control: The Lynching and Execution of Blacks in North Carolina, 1889–1918," *Law and Society Review* 21, no. 3 (1987): 361–374.

Poe-Yamagata, Eileen. *And justice for some: Differential treatment of minority youth in the justice system.* Darby, PA: Diane Publishing, 2009.

Pollner, Melvin. *Mundane reason: Reality in everyday and sociological discourse.* Cambridge University Press, 2010.

Pratt Harris, Natasha C., Michael M. Sinclair, Cynthia B. Bragg, Nicole R. Williams, Kalfani N. Ture, Belinda D. Smith, Isiah Marshall Jr., and Lawrence Brown. "Police-Involved Homicide of Unarmed Black Males: Observations By Black Scholars in The Midst of The April 2015 Baltimore Uprising." *Journal of Human Behavior in the Social Environment* 26, 3–4 (2016): 377–389.

"Pursuing Corrupt Cops," *The New York Times*, December 30, 1993, https://search-proquest-com.famuproxy.fcla.edu/docview/429388982?OpenUrlRefId=info:xri/sid:primo&accountid=10913

Rabb, Selwyn. "Policing the Police: Report Says Police Tolerate Corruption," *The New York Times*, January 2, 1994, https://search-proquest-com.famuproxy.fcla.edu/docview/429440041?OpenUrlRefId=info:xri/sid:primo&accountid=10913

Rao, Sammeer. "Its Been 96 Years Since White Mobs Destroyed Black Wallstreet," *Colorlines*, May 31, 2017. https://www.colorlines.com/articles/its-been-96-years-white-mobs-destroyed-tulsas-black-wall-street.

Rashawn, Ray, Marsh, Kris, and Connor Powelson. "Can Cameras Stop the Killings? Racial-Differences in Perceptions of the Effectiveness of Body Worn Cameras in Police Encounters." *Sociological Forum* 32, no. 51 (2017): 1032–1050.

Rattan, Aneeta, Levine, Cynthia S., Dweck, Carol S., and Jennifer L. Eberhardt. "Race and the Fragility of the Legal Distinctions between Juveniles and Adults." *PloS One* 7, no. 5 (2012): 1–5.

Rector, Kevin. "De Sousa's Resignation Means No Severance, But He Will Receive Accrued Leave According to His New Contract," *The Baltimore Sun*, July 18, 2018, http://www.baltimoresun.com/news/maryland/crime/bs-md-ci-de-sousa-payout-20180515-story.html#

Richardson, L. Song. "Police Racial Violence: Lessons from Social Psychology." *Fordham Law Review* 83, no. 6 (2015): 2961–2976.

Roberg, Roy R., Jack L. Kuykendall, and Kenneth Novak. *Police management.* Los Angeles: Roxbury Publishing Company, 2002.

Robertson, Campbell. "History of Lynchings in the South Documents Nearly 4,000 Names," *The New York Times*, February 10, 2015. https://www.nytimes.com/2015/02/10/us/history-of-lynchings-in-the-south-documents-nearly-4000-names.html

Robertson, Ray V. ed. *Blacks Behind Bars: African Americans, Policing, and the Prison Boom.* San Diego, CA: Cognella Publishing, 2014.

Robinson, Michael A. "Black Bodies in the Ground: Policing Disparities in the African American Community-An Analysis of Newsprint from January 1, 2015 through December 31, 2015." *Journal of Black Studies* 48, no. 6 (2017): 551–571.

Robles, Frances and Jose A. Del Real. "Stephon Clark Was Shot 8 Times Primarily in His Back, Family-Ordered Autopsy Finds," *The New York Times*, March 30, 2018, https://www.nytimes.com/2018/03/30/us/stephon-clark-independent-autopsy.html

Romig, Hillary. "5 Reasons Why A Police Department Needs An in Car Video System," *PoliceOne*.com, January 3, 2018, https://www.policeone.com/police-products/body-cameras/articles/468485006-5-reasons-why-a-police-department-needs-an-in-car-video-system/

Rosenberg, Eli. "Police Bodycam Shows Officer Fatally Shoot a Man Who Ran. Prosecutors Say it was Justified," *The Washington Post*, October 7, 2017. https://www.washingtonpost.com/news/post-nation/wp/2017/10/07/police-bodycam-shows-officer-fatally-shoot-a-man-who-ran-prosecutors-say-it-was-justified/?utm_term=.f7efc4eba6c9.

Russ, J. "The 1943 Detroit Race Riot," *Walter P. Reuther Library Wayne State University*, June 12, 2012. https://reuther.wayne.edu/node/8738

Rutbeck-Goldman, Ariela, and L. Song Richardson. "Race and Objective Reasonableness in Use of Force Cases: An Introduction to Some Relevant Social Science." *Ala. CR & CLL Rev.* 8 (2017): 145.

Savali, Kirsten W. "Racists Prove That They Care More about Gorillas than Black Children," *The Root*, June 1, 2016, http://www.theroot.com/articles/culture/2016/06/harambe-cincinnati-zoo-black-children/

Schomerus, Georg, Susanne Stolzenburg, Simone Freitag, Sven Speerforck, Deborah Janowitz, Sara Evans-Lacko, Holger Muehlan, and Silke Schmidt. "Stigma as a barrier to recognizing personal mental illness and seeking help: a prospective study among untreated persons with mental illness." *European Archives of Psychiatry and Clinical Neuroscience* (2018): 1–11.

Scott, John C. "The mission of the university: Medieval to postmodern transformations." *The Journal of Higher Education* 77, no. 1 (2006): 1–39.

Skogan, Wesley G. "Concern about crime and confidence in the police: Reassurance or accountability?." *Police Quarterly* 12, no. 3 (2009): 301–318.

Skolnick, Jerome Herbert and James J. Fyfe. *Above the Law: Police and the Excessive Use of Force*. New York: Free Press, 1993.

Smith, Brad W. and Malcolm D. Holmes. "Community Accountability, Minority Threat, and Police Brutality: An Examination of Civil Rights Complaints." *Criminology* 41, no. 4 (2003): 1035–1064.

Solorzano, Daniel, Miguel Ceja, and Tara Yosso. "Critical Race Theory, Racial Microaggressions, and Campus Racial Climate: The Experiences of African American College Students." *Journal of Negro Education* 69, no. ½ (2000): 121–136.

Spence, Lester K. "Images of black people in general, and black men in particular, have long." *Contours of African American Politics: Volume 2, Black Politics and the Dynamics of Social Change* (2017): 281.

Spencer, Katherine, Charbonneau, Amanda, and Jack Glaser. "Teaching and Learning Guide for Implicit Bias and Policing." *Social and Personality Psychology Compass*, 9, no. 12 (2015): 705–708.

Spencer, Robyn Ceanne. "Engendering the Black Freedom Struggle: Revolutionary Black Womanhood and the Black Panther Party in the Bay Area, California." *Journal of Women's History* 20, no. 1 (2008): 90–113.

Spielman, Fran. "Disgraced Chicago Cop Jon Burge Breaks Silence, Condemns $5.5 million Reparations Fund," *Chicago Sun Times*, April 17, 2015. https://chicago.suntimes.com/news/disgraced-chicago-cop-jon-burge-breaks-silence-condemns-5-5-million-reparations-fund/

Starr, Terrell Jermaine. "Community Policing is Not the Solution to Police Brutality. It Makes it Worse," *The Washington Post*, November 3, 2015, https://www.washingtonpost.com/posteverything/wp/2015/11/03/community-policing-is-not-the-solution-to-police-brutality-it-makes-it-worse/?noredirect=on&utm_term=.498975d7899a

Stoughton, Seth. "Law Enforcement's 'Warrior' Problem." *Harvard Law Forum*, 128 (2015): 225–235.

Strauss, Anselm, and Juliet M. Corbin. *Basics of qualitative research: Grounded theory proce-dures and techniques*. Sage Publications, Inc, 1990.

Stevenson, Bryan. 2015. *Just Mercy: A Story of Justice and Redemption*. New York, NY: Spiegel & Grau, 2015.

Study.com (2018). Excessive Force: Definition, Cases & Statistics. Retrieved from: https://study.com/academy/lesson/excessive-force-definition-cases-statistics.html

Sulzberger, A. G. "As Survivors Dwindle, Tulsa Confronts Its Past," *The New York Times*, June 19, 2011. http://www.nytimes.com/2011/06/20/us/20tulsa.html.

Swaine, John, Oliver Laughland, James Lartey, and Ciara McCarthy. "Young Black Men Killed by Police at Highest Rate in Year of 1,134 Deaths," *The Guardian*, December 31, 2015, http://www.theguardian.com/us-news/2015/dec/31/the-counted-police-killings-2015-young-black-men?CMP=share_btn_fb.

Sweeney, Annie. "Inside the Failed Prosecution of Dante Servin," *The Chicago Tribune*, July 3, 2015, http://www.chicagotribune.com/news/ct-dante-servin-acquittal-met-20150626-story.html

Taylor, Steven J., Robert Bogdan, and Marjorie DeVault. *Introduction to qualitative research methods: A guidebook and resource*. John Wiley & Sons, 2015.

"The Black Panther Party for Self-Defense," *Socialist Alternative*, May 27, 2018. https://www.socialistalternative.org/panther-black-rebellion/the-black-panther-party-for-self-de-fense/

The Blind Side. Directed by John Lee Hancock. Los Angeles, CA: Alcon Entertainment, 2009.

The Blog. U.S. Laws Protect Police But Endanger Civilians, January 29, 2017, Accessed on July 20, 2018, https://www.huffingtonpost.com/the-conversation-us/us-laws-protect-police-wh_b_9018144.html

The Littlest Rebel. Directed by David Butler. Los Angeles, CA: 20th Century Fox, 1935.

Tonry, Michael. *Punishing Race: A Continuing American Dilemma*. New York: Oxford University Press, 2012.

Troy, Gil. Filming Rodney King's Beating Ruined His Life, March 3, 2016, Accessed on July 31, 2018, https://www.thedailybeast.com/filming-rodney-kings-beating-ruined-his-life

Turner, Caroline S. "Incorporation and Marginalization in the Academy from Border toward Center for Faculty of Color?" *Journal of Black Studies* 34, no. 1 (2003): 112–125.

Tyler, Tom R. "Procedural Justice and Policing: A Rush to Judgment?" *Annual Review of Law and Social Science*, 13 (2017): 29–53.

Tyler, Tom R., and Jeffrey Fagan. "Legitimacy and cooperation: Why do people help the police fight crime in their communities." *Ohio St. J. Crim. L.* 6 (2008): 231.

Tyler, Tom R., Goff, Phillip Atiba, and Robert J. MacCoun. "The Impact of Psychological Science on Policing in the United States: Procedural Justice, Legitimacy, and Effective Law Enforcement." *Psychological Science in the Public Interest* 16, no. 3 (2015): 75–109.

Umoja, Akinyele Omowale. "Repression Breeds Resistance: The Black Liberation Army and the Radical Legacy of the Black Panther Party." *New Political Science* 21, no. 2 (1999): 131–155.

US Legal. Excessive Force Law and Legal Definition. Retrieved from: https://definitions.uslegal.com/e/excessive-force/

Vera, Amir. "Officers Muted Body Cameras in Stephon Clark Shooting. Why?," *CNN*.com, March 26, 2018, https://www.cnn.com/2018/03/25/us/sacramento-shooting-body-camera/index.html

Vick, Michael. Wikipedia, Accessed on July 28, 2018, https://en.wikipedia.org/wiki/Michael_Vick

Vick, Mike. Dogfighting TV Commercial (March 30, 2012), Accessed on July 28, 2018, https://www.youtube.com/watch?v=rk3TbAUDBd8

Villenas, Sofia. "The Colonizer/Colonized Chicana Ethnographer: Identity, Marginalization, and Co-Optation in the Field." *Harvard Educational Review* 66, no. 4 (1996): 711–732.

Wadman, Robert C. and William Allison. *To Protect and to Serve: A History of Policing in America*. Upper Saddle River, NJ: Pearson College Division, 2004.

Walker, April. "Racial Profiling-Separate and Unequal Keeping the Minorities in Line-The Role of Law Enforcement in America.". *Thomas L. Rev.* 23 (2010): 576–619.

Walker, Samuel, Spohn, Cassia, and Miriam DeLone. *The Color of Justice: Race, Ethnicity, and Crime in America*. 4th ed. Belmont, CA: Wadsworth, 2007.

Walker, Samuel, and Charles M. Katz. *Police in America*. McGraw-Hill, 2012.

Ward, Geoff K. *The Black Child-Savers: Racial Democracy & Juvenile Justice*. Chicago, Illinois: Chicago University Press, 2012.

Ware, Lawrence. "#NeverForget: 100 Years Ago, East St. Louis Was on Fire," *The Root*, July 2, 2017, https://www.theroot.com/neverforget-100-years-ago-east-st-louis-was-on-fire-1796490406

Washington, Harriet A. *Medical Apartheid: The Dark History of Medical Experimentation on Black Americans from Colonial Times to the Present*. New York: Anchor Books, 2006.

Waytz, Adam and Juliana Schroeder. "Overlooking Others: Dehumanization by Commission and Omission." *TPM: Testing, Psychometrics, Methodology in Applied Psychology* 21, no. 3 (2014): 1–16.

Weill, Kelly. " Baltimore Cops Caught Turning Off Body Cameras Before 'Finding' Drugs," Daily Beast, August 1, 2017, https://www.thedailybeast.com/baltimore-cops-turned-off-body-cameras-before-finding-drugs.

Weitzer, Ronald. "American Policing Under Fire: Misconduct and Reform." *Society* 52, no. 5 (2015): 475–480.

Weitzer, Ronald. "Racialized Policing: Residents' Perceptions in Three Neighborhoods." *Law & Society Review* 34, no. 1 (2000): 129–155.

Wendt, Simon. "They Finally Found Out that We Really Are Men: Violence, Non-Violence and Black Manhood in the Civil Rights Era," *Gender and History* 19, no. 3 (2007): 543–564.

Whack, Erin Haines. "Philadelphia Moving Statue of Controversial Ex-Mayor Frank Rizzo," *USA Today*, November 4, 2017. https://www.usatoday.com/story/news/nation-now/2017/11/04/philadelphia-moving-statue-controversial-ex-mayor-frank-rizzo/832309001/

White, Michael D. *Police-Officer Body-Worn Cameras: Assessing the Evidence*. U.S. Department of Justice: Office of Justice Programs Diagnostic Center, Washington, D.C., 2014.

Wicentowski, Danny. "First Hand Accounts Show the Horror of East St. Louis' 1917 Race Riot," *RiverFrontTimes*, June 28, 2017, https://www.riverfronttimes.com/newsblog/2017/06/28/first-hand-accounts-show-the-horror-of-east-louis-1917-race-riot

Wilson, John Jay and Ron Wallace. *Black Wallstreet*. New York: Seaburn Publishing Group, 2004.

Wing, Nick. (2017). If Most Police Officers Are 'Good Cops,' These Are Even Better. Retrieved from https://www.huffingtonpost.com/2015/01/13/police-support-protests_n_6419220.html

Wing, Nick. "We Pay A Shocking Amount for Police Misconduct, and Cops Want Us to Accept It. We Shouldn't, *The Huffington Post*.com, May 29, 2015, https://www.huffingtonpost.com/2015/05/29/police-misconduct-settlements_n_7423386.html

Wolfe-Rocca, Ursula. "Cointelpro: Teaching the FBI's War on the Black Freedom Movement," *Rethinking Schools*, Vol. 30, no. 3, 2016. https://www.rethinkingschools.org/articles/cointelpro-teaching-the-fbi-s-war-on-the-black-freedom-movement

Woods, Baynard. "'Ferguson Effect' Did Not Impact Crime in Baltimore-But 'Gray Effect' May Have," *The Guardian*, March 15, 2016. http://www.theguardian.com/us-news/2016/mar/15/ferguson-effect-baltimore-freddie-gray-effect-crime.

Workneh, Lilly. "The Unforgettable Images Expose the Horror of the Tulsa Race Riots," *Huffington Post: Black Voices*, June 2, 2016. https://www.huffingtonpost.com/entry/tulsa-race-riots_us_574fc3aae4b0ed593f134a92

Young, Thomas. "40 Years Ago, Church Committee Investigated Americans Spying on Americans," *Brookings Now*, May 6, 2015. https://www.brookings.edu/blog/brookingsnow/2015/05/06/40-years-ago-church-committee-investigated-americans-spying-on-americans/

Index

accountability of police: increase in police brutality, 160; police maltreatment of blacks and, 123, 125, 127; recommendations to improve, 160. *See also* University Accountability of Law Enforcement Theme

Affirmative Theme, 142n32; discussion of, 115; in question 4 findings, 74–77, 115

aggressive behavior. *See* Personal Experience with Aggressive Behavior Theme

Alvarez, Anita, 159

Anderson, Claud, 163

Ariel, Barak, 157

Armour, Jody David, 7

Atesiano, Raimundo, 149–150

Beck, Elwood M., 23

Becker, Sarah, 8

Bell, Derrick, 4

Beyoncé. *See* Knowles, Beyoncé

Birth of a Nation, 6

Biscayne Park Police Department, 149–150

Bjorhus, Jennifer, 27

black activists: as anti-police, 2; Black Lives Matter, 2, 10; college student, 2; excessive police force and, 1, 2; police killings of black men and, 10

The Black Campus Movement: Black Students and the Racial Reconstitution

of Higher Education, 1965–1972 (Kendi), 2

black children: inability to be children of, 10–14, 16; media treatment of killing of, 9, 12–13, 16; police killings of, 11–12, 14, 16; police perceptions of, 10, 105–106; school disregard and criminalization of, 5–6

black children's lives, devaluation of, 10–13; police killings and, 14, 16

black college student activists, 2

black college student perceptions of police: overview, viii, 2, 3; as racists, 105; as white supremacists, 105. *See also* study of black college student perceptions of police

black college students, interactions with police: as negative, 2; as stressful, 2–3. *See also* study of black college student perceptions of police

black criminals: Ferguson Effect and, 9–10. *See also* perceptions of black criminality

black families: excessive police force against blacks and structure of, 125; police killings of blacks and blaming, 11–12, 13, 16; war on drugs and, 159

black juvenile offenders, perceptions of, 13

black lives, devaluation of, 15; black children, 10–13, 14, 16; police killings and, 14, 16; white lives valuation

183

About the Authors

Ray V. Robertson, Ph.D. is an Associate Professor in Sociology at Florida Agricultural and Mechanical University (FAMU). Dr. Robertson's research and teaching interests relate to Crime and Deviance/Criminology, Social Inequality/Stratification, Race/Ethnicity, Black Seminoles, African American College Student Adjustment, and Police Brutality. He is a member of Omega Psi Phi Fraternity, Inc. In his spare time, he enjoys exercising, reading African history books, and Brazilian Jiu-Jitsu.

Cassandra D. Chaney, Ph.D. is a Professor in Child and Family Studies at Louisiana State University (LSU). Professor Chaney examines the experiences of Blacks in America, and conducts research that relates to: (a) Religion and Black Families; (b) Romantic Relationships of African-Americans; (c) Strong African-American Marriages and Families; (d) Media Representations of African-Americans; and (e) Social Realities of African-American Families. Given the unique socio-historical challenges of Black families, her research provides recommendations regarding how policy can better meet the needs of Black families who experience heightened rates of incarceration, unemployment, weakened family structures, and racism. Most important, her scholarship is rooted in a strengths-based perspective and emphasizes how Black families remain resilient in the face of these challenges. In addition to publishing over 80 manuscripts in various journals in the United States and abroad, she has also presented her research during many local, state, and national conferences. She has contributed chapters for over 10 book volumes relating to the topics of African American community sentiment regarding marriage, marriage promotion, strong Black marriages, and the racial experiences of Black professors at Predominantly White Institutions (PWIs). Dr. Chaney is the Associate Editor of the *Journal of Hip-Hop Studies* (JHHS), and is on the editorial boards of *Family Relations*, *International Journal of Crisis Journalism*, the Editorial Manager of *PLOS One*, and is Review Board Member of *Social Work Online*. She published the co-edited book *Black Women in Leadership: Their Historical and Contemporary Contributions* with Dr. Dannielle Joy Davis (Peter Lang Publishers) which explores the leadership experiences of Black women within macro level (such as education, industry, and social services) and micro level (such as family and individual churches) contexts. This interdisciplinary work examines leadership practices, highlighting the historical and current triumphs and barriers of Black women in these roles. Currently, Dr. Chaney is writing a co-authored book related to the characteristics of strong Black marriages and community perceptions of law enforcement. In her spare time, she enjoys travelling, reading, hiking, and is a Zumba enthusiast.